In *The Last of the Giants* George Otis. sive look at current events in the light of underlying spiritual realities.

While Satan's army is powerful, it is not impregnable. Through compelling vignettes, Otis shows how God is already at work punching holes in enemy strongholds. He introduces the idea of *spiritual mapping*, which involves superimposing our understanding of forces and events in the spiritual domain on places and circumstances in the material world.

By viewing world events in light of Scripture, Otis proposes that the armies of the Lord and the last giants in the armies of Satan are lining up to meet in a final battle at the probable site of the Garden of Eden.

"*The Last of the Giants* is truly a remarkable picture of the unfolding of God's plan in this incredible generation of change. What George Otis, Jr., foresaw as happening in the Soviet Union many months before the events actually transpired convinces me his insights on the giant of Islam ought to be considered very carefully. I've sent *The Last of the Giants* to all directors of our seventy global offices of Every Home for Christ because of my conviction that George Otis, Jr., has uniquely seen into the future regarding the wonder years of world evangelization that I believe lie just ahead for a praying Church."

Dick Eastman, President
Every Home for Christ

"George Otis, Jr., is one of the really God-graced and gifted young leaders who are rising. He has the respect of the larger Christian community born out of expertise and spiritual dedication."

Pastor Jack Hayford
The Church On The Way

"In a time of veritable explosion of information concerning strategic-level spiritual warfare, *The Last of the Giants* stands tall. George Otis, Jr., has emerged as the pioneer of a provocative new field known as spiritual mapping and this is its basic textbook. I use it in my seminary courses."

Dr. C. Peter Wagner
Fuller Theological Seminary

"Do yourself a favor and read this thought-provoking book. It is timely and terrific. Expect to be challenged, instructed, inspired, convicted and changed. I was."

Joy Dawson
Youth With A Mission

"George Otis, Jr., is a true prophetic visionary leader...."

Dr. Paul McKaughan, Executive Director
Evangelical Foreign Missions Association

"In an era when many have forgotten that we are commanded to love God with our whole mind, George Otis, Jr.'s, book is noteworthy for its scholarship and intellectual power. But more than a mere academic report, it is a call to action in fulfilling the Great Commission."

Former U.S. Senator Bill Armstrong

"This book reads like a comprehensive intelligence report on the spiritual state of the world. This is must reading for our national leaders — and anyone who wants a glimpse of God's 'New World Order.' "

Chaplain James M. Hutchens
Brigadier General (ret.), Army Reserve National Guard
Special Assistant to the Chief of Chaplains

"George Otis, Jr., skillfully assembles compelling evidence that we are the generation that may wrangle the most ferocious spiritual battle of all time.... I highly recommend *The Last of the Giants* to all who want to become active participants for Christ in today's quickly changing physical and spiritual world."

Dr. Ted Yamamori, President
Food for the Hungry

THE LAST
OF THE
GIANTS

GEORGE OTIS, JR.

Chosen Books

A Division of Baker Book House Co
Grand Rapids, Michigan 49516

Unless noted otherwise, Scripture quotations in this publication are from The New King James Version. Copyright © 1979, 1980, 1982 Thomas Nelson, Inc., Publishers.

Scripture texts identified NIV are from the Holy Bible, New International Version, copyright © 1973, 1978, 1984 International Bible Society. Used by permission of Zondervan Bible Publishers.

Scripture quotations identified NASB are from the New American Standard Bible, copyright © The Lockman Foundation 1960, 1962, 1963, 1968, 1971, 1972, 1973, 1975, 1977.

Verses marked TLB are taken from *The Living Bible*, copyright © 1971 by Tyndale House publishers, Wheaton, Ill. Used by permission.

Scripture quotations identified KJV are from the King James Version of the Bible.

Library of Congress Cataloging-in-Publication Data
Otis, George, date
    The last of the giants / George Otis, Jr.
      p.   cm.
    Includes bibliographical references.
    ISBN 0-8007-9192-4
    1. Bible—Prophecies—Middle East.   2. Missions to Muslims.
I. Title.
BS649.N45085   1991
220.1'5—dc20   91-21233
                                        CIP

A Chosen Book
Copyright © 1991 by George Otis, Jr.
Chosen Books are published by Fleming H. Revell
a division of Baker Book House Company
P.O. Box 6287, Grand Rapids, MI 49516-6287

ISBN: 0-8007-9192-4

Ninth printing, February 1999

Printed in the United States of America

For current information about all releases from
Baker Book House, visit our web site:
http://www.bakerbooks.com

This book is dedicated first of all to my wife, Lisa, and to my three sons, Brendan, Brook and Daron. Thank you for your patient contributions to a lengthy cause.

This book is also dedicated to the millions of spiritually thirsty Muslims around the world, and to the faithful men and women who have deemed it their reasonable service to bring them the Water of Life.

Acknowledgments

The respected Bible teacher Campbell McAlpine once said that the largest room in the world is the room for improvement. This truth is certainly applicable to this book. Despite its many flaws, however, it is a start; and as they say, *nothing ventured, nothing gained*. It is my hope that, in time, the Holy Spirit and thoughtful readers will provide me with enough constructive feedback to allow for a healthy remodeling project.

In the meantime, I have many people to thank.

First and foremost are the scores of faithful intercessors who watched over this project from gestation to birth. Notable among these are my wife, Lisa, and her prayer partner, Jan Gaffney, my mother, Virginia Otis, and all of the wonderful women of the Lydia Fellowship.

I am also profoundly grateful to my associate Jacqueline Brown and to Chosen editors Jane Campbell and Ann McMath whose sensitivity, encouragement and insights throughout a complex and, at times, hectic project made things a good deal easier.

Thanks are also due to David Aikman for his timely leads and observations, and to Patrick Johnstone, David Barrett, John Robb and Patrick Sookhdeo for their hospitality and research support. Were it not for space and security considerations, many others could be mentioned here as well.

Lastly, thanks to Dick Hochreiter, a genuine unsung hero, whose early financial assistance allowed us to proceed with necessary field research.

Contents

Foreword   **15**

Preface   **19**

Introduction: The Earth Is the Lord's   **21**

Surrealistic Nights and Smoking Cities: Colliding with
Reality

The Numbers Expedition: Most Saw Grasshoppers

Weeping in the Wilderness: The Dispensability of a
Generation

1: The Three Understandings   **31**

Where Are We Going from Here?

Understanding the Times We Are Living In

Understanding the Spiritual Battlefield We Are Fighting On

Understanding God's Ways

2: The Decade of Transition   45

Intercessory Prayer, the Tripwire of Change
The Kremlin Plague
With a Great Fall: The Miracle of Eastern Europe
The New Spiritual Superpowers

3: The Strongest of These   61

Revelations and Bewitchments: The Mystical World
    of Islam
Zealots of the Crescent
Oil: The Treasure Chest of Allah
The Revolution Heads West
Watching the Infidels: The Monitoring of Christian
    Missions

4: Spiritual Mapping   84

Spiritual Borders: Invisible Boundaries of the Will
Spiritual Territoriality and Human Systems
Establishing Beachheads and Renewing Allegiances
Spiritual Capitals: Identifying the Real Centers of Power
Spiritual Fronts: The 10/40 Window
The Garden of Dreams

5: By the Rivers of Babylon   103

The Peacock Angel
Omens, Ghosts and Ziggurats: A Tale of Four Cities
Reviving the Spirit of Babylon
Arabian Nights of Terror
The Aftermath of War

6: The Reemergence of the Prince
of Persia   120

Establishing God's Government
Revisiting the Valley of the Assassins

The Association of Militant Clerics: Exporting the Politics
of Hate
Under the Temples of Baalbek: Little Teheran and the
Hizballah
The Dangers of the Ungodly Path

7: Closing on Eden   142

The Shrinking Frontier
Open Doors and Windows of Opportunity
Kairos, Muslims and the Supernatural
Facing the Last of the Giants

8: The Transformation of Magog   169

Perestroika in Peril: The Dissolution of the Soviet Empire
Soviet Muslims: Swelling Ranks of Discontent
Fuel for the Fire: International Islamic Support
The Mosque and the Popular Front
Backlash: *Pamyat* and the Rise of Russian Fascism
Return of the Basmachi: Walking the Precipice of Way

9: Days of Rage and Wonder   199

Apostasy and Desecration: Provoking the Ultimate *Jihad*
Black Hundreds and Green Flags: Forging the Ezekiel
Alliance
Gog and the Spirit of Totalitarianism
The Expected One: Al-Mahdi and His Miracles
Two Reapers, Three Frogs and Seven Angels: On the Eve
of Armageddon

10: Responding to the Times: A Strategic
Checklist   223

Pulling in the Right Direction: Identifying and Targeting
Key Harvest Fields

Pulling Together: The Case for Partnerships
Pulling Out the Stops: Adequately Financing the
Campaign
Pulling Strings: The Role of Prayer and Spiritual Power
Pulling It Off: Cultivating an Activist Mentality

Epilogue: Risky Safety   **259**

Open Doors and the Gates of Hell
No Fair Fights

Appendix: Islamic Beast Theory   **267**
Selected Bibliography   **269**

"Write down the revelation
  and make it plain on tablets
  so that a herald may run with it.
For the revelation awaits an appointed time;
  it speaks of the end
  and it will not prove false.
Though it linger, wait for it;
  it will certainly come and will not delay."

Habakkuk 2:2–3 (NIV)

Foreword

Ever since the very earliest days of the faith, Christians have been admonished down through the centuries to equip themselves for "spiritual warfare." The New Testament verse often cited to underline this is from the letter of Paul to the Ephesians, chapter 6, verse 12: "For our struggle is not against flesh and blood, but against the rulers, against the authorities, against the powers of this dark world and against spiritual forces of evil in the heavenly realms" (NIV). For many believers, undoubtedly, this idea is a little frightening. It's hard enough, he or she might say, coping with the ordinary pressures and challenges of life without having to worry about the spiritual minefields that the dark forces of the universe may have laid in our path to waylay seekers of truth and righteousness. The fact is, though, that all great men and women of the Christian faith have walked and worked in an awareness that the major spiritual achievements throughout history have come as a result of victories won through prayer and faith against very real, albeit unseen, spiritual adversaries.

An awareness of this spiritual dimension is hardly limited to the writers of the New Testament. Vivid glimpses of the spiritual forces both obeying and opposing God crop up in unexpected places in the Old Testament, too. One of the most remarkable, to me, is in the tenth chapter of the book of Daniel, where an angel visits Daniel three weeks after Daniel started to fast and pray, and reveals an astounding insight into unseen spiritual warfare. The angel says that he was held up by resistance from "the prince of the Persian kingdom."

Who was this nefarious individual? Obviously, he was a spiritual rather than a human being. It is only reasonable to assume that he is one of the "rulers" cited in Paul's letter to the Ephesians, a supernatural being of local geographic authority who resists the emissaries of God—i.e., angels—and who owes his allegiance to the devil himself.

If, as it seems reasonable to assume, the "rulers" such as the one who delayed the angelic visitation to Daniel exercise power in many different areas of the world, then some of the world's most intractable problems may be due at least partly to spiritual forces behind the scenes rather than merely the obvious "overt" factors such as geography, history and political conditions.

To some, this point may seem so obvious as to be merely banal. To others, it may be quite startling. But for both categories of readers of this book, what George Otis, Jr., has attempted is truly interesting. He suggests that there are identifiable geographic locations where not only wickedness in human form seems particularly apparent (in Mesopotamia, for example, the birthplace of modern Iraq), but where resistance to the free profession of the Christian faith is particularly virulent. He also links certain non-Christian religious faiths and practices to certain geographical regions, implying that there is a continuity of spiritual influence (in these cases quite negative ones) even when the overt form of religious expression changes over the centuries. Thus, for example, he suggests that the extreme violence associated with so much of Iraq's history in both ancient and modern times may be connected with the malevolent deities worshiped by the ancient Mesopotamians in biblical times.

This is an important insight. For one thing, it removes from Christians the need to identify other religions as the "enemy."

Otis, as a Christian, obviously believes that the Christian faith is God's true revealed message to the human race. But if, as he suggests, opposition to that faith, particularly when it is violent or even murderous, constitutes not so much local cultural quirkiness as the expression of actual demonic powers at work, then the victims of the violence are not merely Christian believers but all who have come under the influence of those dark powers in a given cultural or geographic setting.

Much of this book concerns Islam. It is important to recognize that Otis is not at all attacking Islam as such, but merely suggesting that dark underlying spiritual forces have in some instances turned particular groups of Muslim believers into harsh antagonists of all opposing religious views. The corollary of this view, of course, is that some self-styled Christian groups in historical times have also behaved in ways that could only be described as demonic. Islam remains a very powerful, coherent religion, and its continued global vitality obviously impinges on the effectiveness of Christians who seek to make the faith of the Gospel of Jesus Christ known at least equally well in all parts of the world. What Otis achieves, I believe, is a sense of the spiritual warfare that lies beneath all major clashes of values around the world.

The book is pioneering and, in some respects, experimental. Yet it is well-documented, well-written and truly fascinating. Otis has a great gift of culling different pieces of information from a variety of sources and then drawing intriguing connections between them.

The book is one of the first efforts to explore the world of spiritual darkness in a global context. Otis has coined the term *spiritual mapping* to denote this exploration. He will also doubtless provide greater detail in later works of how he believes the system operates. He is appropriately modest in his conclusions and refreshingly undogmatic in his analysis. Those qualities alone make this book a major and valuable contribution to an extremely important subject.

David Aikman
Washington, D.C.
May 1991

Preface

The Last of the Giants paints a well-researched, poignant sketch of the times in which we live, quite possibly man's final season. George Otis, Jr., has assembled compelling evidence that we are the generation that may wrangle the most ferocious spiritual battle of all times.

The topic of spiritual strongholds may be foreign to many who read this book. In a lively and fast-paced style, George removes the shroud of mystery surrounding spiritual warfare. He underscores the need to meet the future with sharp eyes and intellect—to see world events as they really are rather than how they appear to be. He challenges us to be like the children of Issachar in 1 Chronicles 12:32: ". . . Men that had understanding of the times, to know what Israel ought to do."

Jesus commanded us to be lights in the world, saying that spiritual battles are not only inevitable but will escalate during the final days. We cannot afford to falter or accept battle plans from anyone but God. The near future holds a final epic battle that

Christians must not watch from living rooms and churches. We Christians must act upon the message of this book—to become active players by reaching out in both mind and spirit.

I personally have learned much from George's refreshing insights. A brilliant researcher and gifted analyst, he is capable of straining substantial evidence through a clearly focused vision. I highly recommend *The Last of the Giants* to all who want to become active participants for Christ in today's quickly changing physical and spiritual world.

Dr. Ted Yamamori
Chairman, Spiritual Mapping Track
A.D. 2000 Movement
Adjunct Professor of Sociology
Arizona State University

Introduction

The Earth Is the Lord's

The earth is the Lord's, and all it contains, the world, and those who dwell in it.

Psalm 24:1 (NASB)

Living thus in the twilight of a spent civilization, amidst its ludicrous and frightening shadows, what is here to believe?

Malcolm Muggeridge[1]

If we are honest, most of us will admit to the fact that there are occasions when we are frankly baffled by the meaning of particular Scriptures. We read the words, but we have not yet come to "know" them as companions. They are like the elegant wedding gifts bestowed on us proudly by wealthy relatives; other than the fact that we believe them to be valuable, and that they make us feel good when we see them, we are not precisely sure what is to be done with them.

The most common explanation for this is that our reading of Scripture has been so cursory that we have failed to grasp meaning that is plainly evident. We have not taken the time, as they say, "to smell the flowers." Dutiful reading—the act of scanning holy pages so as to fulfill certain self-imposed quotas—rarely has revelation in mind as a destination. Understanding is also difficult to come by when the scope of our reading is so limited that we forfeit the interpretive benefit of other related passages.

On other occasions, certain Scriptures stump us because they appear at odds with surrounding reality. The "facts," as recorded by our five senses, seemingly fail to corroborate the assertions of these biblical declarations, promises and prophecies. At times the dilemma can be pronounced and uncomfortable. Not wanting to doubt the Word, but also not wishing to live in the abstract, we strive to break the code of these mysteries through a season of prayer and meditation. If we press on with diligence, God has promised to reward us with truth. If we capitulate to apathy, however, we are left with the crusts of unexplained paradoxes and the strong temptation to exchange dynamic intimacy with Christ for mere forms of godliness.

While it would seem logical that the most commonly encountered dilemmas would relate to passages containing theological complexities or specific (and seemingly unfulfilled) promises, my own struggles, surprisingly enough, surfaced in connection with Psalm 24:1—a verse considered so sublime and reassuring that it frequently adorns Christian posters and stationery:

> The earth is the Lord's, and all it contains, the world, and those
> who dwell in it.   (NASB)

Surrealistic Nights and Smoking Cities: Colliding with Reality

The first time I recall entertaining questions about the meaning of this wonderful psalm was during the course of my initial visit to the Soviet Union in the spring of 1973. I had arrived in Moscow on May 1 (or May Day, as this workers' holiday is known throughout the Communist world) in order to share the love of Christ with those Muscovites drawn out of their homes for the celebration. It was a memorable experience.

If there is one thing totalitarian governments have proven they are ultimately adept at, it is throwing larger-than-life parties. This day, like every Communist holiday before or since, was no exception.

Festooned in crimson, the entire city had become a stage whose edifices were used as elaborate props and whose citizens were carefully choreographed by central planners. No quarter of this vast metropolis was without some sort of visible holiday reminder.

The grand centerpiece was Red Square. Of the world's premier architectural monuments, perhaps only China's Tiananmen Square and Washington's Capitol rate comparably when it comes to dazzling visitors with the trappings of human power. By eight o'clock that evening, despite the fact the day's festivities were winding to a close, thousands of people continued to mill about this magnetic pole of the Communist world. The grandeur, especially at night, was awe-inspiring.

At the same time, as I looked at the Kremlin sitting mysteriously behind thick red-brick walls, it struck me as a rich visual metaphor of Soviet society. Like the proletariat rank and file around me, about all I could see of the ruling palace was the green dome of the Supreme Soviet building with the hammer and sickle flag fluttering rhythmically above it in the breeze. Illuminated against a darkened sky, it was easy to see how Muggeridge could have referred to this terrible banner as "a pool of blood." Turrets situated at the corners of the sprawling complex hoisted five-ton red stars high into the air to frame the picture.

On the other side of the square, beyond the adorned onion domes of St. Basil's Cathedral, my eyes focused upon a massive floodlit billboard that cast four-story images of Marx, Engels and Lenin in dramatic and surrealistic poses. From this elevated platform these architects of the modern Communist movement hovered as mute observers over their kingdom's most regal acres.

As I lowered my gaze, I soon realized that the eyes of these revered socialist icons were not the only ones observing me and fifteen other colleagues who had also gathered in Red Square that evening to spread the Good News. Following a time of worship, witness and Scripture distribution, we were suddenly surrounded by the guardians of the realm. Seconds later, large numbers of uniformed militiamen and plainclothes KGB officers pushed determinedly through the crowd to arrest us. As the entire scene pressed in against my senses, the words of Psalm 24 seemed as

remote and abstract as a celestial equation. *The earth is the Lord's?*
I thought. *Maybe. But not Moscow.*[2]

Ten years later, I once again found myself far from home. This
time the venue was Baabda, Lebanon, a hill-hugging community
hosting the nation's presidential palace and affording a command-
ing view of the besieged city of Beirut. Within my line of sight were
a total of eight militias poised nervously on the brink of bloodshed.

The late morning calm was soon pierced by the shrill whine of
an artillery round arching overhead to an unknown destination
below. Instantly the air was filled with the deafening sounds of
war. Buildings in the city's suburbs belched flames and smoke
before crumbling in defeat. As I watched helplessly through a pair
of binoculars, people in the line of fire lurched under the influence
of adrenalin, gesturing warnings frantically, but ultimately unsure
as to where the next round would land.

Despite the heroic efforts of friends and neighbors, in the end
the rockets and tanks did their work. No more than a couple of
miles from my relatively safe mountain perch, buildings and bodies burned. The air that day was heavy with fear and death. As I
breathed it in, I thought again to myself: *The earth is the Lord's?*
Perhaps. But not today, not in Beirut.

In the fall of that year, my wife and I found ourselves preparing
to leave the socialist outpost of Mongolia following an absorbing
three-week visit. Far from any of the world's great seas, Mongolia
lies landlocked between China's northern provinces and the
U.S.S.R.'s Siberian frontier. From the early campaigns of Genghis
Khan to the reports of the intrepid Marco Polo, the outside world
has found itself alternately terrified of and fascinated with this
mysterious Eastern kingdom.

It was not until our train began to pull away from the drab Ulan
Bator station, however, that we first began to realize the degree to
which the experience had immersed our spirits in suffocating spiritual darkness. In the course of dozens of conversations with nationals in apartments, hotel rooms and jostling bus rides across the
Gobi Desert, we had not met a single Mongol who had ever heard
of Jesus.

Research prior to our journey had presented us with the astonishing revelation that Mongolia had not known an established Christian church since Jesus was born in Bethlehem some 2,000 years ago. Now we had faced the truth of it. As our train snaked through the alpine foothills of southern Siberia, we wrestled with mental stowaways that included images of freshly erected spirit cairns in the Gobi Desert, the demonically contorted faces of Buddhist monks inside the Gandan lamasery and, above all, the blank, uncomprehending stares of first-time Gospel hearers.

Once again the words of the psalmist came to me: *The earth is the Lord's, and all it contains, the world, and those who dwell in it.* As the evening fell and the train's metronomic rhythm began to dull the senses, I wondered how this word could possibly apply to the dark void of Mongolia.

While each of these collisions with reality made an impact on my spirit, collectively they forced me to a summit meeting of sorts with the Holy Spirit. A decade of observations had convinced me that these experiences were not unusual, and that in fact very little of the world showed any tangible evidence of belonging to the Lord.

A friend of mine once said that although God is no mark for the rebellious *Why?*, He is always available for the sincere *Why?* While the former is rooted in bitterness and self-indulgence, the latter seeks to learn. If our hearts are right before God, there is no reason to refrain from approaching Him boldly with our inquiries. In fact, failing to deal with questions when they are still the musings of a sincere heart will often lead to their return at a later date as the bitter fodder of a rebellious heart.

My question of the Lord was a simple one: If the earth really was His, then why did there seem to be so little evidence of it? In His goodness, the Lord responded gently. *The earth is Mine*, He said, *in the same manner that Canaan belonged to Israel—it is rightfully owned, but unpossessed. The latter is your responsibility.*

The Numbers Expedition: Most Saw Grasshoppers

The Israelites' first encounter with the Promised Land is recorded in the thirteenth chapter of Numbers. After camping for

nearly a year at the foot of Mt. Sinai, the Hebrews moved north-
ward into the Wilderness of Paran, reaching first the tip of the Gulf
of Aqaba, then the oasis of Kadesh-barnea. From this location just
forty miles south of the Promised Land, Moses, at God's behest,
dispatched twelve tribal leaders to "spy out the land of Canaan."

As the people watched the spies disappear in the direction of the
Negev hill country, their hearts were fired with an anticipation they
had not experienced since they sang to the Lord on the eastern shore
of the Red Sea two years earlier. Could it be that their long, arduous
and supernatural journey was about to come to an end? What tales
would Moses' scouts bring back from the Promised Land?

After forty days out in the field, the expedition returned to the
Hebrew camp at Kadesh-barnea with their report. There, with
Moses and the people gathered before them, they proceeded to
recount their discoveries with a zeal that comes with the knowledge that one has both privileged information and an eager audience. Such was the power of their narration that, within the space
of the next few hours, the entire nation was launched on an emotional roller-coaster ride that would take them from the heights of
hopeful expectancy into a dark free-fall into fear and despair.

The drama was heightened by disagreement among the spies
themselves—although the tension had little to do with the accu-
racy of the report. In fact, as their debriefing began, descriptions
of the land's incredible fruitfulness were supported impressively
by an ample cluster of grapes collected by the team in the Valley
of Eshcol. No one disputed that Canaan was indeed an "exceedingly good land." Nor was there any arguing the facts that the
inhabitants of the land were numerous, physically daunting and
that their cities were well-fortified. From the central highlands to
the Negev, from the Mediterranean Sea to the Jordan River, all
agreed that the Promised Land was occupied by tenants with no
present thoughts of relocating.

It may have been the mention of seeing the Anak giants that
brought Caleb to his feet to silence the first murmurs of concern
among the people. Whatever it was, Caleb clearly sensed it was
time to steer the house of Israel in the direction of faith. For this
captain of Judah there had been enough talk about what had been

seen. It was time to consider what must be *done!* "Let us go up at once and take possession," he declared, "for we are well able to overcome it."[3]

Suddenly Caleb and Joshua found themselves in the awkward position of being faced down by their own expeditionary colleagues. Despite unity over the *facts* of the report, the spies parted company publicly when it came to drawing *conclusions* from these facts. In a vigorous rebuttal to Caleb's challenge to faith, the majority recommended against possession on the basis that the present inhabitants of the land "are stronger than we." To justify their own unbelief, they proceeded to pass on a "bad report" to the children of Israel that, while correct in its description of existing challenges and obstacles, neglected to consider the intentions and capabilities of God.

A revealing admission in the final stanza of the majority report affords clear evidence of the tragically low line of sight maintained by its authors during their sojourn in Canaan. "There we saw the giants," they told the people. "We seemed like grasshoppers in our own eyes, and we looked the same to them."[4]

Ironically, in spite of all their mention in the spies' report, Canaan's formidable giants would in the end have little to do with the Israelites' possession of the "land that [God] had searched out for them."[5] Of far more importance to God (and this was, of course, His real purpose in sending out spies in the first place) was *what else* the Hebrew scouts would see in Canaan. The final scorecard? All saw giants; most saw grasshoppers; two saw God.

Weeping in the Wilderness: The Dispensability of a Generation

> So all the congregation lifted up their voices and cried, and the people wept that night.[6]

Perhaps nowhere else in Scripture is the gall of disappointment documented more vividly. What must this collective mourning have sounded like to the desert Bedouin resting their camels at the Kadesh oasis? The implications of the spies' bad report had settled on the nation like a virulent contagion; and as its fearful poison spread throughout the camp, the night air was filled with the sounds of hope extinguished.

As the evening hours wore on, the congregation's emotions began to darken with the horizon. Disappointment collapsed into dissension and ominous threats of insurrection. Talk began to circulate about selecting a new leader from among the ranks and returning to Egypt. With all its liabilities, predictable servitude was surely better than treading the manifold perils of Canaan.

Crushed by this obscene disintegration of faith a mere forty miles from the Promised Land, Moses and Aaron fell prostrate before their kinsmen. Seeing this, Joshua and Caleb were no longer able to restrain themselves. Ripping their upper garments as a symbol of their profound grief, the young firebrands leapt onto the platform in a last-ditch attempt to reason with the angry masses.

> "The land we passed through to spy out is an exceedingly good land. If the Lord delights in us, then He will bring us into this land and give it to us. . . .
>
> "Only do not rebel against the Lord, nor fear the people of the land, for they are our bread; their protection has departed from them, and the Lord is with us. Do not fear them."[7]

The sad story, of course, is that the people did not listen. With manna still clinging to their beards, this generation that God had elected to drive out the idolatrous inhabitants of Canaan picked up stones instead against those who would keep them from Egypt.

In the end, aside from Joshua and Caleb, none of the mighty host that passed through the waters of the Red Sea and sang of their Deliverer on the other side ever set foot in the land of their inheritance. Having turned their backs on the visible fruits of Canaan, they returned to the desert wilderness where their flesh eventually joined the blowing sands of Sinai. Their demise would prove in graphic terms, and for all ages, the dispensability of a generation—even one chosen and led by God!

Surely there are lessons here for those of us who live at the end of the twentieth century. Some will remind us that the mere fact that a particular nation, people or ministry has been assigned to us as an inheritance is no guarantee that our "possession" of these modern-day Promised Lands will be uncontested. Others will point out that no generation, regardless of how unique and privileged they may fancy themselves, is indispensable to the fulfilling of God's purposes.

I am frequently asked these days whether I believe with the advent of Christian radio and television, flourishing national churches and the current aggressive mobilization of thousands of new mission laborers that the Lord's return will be an event witnessed by this present generation. While it is an interesting question, my response has invariably been, "I simply don't know." Although there are signs that today's international Church has indeed approached the perimeter of the Promised Land, I do not know what we shall do next. It is a moment of destiny. If we determine to confront the giants that would bar our path and plant heaven's flag in the hills and fields across the Jordan, then we may indeed prepare this earth to receive her King. If, on the other hand, we elect to see ourselves as grasshoppers, then we, too, will return to the wilderness while God awaits another generation.

This book has not been written with the intent of persuading Christians that we are entering an extraordinary stage of history— there is ample recognition of this fact already. Rather, it is my hope that the revelations and recommendations contained in the pages that follow will stimulate readers to become participants in, rather than observers of, the work of God in this hour.

There are three main themes woven throughout *The Last of the Giants*—world evangelization, spiritual warfare and the end times. Islam, which is an important component of each of these, also figures prominently in the book. The information you are about to read on these subjects represents the gleanings of more than 3,000 documents, books and interviews, thousands of miles of travel and nearly three years of work. There is a lot of content here. At times it will be grim, at others, exhilarating. Most importantly, for those who take the time to finish this book, it will also be life-changing.

It has been said that information without experience is pretty thin stuff. Accordingly, I have endeavored to "thicken the soup" of this prophetic story with my own encounters and observations. Ultimately, however, it will be up to the reader to take the information contained in this pulp-and-ink messenger and translate it into his or her own life experiences.

Notes

1 Malcolm Muggeridge, *Jesus Rediscovered* (New York, N.Y.: Pyramid, 1974), p. 59.
2 Out of the group of fifteen, nine of us were actually arrested. Following an interesting night of interrogation, we were released to our hotel rooms.
3 Numbers 13:30.
4 Numbers 13:33 (NKJV and NIV).
5 Ezekiel 20:6.
6 Numbers 14:1.
7 Numbers 14:7–9.

1

The Three
Understandings

We have no choice but to think about the future, for the
future is all that is left of life.

Edward R. Dayton

The sons of Issachar . . . had understanding of the
times, to know what Israel ought to do.

1 Chronicles 12:32

In a May 1989 episode of the CBS news magazine
"West 57th Street," a 110-year-old woman remarked to her inter-
viewer: "Listen, honey, I've seen the beginning of everything."
She was almost right.

Up until this century, history was pulled along at an oxen-like
pace. No longer. Since the dawn of the 1900s, mankind has been
hanging onto the reins of progress for dear life. In the post-World
War II era alone the identities and borders of more countries
changed than were changed by all the previous wars in history.[1]
Fully sixty percent, or some one hundred, of the world's current
fraternity of sovereign nations were birthed during this brief time
span.

Recent technological developments have been no less stagger-

ing. So accustomed have we become to the likes of micro-
computers, arthroscopic surgery, compact discs, CAT scans, laser-
guided missiles and space shuttles, it seems inconceivable that
just a few short years ago these marvels were confined to the
thought lives of imaginative engineers—the stuff of science fiction.
As British author Arthur C. Clarke quipped during the 1960s:
"The future isn't what it used to be."[2]

This truth is illustrated perhaps most remarkably by a pro-
nouncement delivered in the early 1970s by the FCC's top educational broadcasting specialist, Dr. Robert Hilliard: "At the rate
at which knowledge is growing, by the time the child born today
graduates from college, the amount of knowledge in the world will
be four times as great. By the time that same child is fifty years
old, it will be thirty-two times as great, and ninety-seven percent
of everything known in the world will have been learned since the
time he was born."[3] In a more recent interview, Brown University
president Vartan Gregorian revealed that potential knowledge,
meaning available information, is now doubling every five years.[4]
Put into perspective, this means that a daily edition of the *New
York Times* newspaper holds more information than a man or
woman in the sixteenth century had to process in the whole of his
or her entire life.[5]

In the Old Testament, the writings of the prophet Daniel reveal
that in "the time of the end . . . knowledge shall be increased."[6]
Without placing specific time parameters onto this period, it is
safe to say that if the end times are distinguishable by a notable
increase in knowledge, then we have surely entered them.

Where Are We Going from Here?

For four years during the late 1970s, British author Robert
Lacey traveled throughout the kingdom of Saudi Arabia interview-
ing desert Bedouin tribesmen, Islamic scholars, international businessmen and influential members of the royal family. His resulting
book, *The Kingdom,* was published in 1981 and offers a fascinating glimpse into Arabia and the House of Sa'ud. In the latter pages

of the book, Lacey shares a modern Saudi fable about uncertainty known locally as the "Tale of the Taxi."

> A man hailed a taxi one day, and as it drew to a halt the driver asked him where he wanted to go.
>
> "Never you mind," said the man as he got inside.
>
> "Well, which route shall I follow?" asked the driver.
>
> "Never you mind," said the man. "Just drive on and we shall see."
>
> So the taxi set off. When the man wanted to turn right, he told the driver. And when he wanted to turn left, he told the driver. And then he told the driver to stop, paid the fare and got out. He hadn't said where he was going, he hadn't said how he was going to get there, and nobody but he really knew whether that was really the destination he had wanted in the first place.[7]

A similar message, in the form of a riveting axiom, was delivered by Dr. Henry Kissinger to delegates attending the 1980 Republican national convention. "If you don't know where you're going," warned the former Secretary of State, "then any road will take you there."

A logical follow-on to this important truth reminds us that lack of personal or corporate direction can place us at the mercy of others, especially charismatic and opportunistic individuals eager to peddle trendy answers and ideologies. Our aimlessness is an advertisement that we are shopping for direction, and it grants those with a destination in mind the license to "take us for a ride." Venturing into the future without a clear sense of where we are going is a sure prescription for tragedy.

For Christians, this tragedy is compounded by the fact that we are not fulfilling one of God's intended purposes for His Church— that it serve as a spiritual directional beacon for all mankind. According to the late Francis Schaeffer, this intention, manifest first at creation when God gave an attentive Adam and Eve dominion over the earth, "puts a moral responsibility on us"[8] to offer leadership. "You are the light of the world," Jesus said to the early Church. "A city set on a hill cannot be hidden."[9]

The world's need for leadership cannot be underestimated. In a

recent edition of *The Washington Report,* editor Ray Allen recounted an enlightening personal experience he had while addressing an audience of elderly citizens several years ago. "In the
middle of my presentation," Allen wrote, "a woman suffering from
advanced Alzheimer's disease turned to her fellow-listeners, and
with a frightening sense of desperate conviction, cut to the heart of
the matter: 'We need a leader!' she exclaimed. She may have
spoken out of turn, but she certainly was not out of touch with
reality."[10]

The Church of Jesus Christ is God's primary instrument of revelation on earth today. And while we may occasionally find this
fact intimidating, our mandate leaves no room for passive or re-
actionary tendencies. As the people of God we are meant to lead
the parade of history. The question is, do we know where we are
meant to go?

Anyone can observe and report on these turbulent, unpredict-
able times. But deciphering the *implications* of these developments in order to make wise decisions about our lives and our
world is quite another matter. For this we need divine help.

To find this help, we turn to the Word of God, and in particular
to the prophet Daniel whose ancient writings have recently leapt
onto our twentieth-century stage. Reminding us of God's sovereign
oversight, the prophet declares:

> He changes the times and the seasons;
> He removes kings and raises up kings;
> He gives wisdom to the wise
> And knowledge to those who have understanding.
> He reveals deep and secret things.[11]

In keeping with the divine pattern of bestowing added blessings
and responsibilities upon those who have demonstrated good
stewardship, Daniel proclaims here that knowledge—and we
may assume that this knowledge pertains to revelation about tomorrow—will be granted to those who have already cultivated
understanding. An intriguing declaration, and one that raises a
salient question: If understanding is the prerequisite to revelation,
what exactly is it that we must understand?

In short, there would appear to be three crucial elements: 1) *the times we are living in*, 2) *the spiritual battlefield we are fighting on* and 3) *God's ways in evangelism and spiritual warfare*. If the Church fails to concern herself today with these issues, she will have nowhere to lead the world tomorrow. This said, it is worth taking a deeper look at each of these.

Understanding the Times We Are Living In

To rephrase what we have observed, we are living in times of unprecedented change. While it is God who "changes the times and the seasons," it was the Greeks who first coined a word to describe the arrival of these changes. They called it *kairos*. The term, connoting a fullness of time or ripening, is used in Scripture to convey the unique sense of God's timing.

Today, *kairos* moments are all about us—extraordinary events flowing out of heavenly vials of vintage intercession. And though the majority of God's people may not be familiar with the proper term for this fullness of time, they are well aware of the fact that we have entered a unique—and perhaps conclusive—period in history.

The awareness of divine movement in the world, however, must be nurtured. Otherwise, given time, circumstances such as the crumbling of the Berlin Wall and the unprecedented realignment of forces in the Middle East can become all too familiar, reduced to yellowing newsclips stashed in the back of a file cabinet or bundled for the recycler. Understanding the times properly requires that we reach beyond our event-oriented mentalities to cultivate an appreciation for the concept of *spiritual seasons*. If we have indeed entered a new season of divine initiative, we need to understand what this really means. New rules apply, old bets are off, and we cannot return to business as usual—ever.

A quick glance through the pages of Scripture reveals many prescient men and women from whom we can learn about responding to divine initiative in the world. Seeing the future, after all, means nothing if no appropriate action is taken. Conversely, those with no expectations for the future have nothing to drive their present actions. Noah, for instance, saw a coming flood and prepared an ark. Moses saw a coming deliverance and spoke to Pharaoh. Rahab perceived the Israeli conquest of Jericho and hid the spies. Simeon glimpsed a coming Savior and waited for His consolation. Mary sensed the imminence of her son's public ministry and commanded Cana's servants to obey Him. Peter recognized God's desire to release the Gospel to the Gentiles and preached in the home of Cornelius.

Perhaps the most vivid example of biblical prescience is found in the life of Joseph. After a long and unjust incarceration, this young man of God was summarily fished out of the bowels of Pharaoh's prison to interpret his antagonist's bizarre dream. Fortunately for Pharaoh, Joseph knew his stuff and accurately predicted seven years of abundance followed by seven years of famine—pointing out carefully that, while the future in this case was determined by God, *preparation for it was man's responsibility.* His subsequent advice to the Egyptian monarch was prefaced with the admonition "Let Pharaoh take action."[12] Because he had become a prescient believer, Joseph was not only set over all the land of Egypt, but was able to provide sustenance to all the people of the earth.

In addition to being a prerequisite to action, understanding the times has more to do with interpreting the known than seeing the unknown. In 1 Chronicles 12:32 the sons of Issachar are described as men who "had understanding of the times, to know what Israel ought to do." The word *understanding* in this passage comes from the Hebrew word *binah,* meaning "insight," and the root word *byn,* meaning "to distinguish or separate." Both *binah* and its root *byn* are used synonymously with various Old Testament words for wisdom. [13]

If we want to determine where we *should* be going and how to get there, we must petition God in the spirit of the sons of Issachar to add revelatory knowledge to our understanding of the times; to show us the future so that we might prepare responsibly to live and minister in it.

Understanding the Spiritual Battlefield
We Are Fighting On

An equally important pursuit for us today involves reassessing the features of the spiritual battlefield we have been called to fight on. As the times have changed, so, too, has our field of conflict.

Recent battlefield changes reflect both the impact of *kairos* transitions and the sophisticated strategizing of the adversary. These two factors, largely unappreciated by the Body of Christ, must be better understood if the Church is to navigate successfully the perils and opportunities that lie before us in the 1990s.

Kairos events—especially the demise of kings and their ideologies—tend to create spiritual vacuums. A good example of this may be seen today in Eastern Europe where a spent world view, Marxism, has left millions bereft of their spiritual moorings. "We were painted a fantastic future for seventy years," sighed Russian Orthodox priest Anatoli Koljada, "but now we are standing in front of ruins, and we've got nothing."[14] In a popular Moscow literary magazine, leading Soviet writer Victor Astafyev asks: "What happened to us? Who extinguished the light of goodness in our soul? Who blew out the lamp of our conscience . . . ?" In the end Astafyev laments: "They [the Communists] stole it from us and did not give anything in return."[15]

Like a piece of prime property that comes onto the market unexpectedly, spiritual vacuums such as have occurred in Eastern Europe quickly attract competing ideologies eager to "acquire and develop the asset." The Christian Church, unfortunately, often fails to see what is going on in such situations. Two characteristics trip us up. To begin with, we are by nature a celebratory people. As such, we are more inclined to focus our attention on the events that *lead* to spiritual vacuums (the demise of Communism, for instance) than we are on the vacuums themselves. We also tend to be parochial. When we finally recognize and respond to spiritual vacuums, it is often with the assumption that our plans, because they are inherently good, are the only plans in town.

Celebrations, as such, are fine; but if we permit ourselves to become shortsighted in victory, we will likely confront realities down the road that we may not wish to see. A case in point is the recent collapse of the Iron Curtain. Many Christians viewed this remarkable event as the *ultimate* answer to their prayers. As a result, the majority of these same believers failed to detect the far more dangerous spirits that were, at that very moment, climbing through Communism's newly visible breaches.

When the inaugural hole was punched through the wall, the world watched as East Germans saw for the first time what one TV newsman called "the decadent pleasures of Western capitalism." At almost every turn they found shops filled with sophisticated electronic gadgetry and designer fashions, showrooms with shiny Mercedes and BMWs, and theaters filled with graphic images of avarice and sexual indulgence. To these virgin consumers, the West was finally won.

Only weeks later, the word was passed that *Playboy* and *Penthouse* magazines had officially hit the newsstands of Eastern Europe. In the Soviet Union, a Communist official decried the fact that "flocks of teenagers" in the Siberian capital of Novosibirsk were purchasing and examining nude calendars produced by a Soviet private cooperative.[16] In October 1990, MTV arrived on prime time to rock 88 million Soviet households. Infatuated with the toys and secrets forbidden them for so many years, many Soviet youth became charter members of what 33-year-old author/ economist Alexei Izumov called the "Soviet Me Generation."[17]

In addition to improving our ability to discern and react to the spiritual vacuums created by *kairos* transitions, we must go a step further. Our consideration of the modern spiritual battlefield must also take into account the demonic principalities arrayed against us.

In his introduction to *The Screwtape Letters*, C. S. Lewis writes: "There are two equal and opposite errors into which our race can fall about the devils. One is to disbelieve in their existence. The other is to believe, and to feel an excessive and unhealthy interest in them." The point is, there is danger in either ignoring or in fondling evil spirits. Our tendency to gravitate toward one or the other of these extremes is often dictated by our cultural world view.

In his book *Christianity with Power*, Christian anthropologist Chuck Kraft, currently an instructor at the Fuller Seminary's School of World Mission in Pasadena, California, observes that while "all peoples need to deal with the material world, the human world, and the spirit world, different societies choose to emphasize one or two of these areas to the exclusion of the other(s)." More specifically, Kraft points out, "[while] most of the rest of the world is primarily concerned with how to deal with the spirit and human worlds, we in the West are almost exclusively concerned with how to conquer and manipulate the material world."[18]

The practical consequence of this truth is that Westerners, including Bible-believing Christians, generally require an added emphasis on the spiritual domain in order to be brought into balance with what Kraft calls "big R" Reality. As the apostle Paul reminds us, "We are not fighting against people made of flesh and blood, but against persons without bodies—the evil rulers of the unseen world, those mighty satanic beings and great evil princes of darkness who rule this world."[19]

Demonic deceptions, offensives and strongholds are both real and sophisticated and represent a blend of unilateral initiatives against and considered responses to divine deployments. Understanding today's spiritual battlefield means negotiating our way through enemy zones of control or extraordinary influence (strongholds), and grappling with matters such as the strength and purposes of rival belief systems (such as Islam, Hinduism or materialism).

If these systems and strongholds are to be overcome, they must first be identified with precision and then engaged with steadfastness and courage. Those Christians who would approach the conflict with spiritual swagger and clichés should bear two things in mind. First, Satan and his minions have been accomplished practitioners of the art of spiritual warfare from before the foundation of the earth—in other words, long before any of us were even familiar with the term.

Second, while the enemy's ultimate fate may be a sealed issue, there are no indications he will surrender peacefully. Kraft draws attention to the fact that in the eleven months between D-Day (when the Allies invaded Europe) and VE-Day (Victory-in-Europe Day when the Germans finally surrendered), more casualties were reported in the European theater than had been tallied in the entire war up to that point. This, despite the fact that during this period there was no doubt as to who would ultimately win.[20]

Understanding God's Ways

The early Christians, living among eastern Mediterranean populations comprising essentially Jews and pagans, were called by the latter the "third race," a name that they eventually adopted themselves. As Herbert Schlossberg notes in *Idols for Destruction*, as long as they did not think of themselves as belonging to one branch or other of this dual world, they could truly be Christian.[21] What made the Christians extraordinary, however, was not simply their nonconformity, but the fact that they alone truly understood God's ways.

When we talk about understanding God's ways we are referring to the methods He employs to accomplish His will on earth and to what motivates Him in His interactions with mankind. Whatever measure of ministry success we as His people hope to experience, then, must be related to our ability to recognize and appropriate divine thoughts, principles and tools.

Ministry failures, when they occur, are not the result of any diminished capacity on God's part, but are a reflection of the fact that from God's divine perspective it may not be expedient or to His glory to do many things He is *able* to do. In the words of the late John Wright Follette, "It is not always a question: 'Is God able?' but, 'Is it God's will and purpose?' "[22] One of God's ways is obedience, and even though we may be armed with an accurate understanding of the times and our current field of conflict, we cannot afford to march into battle on our own orders.

Given the certainty that God can do anything, our task becomes one of discovering what He *wants* to do. Fortunately, while the Bible reveals that knowledge will increase in the last days, it nowhere suggests that this knowledge will be the exclusive domain of unbelievers. In fact, Joel 2 affirms God's intent to release unique understanding and power to, and through, His people during this time.

When this power and understanding are coupled to personal obedience, the Church truly becomes a force to be reckoned with. But what of our weapons? Certainly those employed by the armies of the world, whether nuclear or conventional, are of little use against either human sinfulness or spiritual powers. Keeping in mind that the ultimate objective of spiritual warfare is the liberation of hearts and minds held captive through sin, the weapons we carry are those of truth, love, martyrdom and the blood of Christ. These, as British author Roger Forster reminds us, "do not destroy by violence, but by revealing the depravity and ugliness of evil for what it is."[23]

As we endeavor to monitor today's horizons for signs of *kairos* and approaching discontinuity, current developments are affording us few opportunities for coffee breaks. Unexpected surprises, profound challenges and exciting new possibilities are appearing everywhere. We are in a meteor shower of change.

While it is unsettling to have our familiar vistas and routines suddenly turned upside-down, it is helpful to remember that change both destroys *and* creates. Its primary agent, crisis, offers us not only a terminus but also a birthplace.

It has been said that responsible Christian living is not easy. And as subsequent chapters will show, the challenge today is perhaps greater than ever before. Marcus Dods, as an old man, said: "I do not envy those who have to fight the battle of Christianity in the twentieth century." Then, after a moment, he added, "Yes, perhaps I do, but it will be a stiff fight."[24]

Now that the people of God have once again reached the perimeter of the Promised Land—the inheritance of the nations promised in Psalm 2:8—a phalanx of formidable spiritual giants has emerged to bar the way. From all appearances, Mr. Dods' predicted "stiff fight" is about to become reality. The '90s have emerged as a decade of unprecedented—and perhaps prophetic—opportunity and conflict for the Church of Jesus Christ. As we will see in the next chapter, it was the '80s that paved the way for this decisive hour by dramatically rearranging the world's familiar political and spiritual landscapes.

Notes

1 Marvin Cetron and Thomas O'Toole, *Encounters with the Future: A Forecast of Life into the 21st Century* (New York: McGraw-Hill, 1982), p. 105.

2 Arthur C. Clarke, *Profiles of the Future* (New York: Warner Books, 1984), p. ix. Note: If a new NASA-Defense Department project stays on line, Americans who marveled 85 years ago at the Wright brothers' flights of fancy on the dunes of Kitty Hawk will shortly witness the maiden flight of an aerospace plane capable of flying up to twelve times the speed of sound. "Travelers will be whisked in two hours or less from an airport runway on one continent to another halfway around the world. Space 'commuters' will fly from the runway directly into orbit, work in space, and then return for a conventional airport landing" [see "The Aero-Space Plane," *The Futurist*, May-June 1988, p. 47]. At the same time, a new communications network, "Skynet 2000," is soon expected to link satellites, lasers and computers in such a way as to make it possible to communicate internationally via pocket telephones and personal TV sets [see Charles Gould and C. R. Gerber, "Skynet 2000" in *Careers Tomorrow* (World Future Society, 1983), pp. 137–142].

In the field of medical research, a team at the Johns Hopkins School of Medicine in Baltimore has achieved a breakthrough recently that, while promising benefits for victims of Alzheimer's disease, strokes or head injuries, also conjures up memories of a B-movie science-fiction horror plot. In the spring of 1990, Dr. Solomon Snyder announced that, for the first time ever, a continuous culture had been developed of human brain cells that divide and multiply in laboratory dishes. Across the country, University of California at Irvine scientists have managed to create sensations of nonexistent odors in animals by feeding signals into their brains. In 1988 Dr. Gary Lynch told the annual meeting of the American Physical Society that advanced versions of the technique could make humans learn faster by pumping information directly into the brain. An alternative application might produce detailed artificial memories, such as a day in Paris or "a night with the lover of your dreams."

As if we were not having enough trouble these days distinguishing the real from the phony, futurists and technicians inform us excitedly that we are on the verge of major breakthroughs in a field known as *cyberspace*, or (oxymoronically) *artificial reality*. Corporate and government scientists are competing to perfect today's systems that allow users to enter an artificial world by wearing special "computerized" clothing. Innovative software programs linked to special gloves and goggles permit budding surgeons, golfers and jet pilots to perfect their craft without losing blood or reputation. Soon architects will be able to "walk" clients into buildings that are yet to be built, and proceed to make desired modifications right on the spot. Other futurists think virtual reality will eventually let people take on (temporarily, at least) other identities. "Right now, the technology is disappointing," comments author Howard Rheingold, "but in ten years, it will change the world."

While artificial reality would seem to be the ultimate performance by modern-day computer wizards, now some analysts are predicting that human and artificial intelligence will form a "partnership to super intelligence" [see Derek Partridge, "Social Implications of Artificial Intelligence" in *Artificial Intelligence: Principles and Applications* (New York: Chapman and Hall, 1986)]. And as humans find ways to expand their global knowledge in the 1990s, the rigor and depth of machines is becoming downright formidable. In 1990, AT&T unveiled the world's first optical microprocessor, a technological breakthrough that could increase the capabilities of computers and telephone networks by at least 10,000 times over current levels. Not to be outdone, IBM scientists announced recently that they have succeeded in manipulating single atoms—a development that could lead eventually to ultraminiaturized electronic components and supercomputer performance out of desktop machines.

3 Dr. Robert Hilliard, quoted in *Future Shock* (New York: Random House, 1970), p. 157.

4 Dr. Vartan Gregorian interviewed on Bill Moyers' "World of Ideas," November 15, 1988.

5 Bell Laboratories report quoted on "World of Ideas," November 15, 1988.

6 Daniel 12:4 (KJV).

7 Robert Lacey, *The Kingdom—Arabia & the House of Sa'ud* (New York: Harcourt Brace Jovanovich, 1981), p. 521.

8 Dr. Francis Schaeffer, *Genesis in Space and Time* (Downers Grove, Ill.: InterVarsity Press, 1972), p. 48.

9 Matthew 5:14 (NASB).
Note: When earth's first family failed in their initial responsibility, God eventually established a new instrument of revelatory leadership. Israel, the fulfillment of God's covenant with Abraham, was to be lifted up as "a standard for the nations" in an essentially pagan world (Isaiah 11:12, NASB). When Israel also failed, Jesus turned to His disciples—the early Church—as a final option.

10 Ray Allen, *The Washington Report*, Vol. VI, No. 4, April 1988.

11 Daniel 2:21–22.

12 Genesis 41:34 (NASB).

13 *Theological Dictionary of the Old Testament*, Vol. II, ed. Botterweck and Ringgren (Grand Rapids, Mich.: Eerdmans, 1975), pp. 99–107.

14 Lawrence Gay, "Idea of Going Home to Failing Economy Fills Troops with Fear," *The Seattle Times*, November 17, 1990.

15 *World Press Review*, June 1989.

16 *Ibid.*, October 1989.

17 *Newsweek*, December 4, 1989.

18 Charles Kraft, *Christianity with Power* (Ann Arbor, Mich.: Vine Books, 1989), p. 87.

19 Ephesians 6:12 (LB).

20 Kraft, p. 172.

21 Herbert Schlossberg, *Idols for Destruction* (Nashville: Thomas Nelson, 1983), p. 329.

22 John Wright Follette, *This Wonderful Venture Called Christian Living* (Asheville, N.C.: Follette Books, 1974), p. 63.

23 Roger Forster and V. Paul Marston, *God's Strategy in Human History* (Wheaton, Ill.: Tyndale, 1974), p. 21.

24 Marcus Dods, quoted by Harry E. Fosdick, in *Christianity and Progress*, p. 48.

2

The Decade of Transition

We could not have planned this [Czechoslovakia's democratic revolution]. We had help from above.
Vaclav Havel, Czechoslovakia's first
post-Communist-era president[1]

"For out of the serpent's roots will come forth a viper,
and its offspring will be a fiery flying serpent."
Isaiah 14:29

In the momentous year of 1979, three seemingly unrelated events placed their bloody fingerprints on the pages of
history: the rise of Iraqi strongman Saddam Hussein, the return of
Ayatollah Khomeini to Iran and, in the final week of December,
the Soviet invasion of Afghanistan. Taken separately, each of these
events would spawn its own unimaginable violence. Together they
would coalesce to usher in the Decade of Transition—and a new
set of spiritual realities.

The Soviet military intervention in Afghanistan, more than any
other single event of the past decade, served to hasten the current
social and economic unraveling of the Soviet empire and Communist system. The first sign of this came in 1980 when riots broke
out in the Soviet provincial capital of Alma-Ata over an attempt by
authorities to bury a slain Soviet Muslim army officer in a cemetery
reserved for Soviet war heroes. Sending Muslims to kill fellow

Muslims in a dubious war was bad enough, but burying a Muslim next to atheists would rob him of his only genuine reward— paradise![2]

As the war effort progressed from months to years, the ominous shadows of popular discontent and economic debt lengthened considerably. This growing disillusionment with the war was reflected in a survey conducted by Radio Liberty, which found that only one-quarter of those polled approved of Soviet policy.[3] Many citizens, particularly in the U.S.S.R.'s Muslim republics, lost faith in the Communist leadership altogether. "They are souls lost in a sea of doubt," remarked a student at the Mir-Arab Islamic seminary in Bukhara. "They have just discovered that man-made beliefs could also be destroyed by men."[4]

Economically the war was a disaster. In addition to triggering a steep rise in the rate of inflation, the conflict also led to a quadrupling of Soviet national debt. Annual budget deficits grew an astonishing 767 percent between 1979 and 1989. In his samizdat writings from the city of Gorky in the early 1980s, the late Nobel Peace Prizewinner Andrei Sakharov blamed the Afghanistan debacle frequently for what he termed "the general upsetting of the world equilibrium."[5]

In 1960, Soviet Premier Nikita Khrushchev predicted that within two decades—or by the year 1980—the building of socialism would be completed and the era of Communism would be ushered in.[6] Instead, with the full escalation of the war in Afghanistan, 1980 gave birth to the decade in which world Communism would go into severe convulsions. In March 1990, CIA director William Webster, in a rare appearance on Capitol Hill, declared that "Communist parties and Marxist doctrines are collapsing or already lie in ruins."[7]

But if Communism was indeed descending from its lofty heights, the Western world, including both church and state, found little time to celebrate. New concerns now occupied the thoughts of global-minded politicians, businessmen, journalists and missionaries. Out of the seething cauldron of Central Asia, an old force, Islam, was demonstrating a new and formidable muscularity. Even before the Soviet decision to withdraw from Afghanistan in 1988—

which most Muslims did not hesitate to see as a defeat for Russia and a triumph for Islam—regional leaders like Saddam Hussein, Gulbuddin Hekmytar, Zia ul-Haq and, most of all, Iran's militant ayatollahs, were inciting Muslims to stand up and be counted.

The results were explosive. As one European publication put it, "In 1914, 1939, or 1970 it did not much matter what was thought in the bazaars of Persia or Algeria—let alone Yemen or Kuwait. Today it is crucial."[8] By 1989 religious zeal had become king, and the transition out of the sterile Marxist-atheist era was virtually complete.

While we will shortly have an "up-close and personal" introduction to Islam and several other spiritual superpowers that emerged in the wake of Communism's indecorous demise, it is worth taking a few moments beforehand to appreciate the forces at work behind the scenes during the recent Decade of Transition. For despite all its technological innovation, bald greed and hypnotic fanaticism, the reign of the '80s will ultimately be remembered by historians as the decade in which the Red Storm rose up—in Eastern Europe and beyond—and blew its own house down.

Intercessory Prayer, the Tripwire of Change

To understand how recent events in Eastern Europe came about requires a quick journey back to the future—or, more specifically, to the book of Revelation. Here, in the pages of John's remarkable end-time vision, we are afforded, perhaps more clearly than anywhere else in Scripture, a glimpse into the mysterious relationship between intercessory prayer and *kairos* events.

We read, for instance, of "golden vials" that are used in heaven to collect the prayers of the saints.[9] In some profound and intricate way, the tears, travail and fastings of God's faithful are transformed upon their arrival in the spiritual dimension into pleasant and compelling odors; and as Revelation 8:1–6 suggests, the overflow of these receptacles represents the tripwire of change.

> When He broke the seventh seal, there was silence in heaven for about half an hour. And I saw the seven angels who stand before

God; and seven trumpets were given to them. And another angel came and stood at the altar, holding a golden censer: and much incense was given to him, that he might add it to the prayers of all the saints upon the golden altar which was before the throne. And the smoke of the incense, with the prayers of the saints, went up before God out of the angel's hand. And the angel took the censer; and he filled it with the fire of the altar and threw it to the earth; and there followed peals of thunder and sounds and flashes of lightning and an earthquake. And the seven angels who had the seven trumpets prepared themselves to sound them.

In a response to this remarkable passage, Walter Wink writes:

> Heaven itself falls silent. The heavenly hosts and celestial spheres suspend their ceaseless singing so that the prayers of the saints on earth can be heard. The seven angels of destiny cannot blow the signal of the next times to be until an eighth angel gathers these prayers . . . and mingles them with incense upon the altar. Silently they rise to the nostrils of God.
>
> Human beings have intervened in the heavenly liturgy. The uninterrupted flow of consequences is dammed for a moment. New alternatives become feasible. The unexpected becomes suddenly possible, because God's people on earth have invoked heaven, the home of the possibles, and have been heard. What happens next, happens because people prayed. The message is clear: History belongs to the intercessors.[10]

A good example of how this process works on the human stage was on display recently in Czechoslovakia, a reborn nation where God is credited with playing a decisive role in the disintegration of Communism. Longsuffering Czech Christians refer to emerging evidence that the Soviet KGB was secretly, and astonishingly, working alongside the Czech public in their efforts to bring down the hard-line regime of Gustav Husak. Milan Hulik, an investigator for the Czechoslovak parliamentary commission probing the plot, told the BBC, "All the facts point to KGB connivance. We cannot reach any conclusion other than the whole affair had been given the blessing of the Soviet political leadership."[11] Local Christians also believe that the mild winter of 1988–1989 was an act of God that made it possible for hundreds of thousands of people to get out and participate in public demonstrations.

The Kremlin Plague

Most observers agree that, despite his problems at home, Soviet President Mikhail Gorbachev was the individual most responsible for the cavalcade of change during the Decade of Transition. What is not so widely known is the story of his positioning for this historic role.

In fact, the *kairos* implications of this development hung thickly in the air. As *U.S. News & World Report* declared back in 1987, "He [Gorbachev] got to the top almost miraculously."[12] With so many intercessors having petitioned God faithfully with respect to the burden of Communism, the circumstances were reminiscent of the Israelites' cries to Jehovah during the Egyptian captivity. In both instances, the heavenly vials of human intercession over-flowed before the throne of God and the Almighty responded by "removing and raising up kings."[13]

Unfortunately, like their predecessor Pharaoh, the hard-line members of the Soviet Politburo had no intention of acknowledging God's power or authority. Thus, in the waning days of 1980, a veritable plague descended upon the Kremlin. Beginning with the death of Soviet Premier Alexei Kosygin the week before Christmas, top Communist Party officials soon became something of an endangered species. Next on the list was long-time Party boss Leonid Brezhnev, who died in November 1982. Two months later, he was followed to the grave by Soviet President Nikolai Podgorny. When the Kremlin old guard persisted in their deceit, atheism and repression, the shadow of death returned to Moscow in February 1984 claiming the life of Party chairman and former KGB head Yuri Andropov. In December it enveloped hard-line Defense Minister and Politburo member Dimitri Ustinov.

The Politburo's stubbornness was eventually broken when, three months after the death of Ustinov, yet another Party chairman, Konstantin Chernenko, gave up the ghost. Embarrassed by the perpetual parade of state funerals, the ruling hierarchy tapped a relative newcomer, Mikhail Gorbachev, to lead the country. With that, the dying stopped. Now that God finally had His man, the Angel of Death was invited to sheath his well-worn sword.

With a Great Fall:
The Miracle of Eastern Europe

In Bratislava, Czechoslovakia's industrial capital on the Danube, 68-year-old Ilonka, a Catholic nun since she was a girl, bustled about her basement apartment preparing supper. Her brisk movements offered no hint of the ten years of forced labor she had undergone for refusing to renounce her vows during the Stalinist 1950s.

As the other nuns gathered around the richly laid table and bowed their heads to pray, one of them looked up and with a puzzled expression asked: "Should we close the windows before we sing?" Sister Ilonka leaned her head back and started to laugh heartily. "Leave them open," she said. "The Communists are gone."[14]

Gone, yes. But one might be surprised to find out just *where* they have gone. In the case of the 55-year-old son of former Soviet leader Nikita Khrushchev—who in the early 1960s declared to the Western world, "We will bury you"—it was to Harvard University, where he spent the fall of 1990 teaching a seminar. In the months leading up to East Germany's reunification with the West, deposed Party boss Erich Honecker, whose hard-line Communist regime had harassed Christian believers for years, suddenly found himself declared homeless by the state and, in an ironic twist of fate, taken in by a Lutheran family.[15]

It has been said that hope is the oxygen of life—remove it, and people will suffocate in despair. For East Europeans living during the Stalinist era, that almost happened. And more than anything else, it was the memory of those soul-quenching years that prompted the unbridled displays of emotion that emerged during the heady days of 1988–1990. Certainly the more than 100,000 Czechoslovaks, many waving American flags, will never forget the

November night in 1990 when they joined President George Bush on Wenceslas Square to sing "We Shall Overcome" in commemoration of the first anniversary of their successful revolution against Communist tyranny.

Nor will an estimated one million East and West Germans soon forget the moment when they joined their voices in an emotion-laden chorus of the national anthem to celebrate the reunification of their country some 45 years after it was split up as a spoil of World War II. Awash in floodlights and fireworks, delirious throngs of celebrants danced through the night under Berlin's once-again-historic Brandenburg Gate.

Across Eastern Europe images of Communist power continue to be chiseled away. In Bucharest, Romania, several hundred citizens cheered recently as workers felled a seven-ton statue of Lenin that dominated a huge plaza in the capital. It took two days and an army of jackhammers before the symbol of the man who for decades was a virtual deity was finally brought down, suggestively, by a huge crane with a noose.

Similar demolitions have taken place in Bulgaria where, one by one, venerated Communist symbols have been shed. Gone is a large red star that shone from the top of Party headquarters; and from the square mausoleum near the Socialist building, gone, too, are the ashes of Georgi Dimitrov, the country's first leader after the 1940s Communist takeover.[16] In Banska Stavnica, Czechoslovakia, the platform in the middle of the town that once upheld an enormous bronze head of Lenin now stands empty. The head, like many other hammer-and-sickle icons and Stalinist statues, now lies forgotten in a forest that students call "The Village of the Ridiculous."[17]

Furthermore, just to prove that in Eastern Europe nothing is sacred anymore, several of the new democratically fueled governments have determined that the names of their countries could also stand refurbishing. Thus, in 1989, Hungary and Poland dropped the word *People's* to become, simply, the Republic of Hungary and Republic of Poland. In January 1990, Czechoslovakian President Vaclav Havel proposed dropping the word *Socialist* from his country's formal name. Even the Soviets are warming to the idea and have proposed the "Union of Soviet Sovereign Republics" as an alternative to the familiar U.S.S.R.[18]

Without question it is religion that has energized the transformation of Eastern Europe and, to a lesser extent, the U.S.S.R.—a reality that would have left Karl Marx dumfounded. Marx saw religion as a convenient escape from the world's misery. It is, he wrote, "the sigh of the distressed creature . . . the opium of the people."[19] In practice, however, Marx's feared opiate has become more like a selective multivitamin. "Our atheists were like snow in the spring," mused Father Stanislovas, a Capuchin monk in the Lithuanian village of Paberze, "they melted away."[20]

The New Spiritual Superpowers

As the spiritual balance of power in the world shifted steadily away from Marxist-atheism in the 1980s, it became increasingly clear that a new order of powerful competitors was vying for pre-eminence.

None of these challengers was new in the sense of not having any previous influence in the world. To the contrary, all three of these new spiritual superpowers—Islam, Hinduism and materialism—had long rap sheets extending all the way back to the beginning of recorded history. What *was* new was the arrogance and seeming sudden muscularity promenaded by these systems.

Hinduism

For its part, Hinduism over the last 25 years has shown increasing signs of shedding the passive teachings of Mahatma Gandhi in favor of an increasingly militant posture. Not long ago, Baikunth Lal Sharma, general secretary of the one-million-member Vishwa Hindu Parishad (VHP) organization, declared to the press: "Our tolerance has been taken as weakness. It is high time we show that Hindus aren't weak."

To prove their point, VHP's youth wing is trained in Indian martial arts, as well as judo and karate. "If someone challenges us we will not spare him," warns Sharma.[21] Other right-wing Hindu political parties and movements, like "Shivaji's Army," display open sympathy with Nazi ideology. At rallies and marches across the Indian subcontinent, fundamentalists scream with fervor, "Be a Hindu, or get out of India!"

India's Christians, many of whom have felt the wrath of this new zealotry, say that the Hindu leadership resents Christianity's growing popularity in certain sectors of the country and have, accordingly, launched their own counter-missions. The VHP's re-conversion program is called "Operation Homecoming," and their monthly *Hindu Vishva* is replete with reports on reconversions to Hinduism from Christian and Muslim communities in India.[22] The program, which began several years ago, was linked to a nation-wide revivalist goal to reconvert 100,000 people by 1990.

Christian Mission magazine reported recently that the well-known Swami Lakhman has begun traveling throughout India in an attempt to reconvert 50,000 Christians who once were Hindus. In his motorcade, he carries with him the statue of the Hindu god Jagannath, which means "God of the World." Indians who do not bow before the idol are harassed or attacked by Hindus. Lakhman also reportedly encourages local Hindus to destroy Christian churches. Whether or not this is true, after the Swami's crusade in one area, fifteen church meeting places were heavily damaged, and at two locations in the Daringabidi region bombs were deto-nated outside sanctuaries.[23]

In 1989, police in Nepal beat the pastor of a village church before dragging several of his parishioners to a Hindu temple where they were forced to bow before idols.[24] A decade earlier, in the fateful year of 1979, thousands of Hindus from around the world gathered at Allahabad, one of India's major holy cities on the Ganges River in northern India. The meeting was convened by the VHP—an organization described by one Eastern cult special-ist as the Hindu equivalent of Christianity's World Evangelical Fellowship. *Update*, a quarterly journal on new religious move-ments, quotes a speaker at the Allahabad World Congress on Hinduism as saying, "Our mission in the West has been crowned with fantastic success. Hinduism is now becoming the decisive world religion, and the end of Christianity has come near. Within another generation there will be only two religions in the world, Islam and Hinduism."[25]

While this prediction appears overly optimistic, it is true that since the 1960s India-based organizations have been engaged in the large-scale export of Hindu spirituality. Cashing in on the disillusionment of the Western mind, scores of gurus—including such luminaries as the Maharishi Mahesh Yogi of transcendental meditation fame, Swami Prabhupada of the Hare Krishna movement, and Baba Muktananda—have influenced millions. The New Age movement, Hinduism's most recent incursion into Western society, is still gaining momentum.

In 1990 trade publications in the United States reported that 450 acres in central Florida, recently purchased for $20 million, will serve as the site of a new theme park called *Vedaland*. (The Vedas are Hindu scriptures.)[26] Linked to Indian spiritual leader Maharishi Mahesh Yogi and magician Doug Henning, the new park, if it comes off, will be based on the theme of transcendental meditation. Similar parks are said to be planned for the Netherlands, Brazil, Canada and Japan.

Materialism

Though it is not often thought of as a spiritual system or philosophy, and is certainly less structured than identifiable religions like Hinduism or Christianity, materialism nevertheless represents one of the most powerful controllers of human thought and behavior in the world today. That its dangers are not perceived by Westerners to the extent that they are by inhabitants of the two-thirds world (second- and third-world countries) is explained by the fact that Westerners are largely ensconced in its trappings.

In actuality, materialism is accompanied by a full complement of religious symbols if one is prepared to see them. There are "holy places" such as Beverly Hills, Paris and Monte Carlo where the rites of materialists are pursued just as intentionally as those performed by Christian faithful in Rome or Muslims in Mecca. Lesser shrines, in the form of shopping malls, nightclubs and resorts, can be found almost anywhere in the Western world. Furthermore, the idols worshiped by materialists easily rival the pantheons found in the animist or Hindu worlds. British journalist William Rees-Mogg asks: "Who can deny that the New York of Donald Trump is a modern Vanity Fair where the towering temples are dedicated to the great god Mammon? As an idea," Rees-Mogg continues, "this materialism . . . is a form of idolatry, a breach of the first commandment, 'Thou shalt have no other gods before me.' It was the leading idolatry of ancient Rome as much as it is of modern New York."[27]

As a new spiritual superpower, materialism roared to life in the Decade of Transition on the back of a new creed: *greed.* In its retrospective on the '80s, *People* magazine splashed across its cover: *Ready, set, go-for-it! From greed to glasnost, brash was beautiful & the only sin was not to win.* Incarnating this philosophy on film, actor Michael Douglas (who portrays the ruthless speculator Gordon Gekko in the movie *Wall Street*) declares to the Teldar stockholders: "The point is, ladies and gentlemen, that greed, for lack of a better word, is good. Greed is right. Greed works. Greed clarifies, cuts through and captures the essence of the evolutionary spirit. Greed, in all of its forms. Greed for life—for money, for love, for knowledge—has marked the upward surge of mankind."[28]

Just fantasy? To attract students, colleges in the U.S. are now taking pains to advertise the fact that every dorm is outfitted with VCRs and MTV, microwave ovens, tanning beds and phone service food delivery. Even this, however, is not always enough—at least it wasn't for some students at Ohio State University who, in 1989, demonstrated because there were not enough brands in condom-dispensing machines on campus.[29]

One of the primary rites of materialism—consumerism—is vigorously promoted through the system's chief valuesmith, television. Advertisers, the gurus of consumerism, speak about how they are only fulfilling needs by providing information about where and how people can achieve satisfaction for their needs. But as former advertising executive Jerry Mander observes, "If we take the word 'need' to mean something basic to human survival—food, shelter, clothing—or basic human contentment—peace, love, safety, companionship, intimacy, a sense of fulfillment—these will be sought and found by people whether or not there is advertising. In fact, advertising intervenes between people and their needs, separates them from direct fulfillment and urges them to believe that satisfaction can be obtained only through commodities."[30]

"Nothing," the advertisers say, "makes you feel as good as gold." Diamond jewelry must be purchased to satisfy "a woman's craving for elegance." Loreal's Preference hair coloring might cost a bit more, but, the actress coos, "I'm worth it." Alcohol, automobile and especially clothing advertisers consistently sell the attractiveness of a lifestyle rather than the functions of a product. Thus, flamboyant tennis pro Andre Agassi is employed to persuade his essentially younger audiences that "image is everything." How far has it gone? Seattle's local news station KOMO reported in October 1990 that it is now possible to purchase outfits, cologne and even Dom Perignon—for your dog.

In its monthly publication *Investment in Tomorrow*, Stanford Research Institute catalogs new areas where human feeling can be converted into needs. Jerry Mander reports that "one SRI category of market opportunity was particularly poignant: 'self-discovery and inner exploration.' Now," he says, "we are so outwardly focused that inner experience has itself entered the realm of scarcity, making it packageable and capable of being sold back to us as a commodity. Our inner lives are now promotable as products. We get to buy back what we already had."[31]

Given the staggering abundance of Western materialistic culture, the incidence of unfulfillment is telling. Tocqueville spoke of "the strange melancholy often haunting inhabitants of democracies in the midst of abundance."[32] Why? In this modern day, the answer has much to do with the fact that we are inundated with so many media images of appetites gratified that we mistakenly assume, in the words of Ronald Berman, that "we are now not alone entitled to the pursuit of happiness, but to its actual capture."[33]

The essence of materialism—and its great lie—is that man must live for his own sake. Rather than embracing happiness as the byproduct of obedience to God, the achievement of his own happiness becomes the highest moral purpose. In this process of striving to find, or make, one's own happiness, *things* take on great importance. Their role, in the religion of materialism, is to provide those who possess them with a sense of control over their physical surroundings. "They are the things that can be seen," writes Charles Kraft, "and [thus be] used to gauge our superiority over others in the race to get even more goodies."[34]

Whereas, for the Puritans, "a godly man worked diligently at his calling not so much in order to accumulate personal wealth as to add to the comfort and convenience of the community—because 'God hath made man a Sociable Creature.'"[35] Relationships today are maintained only for as long as they can be mined successfully for personal benefit. Altruism and *agape* love are throwbacks to an earlier age. "Just as life is an end in itself," declared the late materialist savant Ayn Rand, "so every living human being is an end in himself, not the means to the ends or the welfare of others."[36]

Thus, the amorality displayed in a CBS "60 Minutes" episode about a deadly, taxpayer-supported drug "shooting gallery" located in a park adjacent to wealthy Swiss banks in Zurich should come as no surprise.[37] Nor should the message contained in a political cartoon published recently in the Orlando *Sentinel*, which showed a Communist Chinese official standing in a square strewn with crushed bicycles and bodies. Addressing a Western businessman, he says: "We have lifted martial law." To which the businessman replies: "And a humane action that was, sir. Now, can I interest you in some new bicycles?" In the religion of materialism, the conscience must frequently be sacrificed on the altar of expediency.

At the end of the twentieth century, materialism has become a clear and present danger—and not just in the U.S., Japan and Western Europe. The Decade of Transition has seen the sermon of comfort-through-consumption spread around the world. Deliveries to the two-thirds world have succeeded because, while citizens of Indonesia, Brazil, Saudi Arabia and the Soviet Union can see materialism's faults, many cannot resist its lures. Echoing this thought, social columnist Liz Smith conjectured in a recent interview with CBS newswoman Connie Chung that "maybe wretched excess, through the miracle of television, is what made some of these Communist countries decide they want to be capitalist, too."

Perhaps the biggest concern of all, however, is that materialism has worked its way past the moral and theological sentries of the Christian Church. In many circles, style has now replaced substance, financial or numerical success is confused with spiritual anointing, and "servant" ministers are willing to sell their services for "ten shekels and a shirt." Churches are increasingly evaluated for the efficiency of their parking procedures, and psalmists and worship leaders are being replaced on the platform by Jesus Christ's superstars.

"For all their fierce reputation," writes Gary Kinnaman, "lions rely on their subtlety as much as their strength . . . [and] like a lion, Satan is looking for unsuspecting victims."[38]

The prophet Amos put it this way:

> Woe to you who are complacent in Zion. . . . You lie on beds inlaid with ivory and lounge on your couches. You dine on choice lambs and fattened calves. . . . Therefore you will be among the first to go into exile; your feasting and lounging will end.
>
> Amos 6:1, 4, 7 (NIV)

If, with their chameleon-like natures, materialism and Hinduism represent more insidious threats to the mission of the Church, Islam is a no-nonsense locomotive. Rather than relying on subtlety, the religion of Muhammad stalks its objectives through relentless force. Of all the spiritual superpowers facing the Church at the end of the twentieth century, the strongest, and certainly the most visible, of these is Islam.

Notes

1 IICS Update, "Eastern Europe Welcomes IICS," summer 1990.
2 Amir Taheri, *Crescent in a Red Sky: The Future of Islam in the Soviet Union* (London: Hutchinson & Co., 1989), p. xiv.
3 Taras Kuzio, "Opposition in the USSR to the Occupation of Afghanistan," *Central Asian Survey*, Vol. 6, No. 1, 1987, p. 100.
4 Taheri, p. x.
5 Kuzio, p. 105.

6 Taheri, p. 207.

7 "CIA Director: Soviet Threat Fades," *The Seattle Times*, March 2, 1990.

8 Special Office Brief, Moreton in Marsh, England.

9 Revelation 5:8.

10 Walter Wink, "History Belongs to the Intercessors," *Sojourners*, October 1990.

11 "Did KGB Engineer Fall of Czech Communists?" *The Seattle Times*, May 31, 1990.

12 Henry Trewhitt, "The Risks of a New Revolution," *U.S. News & World Report*, October 19, 1987.

13 See Daniel 2:21 and Job 12:19.

14 "This Year Spring Blossoms in Czechoslovakia," *The Seattle Times*, June 3, 1990.

15 Even these stories, however, do not fully illustrate how far the mighty have fallen. In Czechoslovakia, just six months after Soviet tanks began rolling out, the citizens of Prague cheered as the Rolling Stones came in. As close to 100,000 people listened to the sweaty rhythms of the West, a gigantic red tongue in a huge mouth—the Stones' traditional logo—appeared atop a hill where a statue of Soviet dictator Josef Stalin once stood. Humor has also been employed to demonstrate the profound changes that Mikhail Gorbachev has unleashed in Eastern Europe. During the Khrushchev and Brezhnev regimes, Soviet domination over the region was tested by a series of popular revolts in East Germany, Hungary, Czechoslovakia and Poland. Each uprising was ruthlessly suppressed. Publicly, the Soviet Union justified its right to interfere in Eastern Europe by what became known in the West as the "Brezhnev Doctrine." In a recent session with Western reporters, however, Soviet spokesman Gennadi Gerasimov said that Moscow had now adopted the "Frank Sinatra Doctrine." Every country should be able to say, "I do it my way" ("A New Order Emerges in East Europe," *The Seattle Times*, November 12, 1989).

16 "For Bulgarians, a Soviet Day Is Largely a Day to Be Ignored," *The New York Times*, November 8, 1990.

17 "This Year Spring Blossoms in Czechoslovakia," *The Seattle Times*, June 3, 1990.

18 "USSR May Drop 'Socialist' from Its Name," *The Seattle Times*, September 9, 1990; March 17, 1991.

19 Karl Marx, quoted in *Karl Marx on Religion* (S. K. Padover, 1974), p. xx.

20 Priit J. Vesilind, "The Baltic Nations," *National Geographic*, November 1990. Note: As a consequence, the monthly *Nauka i Religia* (Science & Religion), launched more than forty years ago as a quasi-official journal of "scientific atheism," has transformed itself into a thoughtful journal about religion and culture in the U.S.S.R. and abroad—a change that editor Karen Melik-Simonian asserts has, in a short period, more than doubled the publication's circulation (Harvey Cox, "The Cross and the Kremlin II," *World Monitor*, December 1989, p. 57). At the same time, the director of Lvov's Museum of Religion and Atheism is putting away his mocking exhibits of Catholic inquisitors and raving Pentecostals, and soliciting advice from local religious leaders on how best to present an objective history of faith ("Museum of Atheism Exorcises Its Tortured View of Religion," *The Independent*, August 31, 1989).

21 "From Moksha to Militancy," *Asiaweek*, July 15, 1988.

22 C. V. Matthew, *Neo-Hinduism: A Missionary Religion* (Madras, India: Church Growth Research Center, 1987), p. 45.

23 In an apparently unrelated incident in April 1989, Hindu demonstrators burned and bombed 22 churches and several Christian schools in Nowrangpur (*Christian Mission*, September/October 1989 and March/April 1988).

24 Herbert Schlossberg, *A Fragrance of Oppression: The Church and Its Persecutors* (Westchester, Ill.: Crossway, 1991).

25 C. V. Matthew, p. 6.

26 The Vedas are Hindu scriptures encompassing such works as the Bagavadgita and the Upanishads.

27 William Rees-Mogg, *The Independent*, June 11, 1990.

28 Later on, in a conversation with his young sidekick, Charlie Sheen, Douglas adds: "It's all about bucks, kid, the rest is conversation."

29 Bob Fryling report at InterVarsity Planning Conference.

30 Jerry Mander, *Four Arguments for the Elimination of Television* (New York: Quill Books, 1978), p. 127.

31 *Ibid.*, p. 130.

32 Alexis de Tocqueville, "Why the Americans Are So Restless in the Midst of Their Prosperity," *Democracy in America*, eds. J. Meyer and A. Kerr (New York: Doubleday, 1969).

33 Ronald Berman, "Feeling Unfree," *On Freedom*, ed. Dr. John Howard (The Rockford Institute, 1984), p. 100.

34 Charles Kraft, *Christianity with Power* (Ann Arbor, Mich.: Vine Books, 1989), p. 29.

35 Christopher Lasch, *The Culture of Narcissism* (New York: Warner Books, 1979), p. 108.

36 Ayn Rand, *The Virtue of Selfishness* (New York: Signet Books, 1964), p. 27.

37 CBS *60 Minutes*, "Needle Park," aired June 3, 1990.

38 Gary Kinnaman, *Overcoming the Dominion of Darkness* (Tarrytown, N.Y.: Chosen Books, 1990), pp. 42–43.

3

The Strongest of These

Over the next forty years, populist Islam is going to be the most important ideological force in the world.
Professor James Bill, University of Texas[1]

The Muslims of today have heard your call, Back to Islam! Back to Qur'an! Back to Jihad and martyrdom!
From a poem entitled "O, Imam Khomeini" published on the sixth anniversary of the Islamic Republic of Iran[2]

I want to become a bomb to destroy Tel Aviv and Washington!
Jordanian youth during BBC war coverage in Amman[3]

In the century following Muhammad's death, Islam spread from Spain to India and, in the process, embraced more territory than did the Roman Empire. Now, after a period of Western colonial domination, Islam is again on the move.

As the world's fastest growing religion, Islam is predicted to double in size somewhere around the year 2020. If estimates hold up, Muslims will at that time number approximately 1.9 billion or 25 percent of humanity.[4] One Islamic researcher reckons there are some 50 million new Muslims each year, thanks to what he refers to as "massive conversion campaigns conducted in more than 120

countries by tens of thousands of missionaries and . . . an exceptionally high birth rate."[5]

In a fall 1988 article, *World Evangelization* magazine revealed
that at a recent Muslim-sponsored missions conference in Los Angeles, organizers proudly announced a goal of winning 50 to 75 million Americans to Islam. Their target, they said, were those "strata
of society suffering from the bankruptcy of the social order." Furthermore, they declared, they wanted it known that they are in North
America for the long haul, willing to invest centuries, if necessary,
to gain their objectives. As models of their persistence, they alluded
to their history of gradually becoming numerically dominant in
Egypt, North Africa and Indonesia. Today, of the cities of the pa-
tristic fathers dotting Asia Minor and North Africa (there are fifteen
with a population of one million), all are solidly Muslim.[6]

While Islam's success may be attributable in part to winning
features such as perseverance, universality and an ability to wed
religious faith with nationalist aspirations, these alone are not
sufficient to explain the growth of Islamic influence in the 1980s.
Islam is essentially a spiritual movement and, as such, it must be
spiritually defined. Behind its many laudable characteristics, such
as self-discipline and community consciousness, lies a darker
side, a side that bears witness to the presence of a deeper source
of empowerment. Throughout much of the Muslim world, the spirits of violence and divination have become familiar houseguests.

Revelations and Bewitchments:
The Mystical World of Islam

To understand Islam fully, one must first understand the times
into which it was born. Muslims themselves refer to this period—
the years prior to about 570 A.D.—as the *jahiliyya*, or the state of
ignorance. While many features of these Arabian "Dark Ages" lie
shrouded in mystery, there is no doubt that the birthplace of Islam
at the time was deeply entrenched in superstition and idolatry.[7]

This much Muslims will agree with readily. What they are not as
willing to accept is the notion that Islam has retained various as-

pects of these early pagan religions. Despite this denial, however, there is substantial evidence—observable in many contemporary Islamic symbols and practices—that this is indeed the case.

Take, for example, the *Ka'aba*, Islam's holiest shrine, which today stands in the center of the Grand Mosque in Mecca. Revered by the pagan Arabs because of the shiny black meteorite stone embedded in one of its walls, orthodox Muslims claim that the Ka'aba was God's house originally built by Adam, repaired by Abraham and restored by Muhammad. Though they decry its pre-Islamic status as the residence for some 360 idols, Muslims have nevertheless retained the whole rite of pilgrimage connected with it.[8]

Every year more than two million Muslims from around the world converge on the kingdom of Saudi Arabia for the *Hajj*, a once-in-a-lifetime pilgrimage to holy Mecca. At nearby Jeddah airport planes land every two minutes with faithful from Senegal, Pakistan, France, the Soviet Union, Indonesia, Turkey and scores of other countries where Muslims are to be found. For these pilgrims the Hajj is an opportunity to take a new name and shed their sins. One prayer said in the Grand Mosque at pilgrimage time is worth 100,000 said elsewhere.[9]

Many returned Hajjis recall the instant their lips touched the Black Stone in the hollow worn by the imprint of millions of reverent kisses down through the centuries. One of those historic kisses was planted by Muhammad Labib al Batnuni who, in the early 1900s, recorded a powerful narrative of the spiritual impact of the Ka'aba:

> The whole assembly stood there [around the Ka'aba] with the greatest reverence before this highest majesty and most powerful inspirer of awe, before which the greatest of souls becomes so little as to be almost nothing. And if we had not been witness to the movement of the body during the *salat*, the raising of the hands during the prayers, and the murmuring of the expressions of humility—and if we had not heard the beating of the hearts before this immeasurable grandeur—we would have thought ourselves transferred to another life. And, truly, we were at that hour in another world. We were in the house of God, in God's immediate presence, and all were with lowered heads and humble tongues and

voices raised in prayer, and weeping eyes and the fearful heart and
pure thoughts of intercession.[10]

Beyond the Ka'aba, the most obvious pagan symbol associated
with Islam is the ubiquitous crescent moon. Originally the symbol
of the powerful Babylonian moon god—who in pre-Islamic times
was also lord of the Ka'aba in Mecca—it was eventually adopted
by early Muslims as the logo of their fledgling religion. And as the
Babylonian calendar was fixed monthly by the new moon to honor
their supreme deity, to this day throughout Islam all months begin
with the visual observation by religious authorities of the new
moon.[11]

Yet another connection between Islam and earlier pagan cultures is found in the accounts of Muhammad's early revelations. Though philosophically opposed to the idolatry and divination that prevailed in western Arabia, there is nevertheless striking
evidence that Muhammad himself walked on the very edge of the
spirit world.

His first recorded encounter with the supernatural came in a
cave on Mount Hara. After some days of meditating alone, Muhammad related that he suddenly became aware of a "presence."
Moments later, he was caught up in a "revelation" that would
prove to be the primal spark of the Islamic religion. There are
indications that at first he thought he had been enveloped by an
evil spirit. He felt extremely cold and shivery and, shaken by
his experience, went home to his first wife, Khadija, who wrapped
him in a blanket and persuaded him that he had not been
possessed.[12]

Subsequent revelations were frequently accompanied by observable manifestations such as pain—in the words of Muhammad, "so
that we perceived it"—or sweating even on cold days. Another
scholar reports that Muhammad would "cover his head" and "snore
as one asleep, or rattle like a young camel."[13] This may well be in
reference to *velatio*, the practice of covering oneself with a garment
to encourage inspiration, which the Qur'an, in surah 73, suggests
that Muhammad did.[14]

In these and numerous other ways, Muhammad appears to have

imitated pagan priests called *kahins* (diviners) who routinely employed dreams, omens and the casting of lots both to interpret the
present and to predict the future. Like the kahins, Muhammad
frequently went into mystical trances, during which he would
speak in a rhythmic and rhyming prose—precisely the style later
manifested in the Qur'an.

Not surprisingly, this intermingling of orthodoxy and spiritism
has remained on through the centuries as a prominent feature
of the Islamic community. Today, of the world's approximately
one billion Muslims, it is estimated that some seventy percent are
practitioners of popular or "folk" Islam."[15]

As anyone who has visited the famed *Jma al Fnaa* (market
square) in Marrakech after dusk can attest, this street-level brand
of Islam can bring curious incongruities. At the same time the
haunting flutes of snake-handlers are charming their vipers for
curious onlookers, the rhythmic drumbeats of nearby Sufi Muslims
are inducing hypnotic religious trances in adepts. While squatting
female tarot card readers deal out garden-variety fortunes, turbaned Islamic scholars dispense wisdom from the Qur'an in the
surrealistic light of hissing lanterns. At virtually every turn, the
strings of classical Islam are intertwined with an elaborate web of
demons, saints, omens and amulets.

The world of folk Islam is also illustrated in the well-known story
of *Aladdin and the Wonderful Lamp*. In the tale, whenever the
fifteen-year-old Aladdin rubbed his magic lamp a genie rose from
its brass spout to do his bidding. While Aladdin and his lamp are
fable, however, not so the genie. *Genie* is the English form of *jinni*,
the Arabic word for a spirit said to be created out of smokeless
flame and possessing tremendous powers, including the ability to
appear in human or animal form.[16] Throughout the Muslim world
jinn are feared as the cause of a multitude of problems ranging
from epilepsy to barrenness. Equally varied are their dwelling
places, which, according to Bill Musk in *The Unseen Face of
Islam*, include brick kilns and rubbish pits in Iran, certain trees,
sharks and crocodiles in the Philippines, marshes, rivers and
wells in Morocco, and ruins, graveyards and toilets in Egypt. Dark
rooms and the black of night are also widely considered to be the

haunts of jinn, and elaborate precautions are taken when one is forced to enter such circumstances.[17]

Unlike classical Islam, which places authority in the hands of those who have completed both preordained courses of study and official apprenticeships, folk Islam recognizes those individuals who are able to demonstrate proven abilities to contain and/or conjure spiritual forces. Many of these mediums, exorcists and healers (such as the Zar cult found throughout Northern Africa and much of the Near East) are only nominally identified with Islam, while others (such as the *pirs* in Pakistan, *marabouts* in West Africa and *walis* in the Arab world) make a concerted effort to incorporate Qur'anic teachings into their exotic arsenals of cures, fortunes and curses.

Virtually all practitioners of folk Islam address routine challenges, such as warding off evil forces and events, through the use of amulets and charms. These range from the popular Hand of Fatima (Muhammad's daughter) to colored beads and elaborate potions. During pregnancy, amulets may be tied around the stomach to strengthen the womb. To protect their newborn from jealous curses such as the "evil eye," Pakistani women wash infants in butter and then blacken their eyes and eyebrows with coal. In many cases, a further step involves holding the Qur'an over the child while prayers are recited in Arabic.

When really serious power is required, however, pirs and marabouts will sometimes solicit the services of fallen angels. The following edited account, shared by a former Qur'anic student from West Africa, illustrates the delicate process involved:

> Demons want a sacrifice before they work for a person. To start the process, a person kills two goats, one in the morning and one in the evening. This done, he then takes out the hearts and eats them. If (through the use of signs) the fallen angel agrees to meet with the person, the latter must say the name of the angel Samharouge 7,777 times in one night. Furthermore, the person wishing to see the demon must not show fear, or he will die. The fallen angel always comes on Friday night.
>
> Arranging contracts with the demons requires another sacrifice consisting of seven colanuts, three eggs, and six balls of ashes.

When this is prepared the person goes into the bush or forest. But
since he does not know where the demon is, he repeats the greeting
"Peace be with you" until he hears an answer. Then he knows the
demon is near.

Invariably the demon will reside in a tree. Consequently, the
person will set his sacrifice/offering at the base of the tree and say:
"I have brought food for you and want to be your friend." Then,
without a human hand touching them, the colanuts and eggs will
disappear up the tree, while the ashes remain on the ground. At this
stage a contract will be established between the person and the
demon concerning both the matters and manner in which the demon
will render assistance.[18]

The influence of the marabout has even been felt in the field of
athletics. While many Western observers were amused at the sight
of "ju-ju" men traveling with Cameroon's surprisingly successful
soccer team at the 1990 World Cup Games, the activities of these
spiritualists are a great cause of concern for the Confederation of
African Football. In several African countries—Cameroon, Zaire,
Kenya, Nigeria and Ghana—football clubs have well-paid marabouts to help them win matches. Some clubs refuse to use official
dressing rooms and gates for fear that these places have been
hexed, and it is not unusual for contests to end prematurely over
allegations of "ju-ju."[19]

Zealots of the Crescent

While the majority of Muslims are generally content to solicit
guidance and protection through dreams, talismans, the venera-
tion of saints and Islamic "witch doctors," others decry such practices. These are the classical Muslims, whose primary goal is to
uphold and extend the influence of Qur'anic law. While it would
appear on the surface that these Muslims, by virtue of their fervent
monotheism, are closer to Christianity in principle and practice
than their more earthy brethren, this notion does not entirely hold
up to scrutiny.

While genuine truth-seekers are clearly to be found among the footsoldiers of Islamic orthodoxy, an emphasis on the letter of the law has led an increasing number of them into fundamentalism where, like Judaism's Pharisees and Christianity's inquisitors and Calvinists, they have been seduced by the notion that in the measuring, torment and dispatch of others, they do God a service. In extreme cases, such as may be found today in Iran, Afghanistan, Lebanon and the Sudan, the spirit of violence has grown into a hideous conflagration of death.

"Islamic society," in the words of Lebanese sociologist Dr. Sania Hamady, "is ruthless, stern and pitiless."[20] While this may sound harsh, even coming as it does from a Muslim, Dr. Hamady knows what he is talking about. In Egypt, for instance, a scholar at Cairo's influential al-Azhar University recently pronounced that AIDS victims should be killed to stop them from harming society—suggesting in the process that such persons be denied food, water and medical treatment.[21] On "Amputation Day" at Sudan's Kober Prison, orderlies wave the severed limbs of wrongdoers charged under *Shari'a* law in front of huge crowds who respond with frenzied chants of *"Allahu Akbar"* and other Islamic slogans.[22]

In Malaysia's Pahang State legislators have legalized mandatory whippings and imprisonment for Muslims who apostasize or preach other religions. In China's Sinkiang Province, eyewitnesses report that apostates—in this case Christian converts from Islam—are tied to the ground while soapy water is poured down their throats over a period of three days in order to wash out evil spirits. They are then forced to endure a week-long crash course in the Qur'an after which they must recant their faith in Christ or face possible exile or death.[23]

Numerous signs, both figurative and literal, suggest that fundamentalist influence is on the rise. During an April 1987 visit to Cairo, for example, I recall encountering, at virtually every turn, posters and bumper stickers that declared, *Islam is the Answer!* The campaign, however, was not all it seemed. Jihan Sadat, widow of slain Egyptian President Anwar Sadat, pointed out that, in many cases, fundamentalists had placed stickers on cars without the owners' consent. "Only a few," she said, "have the courage to take them off."[24]

Fundamentalist intimidation has also had its effect on non-Muslims. Realizing they are being observed by their neighbors, and in order to protect their precarious status, a number of Christian churches in Egypt—including evangelical—have reportedly given money toward the building of mosques.[25] In the Sudan, the two million-member Catholic community has not received a permit to build a church for two decades; Muslim groups are not subject to any such regulation, and mosques and Islamic centers are constructed freely.[26]

Inspired by their success in Iran, Islamic fundamentalists have continued to realize significant political gains in recent years. In June 1988, for instance, the Bangladeshi parliament voted to make Islam the official state religion. That same year Malaysia's Selangor State passed a bill prohibiting non-Muslims from using 35 words and phrases reserved solely for Muslims.[27] In Jordan, the Muslim Brothers had, as of 1990, 32 of the 80 seats in parliament and, in June 1990, the Islamic Salvation Front in Algeria won sweeping victories in municipal and local council elections. Egypt's Muslim Brotherhood dominates the opposition in Egypt's parliament, and the country's medical association and most university staff and student organizations are now controlled by Islamic groups.[28]

In her book *Sacred Rage*, journalist Robin Wright recounts that a French ambassador serving in North Africa explained the potency of fundamentalism in Sunni[29] states by telling the story of a teacher he knew in Algeria. In her English language classes, usually attended by the most Westernized youths, she asked her students to write an essay on the nation they most admired. More than seventy percent wrote about Iran.[30]

Exactly two weeks before the launching of the Decade of Transition, the London Sunday *Telegraph* declared: "The West is facing a resurgent Islam with implacable motives which transcend reason and encompass religious rage and revenge." Six years later, as hijackings proliferated and hostages disappeared in Lebanon, Abdelwahab El Affendi warned in *Arabia* magazine: "We are wit-

nessing the upsurge of anti-Western, radical Islam. It is perhaps
too late for the West to do anything about it, except to sit tight and
brace itself for the tidal wave that will soon hit the ship."

And just what is this surge of rage that is coming? According to
Muslim fundamentalists, it is *jihad* or "holy war"—the means of
spreading Islam among those who will not submit willingly, and
enforcing "true faith" internally against apostates.

Shortly after his return to Iran, the Ayatollah Khomeini proclaimed to adoring multitudes in Teheran: "With a population of
almost one billion and with infinite sources of wealth, you can
defeat all the powers. Aid God's cause so that He may aid you.
Great ocean of Muslims, arise and defeat the enemies of humanity.
If you turn to God and follow the heavenly teachings, God Almighty and His vast hosts will be with you."[31] In many Muslim
nations such as Egypt, Khomeini's message was heard loud and
clear. Captions on banners waved during recent trials of Muslim
fundamentalists in Cairo warned, "The Muslims are coming," and,
"We are going to change the face of the world by Islam, and rule
by the Koran."[32]

In mid-November 1988, Libyan leader Muammar Gaddhafi announced that the global expansion of Islam has entered a "new
stage which distinguishes it in quality and quantity from all efforts
in the past." Speaking from Tripoli, Gaddhafi said the Islamic holy
war will now be carried out by an "International Islamic People's
Commando" charged with the task of conducting Islamic mass
activities.[33]

Precisely what this will mean is yet unclear. What is certain,
however, is that Gaddhafi and other radical Islamic leaders can
count on a cadre of young Muslims ready to pay any price. Ten
days after the Iraqi invasion of Kuwait, for example, a young
Jordanian shrieked to a BBC television reporter: "I want to become
a bomb . . . to destroy Tel Aviv and Washington."[34] Echoing
these sentiments, Hamza, a Lebanese terrorist, declared to Western newsmen: "I want to die before my friends. They want to die
before me. We want to see our God."[35]

Oil: The Treasure Chest of Allah

Perhaps nowhere has the observation that "the rich get richer" been more on the mark than in the kingdom of Saudi Arabia. Already the world's biggest oil exporter, the Saudis in 1990 discovered extensive new reserves of high-quality crude oil that assure ample supply well into the twenty-second century. While Westerners may view all this as little more than a lucky ticket in the geological lottery, many Gulf Muslims see their oil reserves as the treasure chest of Allah.

In the early '80s, the head of Saudi foreign intelligence, Prince Turki al Faisal, told British journalist Robert Lacey: "Arabia is rich today as it has never been before and many simple people in this country believe that this is for one reason and for one reason only—because we have been good Muslims."[36]

One undeniable fact is that the oil boom of the '70s enabled Saudi Arabia, along with the nations of Libya and Iran, to advance Islamic interests worldwide. As the petrodollars piled up, their influence not only reached into dozens of countries, but according to international scholar Daniel Pipes, "seriously affect[ed] many of them."[37]

A major target of this influence has been Great Britain. In the summer of 1987, then Home Secretary Douglas Hurd launched a high-priority inquiry into the intent and impact of millions of pounds flooding into the U.K. from oil-rich Islamic states such as Libya, Kuwait, Iran, Saudi Arabia and Iraq. Most of these foreign funds were, and continue to be, divided into three categories: investment, philanthropy and religious development/propagation. While, on the surface, only the latter of these would appear to be of any real concern to the British or any other Western government, there is strong evidence to suggest that all three of these categories are, in fact, strategically linked.

To begin with investments, there is mounting concern on the part of many Britons that Islamic oil wealth is achieving the same effect in their country that Japanese money is having in the United States. Slowly but surely, major landmarks and institutions are being purchased and controlled by Near Eastern entities with di-

vergent values and loyalties. In addition to the famed Harrods
department store, Middle Eastern companies now either own or
have a stake in such top-class London hotels as the Carlton Tower,
the Sheraton Park, the Churchill and the Montcalm. In fact, during the late 1980s, more than a third of all foreign real estate
transactions in London involved Middle Eastern Arabs.[38]

Another growing area of Muslim influence is the field of investment banking. Beyond the sixty or so Arab banks currently trading
in London, the powerful Kuwait Investment Office holds at least a
five percent stake in the British merchant bank Morgan Grenfell
and, according to the BBC, a 10.5 percent interest in the Midlands
Bank.[39]

In the arithmetic of influence, wealth and population equal political clout; and it is political clout that remains a prime objective
of Muslim strategists both within and outside of Britain. While
there is little anyone can do about the country's growing Muslim
population, the government has made it clear that it intends to
tighten its scrutiny of the relationship between financial contributions from abroad and political action at home.

In the minds of some, however, this intervention may already be
too late. "Islamic inroads are being made in our land with definite
success," observes Mr. Fouzi-Ayoub, an Arab Christian living in
Britain. "It is the declared aim of the Muslim to turn Britain into an
Islamic nation."[40] Lending credence to Mr. Fouzi-Ayoub's fears,
in early 1988 the Iranian-financed Muslim Institute of Britain
hosted a conference in a London hotel to plan the next phase in
spreading the Iranian Islamic revolution. The conference was attended by leaders of extreme Islamic groups from 44 Muslim countries who heard reports of good progress toward fundamentalist
objectives.[41]

At a more recent conference of Islamic leaders, participants
called not only for a "Muslim Parliament," but also for the establishment of a "special relationship" between British Muslims and
Iran.[42]

In September 1989, a group of British Muslims moved out of the
realm of rhetoric to establish the Islamic Party of Britain, the first
Muslim-oriented political party in Europe.[43]

In the categories of philanthropy and Islamic development, not only have the Saudis and other Gulf rulers funded numerous mosques, mission agencies and at least five Islamic magazines in the U.K., they have also employed state funds and private fortunes to bankroll Islamic Studies Centers in several British universities, most notably Oxford and Exeter.[44] While this may appear tame, and even noble, Pipes and others caution that "sizable Saudi contributions for research on Islamic topics have strengthened and publicized the fundamentalist view."[45]

What is more, such research is now getting high-tech help. The London-based Islamic Computing Centre (ICC) has recently computerized Muhammad's sayings, the *hadith*, enabling a single word or phrase to be traced at the press of a button. In creating this new study tool, the ICC has used complex indexing and retrieval software developed by the U.K. Atomic Energy Authority's Harwell Laboratory.[46]

Outside of Britain, the Saudis have used their considerable financial resources to establish or sustain scores of religious, political, business and cultural entities—all intended to advance the cause of Islam. Among the more important of these organizations are the Muslim World League, the International Islamic Federation of Student Organizations, the Islamic Development Bank, the Islamic Conference and the International Islamic News Agency (which, incidentally, was launched with a budget at least twenty times higher than the initial funding for AP or UPI).[47]

The economic strength of Islam is causing especially grave concern for Christians in East Africa. The head of the Anglican Church in Kenya, Manasses Kuria, has openly complained that Muslims are spending millions of petrodollars in Africa to lure Christians into the Islamic faith. When asked to respond to the charge, a spokesman for the Supreme Council for Muslims in Kenya admitted in 1987 that "Kenyan Muslims are [indeed] undertaking major projects involving millions of dollars." Drawing particular attention to plans for new Islamic colleges in Nairobi, Maragua and Eldoret, the spokesman added: "The money to finance these projects [comes] from the Islamic Development Bank and . . . from foreign Islamic donors and local Muslims."[48]

More overtly, while on a state visit to the West African state of

Togo in January 1977, Libya's Muammar Gaddhafi called for a "revolt against Christianity." Ten years later he sounded the same theme in the nation of Rwanda, urging citizens to "wage a holy war so that Islam will spread in Africa." According to the Christian Association of Nigeria, Gaddhafi has called for the establishment of an international Islamic Jihad Fund to finance the effort, and is apparently willing to use Libyan soil as the launch site for any activities.[49] Apparently someone is listening because, in 1990, 24 African governments collaborated to form a new organization called "Islam in Africa" whose purpose is to eliminate Christianity completely from the continent.[50]

While Gaddhafi certainly stands out among modern politicians when it comes to rhetoric, the North African leader has also shown a willingness to put his money—and troops—where his mouth is. In Uganda, for example, Gaddhafi was instrumental (along with Saudi Arabia) in persuading former strongman Idi Amin to convert to Islam, and then in providing money and soldiers to support his regime. During Amin's final days in power, two thousand Libyan troops stood by the dictator ostensibly "to save Islam in Uganda."[51] Gaddhafi is also known to have given millions to a Muslim candidate in Burkina Faso (on the understanding that, if elected, he would apply Shari'a law in the country), and offered the former president of Chad, Francois Tombalbaye, $2 million and an assortment of projects for his country if he would convert to Islam.[52]

Gaddhafi has also established several Islamic mission agencies, perhaps the best known of which is the Conference for the Islamic Call. At present, the Call fields more than 500 missionaries in at least 60 countries. Not to be outdone, the Saudis gave $10 million from 1979 to 1981 to spread Islam in the United States,[53] and have reportedly given millions more since.

The Revolution Heads West

As Islam marches solemnly westward through conversion, immigration and birth, Muslim populations are emerging in sizable numbers. By most accounts, Europe is now home to an estimated ten to twelve million Muslims—many more if one includes those living in Eastern countries such as Yugoslavia, Bulgaria and the U.S.S.R. In Japan, according to a recent Islamic World Congress bulletin, the number of Muslims has doubled since 1977.

France has Western Europe's largest Muslim population, with the vast majority hailing from various North African nations. Officials put the total figure at 2.8 million, though estimates go as high as 4.5 million.[54] In West Germany, the number of practicing Muslims has increased substantially since 1985, and the Central Islamic Institute now predicts the country has approximately two million faithful worshiping in some 900 mosques or places of prayer. In Holland, Islamic converts and schools have sprung up in similar fashion, and in late 1987 the Netherlands became host to Europe's first Muslim television company.[55]

To put these gains in better perspective, it is useful to note that Muslims in the United States currently outnumber members of the Assemblies of God three to one,[56] while in the U.K. there are now more followers of Allah than Methodists and Baptists combined.[57] In France, Muslims represent the nation's second-largest religious group, and boast more adherents than all Protestant denominations put together.[58]

Figures published in the *U.K. Christian Handbook* show that while the Christian churches in Britain and Northern Ireland lose about 100,000 members every year, Islam is expanding at a phenomenal rate. From 1987 to 1988 alone, the Muslim population of Britain grew by nearly 50,000. Three hundred British church buildings have been turned into mosques, including the church that sent William Carey to India. In the Whitechapel area of East London, near where Wesley and Whitefield used to preach, it is Bangladeshi Muslims who now drown out their echoes.[59]

Who is showing interest in the message of Islam? The short answer seems to be those who are fed up with the moral decadence of Western culture, and those who are searching for an unfragmented view of life. Dr. Edward Skinner, the principal psychologist at St. Luke's Hospital in West Yorkshire, said he joined the growing number of British converts to Islam because he felt that in so many Christian churches, and the Church of England in par-

ticular, spirituality had been replaced by a soggy liberal intellec-
tualism that fudged on just about every moral issue. "Islam," he
said, "[offers] that clarity and certainty of doctrine so much of the
Christian world now lacks."[60]

Yusuf Islam, who as pop superstar Cat Stevens performed with
the likes of Jimi Hendrix and Englebert Humperdink and reeled
off eight straight gold records in the late '60s, also believes Islam
is the answer. "I started my quest for peace and enlightenment a
long time ago," he says. "My soul was thirsty for the truth. My
songs became a vehicle for my spiritual search . . . but that still
didn't satisfy me." When he discovered Islam in 1972 (in Mar-
rakesh, Morocco), Stevens said "it was as if someone, somewhere
had switched on the lights."[61]

Not everyone is as sanguine over Islam's role in the West. A
recent BBC survey indicated that sixty percent of the British population think that the major religious issue of the '90s will be Islam
versus Christianity.[62] Imam Khurram Murad, director general of
the Islamic Foundation near Leicester, recently proclaimed: "The
[Islamic] movement in the West should reaffirm . . . the suprem-
acy of Islam in Western society as its ultimate objective, and
allocate it to the highest priority."[63]

In the words of one Arab Christian, "It is a complete miscon-
ception to think that Christianity and Islam can coexist." Convinced that the Islamic tide is rolling in, he warns fellow Christians
that "courteous and vigorous evangelism is urgent."[64] The question is, Will the Church accept the challenge? In Holland, so far,
the Muslim community is unimpressed. "We say: 'Allah is Great,'
[while] they say: 'The guilder [Dutch currency] is great'—not one
of them talks about Jesus."[65]

Although generally less militant than its European counterpart,
North America's Muslim community, some ten to twelve million
strong, is roughly equivalent in size. Should it continue to grow at
its present rate, Islam will likely overtake Judaism as the second-
largest religion in the United States somewhere around the year
2015.[66]

In pursuit of this goal, hundreds of Islamic centers throughout
the U.S. launched a program called "Invitation to Islam" in the

spring of 1989. During this same year, 42 private Islamic schools were opened across the country, and according to the president of the Islamic Society of North America, 300 imams and other Muslim preachers were graduated from Islamic theological colleges in the U.S. These, said Dr. Ahmad Zaki Ahmad, are now working for "Da'awa" (mission) organizations among non-Muslims.[67]

Standing in the line of Muslim evangelistic fire are America's African-American communities. Forty percent of the grocery marts in Chicago's black neighborhoods, for example, are owned by Arabs who use their stores as outposts for Islamic evangelism. Already accounting for about a third of America's Muslim population, blacks are buying Islam, in the opinion of urban expert Ray Bakke, because it is a brotherhood.

When Dr. Bakke took his Christian students on a recent field trip into Chicago's minority communities, one of the first stops was a local mosque where they went in to hear from the resident imam—a former Christian. When asked why he had left Christianity for Islam, the imam (who is black) replied: "Islam offers a way for emasculated men to become something. Christianity, on the other hand, is a welfare religion—Jesus paid it all—and my people don't need that."[68]

A world away from the inner city, on the high plateau of northern New Mexico, lies another important center of Islamic influence. Dar al-Islam, or the Abode of the Faithful, was incorporated in 1980 as the first Islamic village in the United States. Initially established with the financial aid of five Saudi princesses, the center now enjoys the full support of the Riyadh-based World Muslim League. The village's core facilities consist of a mosque, Islamic school, housing and an Institute of Traditional Islamic Studies.[69]

In early 1991, four Muslim businessmen in Talbot County, Georgia, submitted similar blueprints for a planned 194-acre, $100 million Muslim community complete with a college, mosque, shops and homes. If the project is approved, financing will come, as it did in the case of Dar al-Islam, from Muslims in both the U.S. and Saudi Arabia.[70]

Although Islamic propagation efforts in both the West and the two-thirds world have already achieved a significant measure of success, the sobering reality is that, in many respects, the movement is still getting underway. Every year mission training programs in Egypt, Iran, Libya and elsewhere graduate hundreds of new workers to augment an estimated 10,000-member force currently on the field. By way of example, Egypt's Cairo University admits some 100 Muslim students each year specifically for training as missionaries to the Spanish-speaking world. Following graduation, the efforts of these students are then coordinated regionally through events such as the January 1988 Islamic strategy consultation in Bogota, Colombia—a summit attended by about 250 Muslim leaders from throughout Latin America.[71]

In December 1983, a World Muslim League seminar on "Islam in Africa" was held in the West African country of Sierra Leone. A confidential listing of the recommendations developed at this seminar for promoting Islam in Africa—where Islam doubles itself every 25 years[72]—offers interesting insights into Muslim strategic thinking. In addition to strategies dealing with such things as media usage, Islamic relief programs and message contextualization, one recommendation actually urges the conference to pursue a project to rewrite the history of Islam in which it is purified of its faults.[73]

Watching the Infidels: The Monitoring of Christian Missions

The challenge of Islam is immense. Of the world's remaining unreached people, Dr. Robert Douglas of the Pasadena-based Zwemer Institute reckons that one out of every three is a Muslim. As Christian workers and agencies scramble to respond to this challenge, however, they are encountering fierce resistance from Islamic organs of power. In fact, the general secretary of the Muslim World League has gone on record recently declaring Communism, two quasi-Muslim cults and Christian missions to be the worst enemies facing the world of Islam.[74]

In addition to employing strict censorship of incoming mail and broadcasts—in Saudi Arabia, videotaped imports of "The Muppet Show" are confiscated on the grounds that its heroine is a pig[75]—a global monitoring of Christian organizations and their intentions is underway and believed to be coordinated, or at least assisted, by Saudi intelligence.

Not long ago, a Palestinian Arab student in the United States telephoned a worker with an international student ministry the night before she was to leave on a trip to Southeast Asia for the purpose of following up on several students. With great persistence, this student proceeded to ask her where she was going, whom she was going to see and precisely what she was going to do once she arrived in Asia—all this just before he himself was scheduled to leave for Saudi Arabia.

Evidence of Muslim monitoring of Christian activities proliferates in the Islamic media. In a recent Pakistani newspaper editorial, for example, the writer declared that the government should screen workers going to the Persian Gulf countries more carefully because many of them are working to evangelize Muslims there. In *Al Musalmin*, an Arabic newspaper printed in London and distributed throughout Europe, a recent front-page headline read: *Evangelism Convocation in Europe*. The related story, which reviewed a number of ministry details, was adapted from an article written for a Scandinavian Christian newspaper.

Writing in *The Challenge of Islam*, Clifford Denton shares: "I heard one story of how a certain missionary agency found some facts printed in an edition of *Focus* [a magazine published by the Islamic Foundation in Britain] outlining some future plans. It was published in *Focus* before their own Christian missionary publication came out containing the same information." While in England recently, I reviewed several back issues[76] of *Focus*, and found these editions to include the names of at least 17 key evangelical missions leaders, 24 mission organizations and a number of key publications and events.

The message is clear: We are being watched. Given these circumstances, then, it is incumbent upon us not only to conduct ourselves in a manner befitting Christ, but also to recognize that this daily observation extends to legions of unseen powers in the spiritual realm.

Despite the concerns expressed in this chapter, it would be a grave mistake to jump to the conclusion that Muslims—or, for that matter, Hindus, Buddhists or Communists—are somehow the enemies of God and His Church. To the contrary, Scripture makes it clear that each human being is the object of God's undying love and affection. And if they are precious in His sight, how then can they be the enemies of His people?

This is not to say the Church has no enemies. Indeed, her enemies are many, and they are ruthless. But as they are not born of flesh and blood, they may be discerned and engaged only by those who have learned the language and secrets of the spiritual dimension.

Notes

1 "Islam's Militants," *Newsweek*, July 15, 1985.
2 Published by the Islamic Republic News Agency in London; quoted in Clifford Denton, "The Challenge of Islam" (Souldern, England: Institute for Demographic Studies, 1988).
3 Shown in Britain ten days after the Iraqi invasion of Kuwait.
4 Reported on ABCs "Nightline," aired February 15, 1989.
5 John Laffin, "Islam's Clandestine Operations." The Challenge of Islam Series (see footnote 2).
   Note: In their recent study, "The Demography of Islamic Nations," population experts John R. Weeks and Saad Gadalla project the birth rate in Muslim nations is about 42 per 1,000 compared to less than 34 in other developing countries.
6 Conversation with Dr. Sam Wilson, Monrovia, California, December 1987.
7 See Michael Nazir-Ali, *Islam: A Christian Perspective* (Paternoster Press, 1983), pp. 25–28.
8 *Ibid.*, pp. 26–27.
9 Robert Lacey, *The Kingdom—Arabia & the House of Sa'ud* (New York: Harcourt Brace Jovanovich, 1981), p. 515.
10 "Hajj," *Arabia* magazine, September 1982.
11 H. F. Saggs, *The Greatness that Was Babylon* (London: Sidgwick & Jackson, 1962/ 1988), pp. 436–437.
12 Nazir-Ali, pp. 28–29.
13 Paul Duggan in *ReachOut*, Vol. 3, Nos. 1 & 2.
14 There is speculation that Moammar Gaddhafi engages periodically in this same practice in the Libyan desert.
15 Phil Parshall, quoted in Field Update "Folk Islam—Part I" (Joan Rulison for Biola University, fall 1987); see also *Impact*, "Mixing Allah and Amulets," November 1986, and Gail Bennett interview with Dr. Dudley Woodberry in *Pulse*, March 21, 1986.

16 SIM Now, "Jinns, Spells, and Talismans," March–April 1984.

17 Bill Musk, *The Unseen Face of Islam* (Sussex, Great Britain: MARC, 1989), pp. 33–44.

18 Testimony of Lamin Kante, quoted by Rulison (see footnote 12).

19 David Ndifang, "Marabouts in the Muslin World," July 12, 1981.
   Note: Ju-ju is an African word for witchcraft.

20 Quoted by John Laffin in "The Many Faces—and the Heart—of Islam," The Challenge of Islam Series (Souldern, England: Institute for Demographic Studies, 1988).

21 Abdullah al-Mashad, head of the Fatwa Committee of Cairo's al-Azhar University, quoted in *The Independent*, April 7, 1989.

22 Robin Wright, *Sacred Rage, the Wrath of Militant Islam* (New York: Simon & Schuster, 1986), pp. 201–202.

23 "Muslim Converts Brutalized in Urumqi, China," News Network International, November 15, 1989.

24 *Evangelical Missions Quarterly*, Global Report, October 1985.

25 Conversation with Sam Soloman in London, July 1990.

26 Joseph E. Davis, "The Islamization of the Sudan," *America* magazine, November 12, 1988.

27 "Local News—Enactment Against Proselytisation," *Berita*, published by the Christian Federation of Malaysia, April 1988.

28 "Islam's Tide Is Just a Ripple," *The Economist*, June 23, 1990.

29 Comprising about 85 percent of the Islamic community, *Sunni* Muslims are generally considered to be more traditional and less radical than their minority counterparts, the *Shia* (or Shi'ites).

30 Wright, p. 173.

31 From speech given by Ayatollah Khomeini in Teheran on September 13, 1980; quoted in *Islam and Revolution*, ed. Hamid Algar (Berkeley, Calif.: Mizan Press, 1981).

32 Wright, pp. 173, 184.

33 "Gaddafi Intensifies Global Expansion of Islam," Special to News Network International.

34 Statement on BBC television, August 11, 1990.

35 Peter Ross Range, "Islam: Seeking the Future in the Past," *U.S. News & World Report*, July 6, 1987.

36 Lacey, pp. 514–515.

37 Daniel Pipes, *In the Path of God* (New York: Basic Books, 1983), pp. 297–298.

38 *Islam in Britain*, Fifth Edition; published by Christian Support for the Persecuted.

39 Not to mention a 10-percent interest in British Petroleum and 3 percent of Trusthouse Forte. *The London Daily Telegraph*, May 1, 1987; BBC television report, August 7, 1990.

40 *English Churchman*, June 1, 1990.

41 *The Copts*, Christians of Egypt, July 1988; quoted in OMS Outreach "Worldwatch."

42 Afterward, the director of the Muslim Institute, Dr. Kalim Saddiqui, announced to the media: "We have committed ourselves to create in Britain institutions normally associated with a sovereign territorial state. We are an autonomous community, capable of setting our own goals and priorities in domestic and foreign relationships." "Autonomy Vote by UK Muslims," *The Independent*, July 15, 1990.

43 Richard Evans, "Islam! From Invasion to Indenture," *Geographical* magazine, December 1989.

Note: Part of their early agenda has been to press for implementation of a well-publicized Muslim Charter of Demands issued jointly by twenty Islamic organizations in Great Britain.

44 "Islam's Intellectual Challenge," *World Evangelization Information Service*, August 1, 1988.

45 Pipes, p. 304.

46 "Prophet's Sayings Now on Computer," *Arabia*, July 1986.

47 Aslam Abdullah, "Focus on the Muslim Media," *Islamic World Review*, April 1987; see also Pipes, pp. 303–304.

Note: Another important institution, the Islamic States Broadcasting Organization (ISBO), represents the cutting-edge of the Muslim world's international mission effort. Heavily supported by donations from Saudi Arabia, Kuwait, Libya, Pakistan, Iraq, Qatar, UAE, Oman and Malaysia, the ISBO puts out more than 6,100 programs a year (*Arabia*, February 1987). All total, Muslims are now broadcasting from or in 120 countries. (David Barrett & Todd Johnson, *Our Globe and How to Reach It* [Birmingham, Al.: New Hope, 1990], Global Diagram 16, p. 29).

48 Open Doors New Service, December 15, 1987, p. 11.

49 Christian Mission, "Africa News," July-August 1988.

50 Harold Brown (The Religion and Society Report, November 1990), quoted by Herbert Schlossberg in *A Fragrance of Oppression: The Church and Its Persecutors* (Westchester, Ill.: Crossway, 1991).

51 Pipes, p. 320.

52 *Ibid.*, pp. 305, 320.

53 *Ibid.*, p. 320.

54 "Islam's Solemn March West," *Asiaweek*, February 23, 1990.

55 News of Muslims in Europe, No. 39, April 30, 1987.

56 *Update*, "Surprising Facts You Should Know About Islam."

57 "Islam Growing in U.K.," *The Church Around the World*, Vol. 18, No. 1, 1987.

58 George W. Braswell Jr., *Christianity Encounters Islam: Iran and Beyond*; published in Missiology, an International Review, Vol XI, No. 2, April 1983.

59 Robert C. Douglas, "A New Star Over London," *World Christian* magazine, February 1989.

60 "Britons with Faith in Themselves," *The London Daily Mail*, February 6, 1989.

61 Arthur Clark, "On the Road to Find Out," *Aramco World* magazine, May-June 1987.

62 *English Churchman*.

63 Imam Khurram Murad, "The Islamic Movement in the West."

64 *English Churchman*.

65 Paul Verschuur, "Islam Makes Its Mark on Dutch," Jordanian Newspaper-AP, May 1988.

66 Dr. Yvonne Haddad, Islamicist at the University of Massachusetts; quoted in *Eternity* magazine, March 1988.

67 *English Churchman*.

68 Conversation with Ray Bakke, Arrowhead Springs, California, January 23, 1990.

69 An old adobe hacienda is the venue for a variety of programs and seminars, which included, in mid-1986, a training workshop for Muslim teachers co-sponsored by the World Muslim League.

Demonstrating that Islam is not merely a church within the community, but a community integrated with religion, trustee Sahl Kabbani established the Crescent Leasing and Development Company to help create jobs for Dar al-Islam's residents. Crescent leased a portion of the land fronting the highway and used it to erect an inn, restaurant, gift shop and automobile body shop. Another company, *Al-Manjara* (The Builders), leases space from Dar al-Islam and carries out major construction for the center and for clients as far away as Santa Fe and Albuquerque (*Aramco World,* May/June 1988).

70 "Georgia," *USA Today,* March 14, 1991.

71 "Dialogue and Encounter: Latin Muslims," *Latin American Evangelist,* April-June 1988.

72 Mervin Cetron/Thomas O'Toole, *Encounters with the Future,* p. 168.

73 Recommendations Du lleme Seminaire Islamique Mondial sur L'Islam En Afrique, Al-Rabita XXII/3 (December 1983), p. 51.

74 *World Christian News,* November 1989.

75 Lacey, p. 518.

76 Through April 1990.

4

Spiritual Mapping

Men in general judge more from appearances than from
reality. All men have eyes, but few have the gift of
penetration.

Machiavelli[1]

The one who scatters has come up against you. Man the
fortress, watch the road. . . .

Nahum 2:1 (NASB)

Orthodoxy is necessary, but it is not enough. If it is true
that our battle is not against flesh and blood, then we
need spiritual insight and power of our own to make a
fight of it.

Gary Kinnaman[2]

At first glance, the world we live in can appear to be
a complex and bewildering place, a tangled web of borders and
ideologies, agencies and revolutions. Even those things we think
we know something about—such as regional alliances, world religions and the names of certain leaders—are often subject to
sudden and radical transformation.

To help us sort it all out, we generally turn to professional
definers—cartographers (mappers), historians and, most of all,
journalists. By putting their knowledge and experience to work for
us, we hope to make some sense of today's world.

And if the world is inherently the product of human decisions, then the digging and analyses performed by these professionals should indeed supply us with the insight we need. If, on the other hand, the material world does not represent the marrow of reality, then global society is not all that it appears to be, and we need a different kind of evaluative process.

As Christians we have been taught by Scripture and tradition to acknowledge the spiritual dimension as the true nucleus of reality. Human endeavor is a related, but dependent, outer layer. This, at any rate, is what we say. In truth many Christians have become practical atheists—people who conduct their daily lives as if there were no God. Like the nonbelieving world around them they routinely neglect or discount the spiritual dimension.

Christians who do this, it is safe to say, are not choosing consciously to set aside their beliefs. Rather they are frustrated by their seeming inability to master the language and rules of the supernatural. The pressured cadence of modern living crowds out the time God would use to mentor them in the ways of the Spirit. Thus, the spirit realm remains fuzzy, elusive and, at times, irrelevant.

This situation is more dangerous than we might think. For while we can never comprehend reality *absolutely*, we must, as Chuck Kraft says, perceive it *adequately* or we "will not survive long or well."[3] This is especially true in an hour when the spiritual hosts of darkness are deploying for what may prove to be some of *the* consequential battles of history. If we are to emerge from these spiritual encounters triumphantly, we must improve our ability to detect the true circumstances behind the headlines and to identify correctly the authentic centers of power. In short, we must learn to see the world as it really is, not as it appears to be.

This new way of seeing I have labeled *spiritual mapping*. It involves superimposing our understanding of forces and events in the spiritual domain onto places and circumstances in the material world. The result is often a set of borders, capitals and battlefronts that differ notably from those we have come to associate with the political status quo. On this new map of the world, the three spiritual superpowers we have examined—Hinduism, materialism,

Islam—are not entities in themselves. They are, rather, the *means*
by which an extensive hierarchy of powerful demonic authorities
controls billions of people.

Spiritual Borders: Invisible Boundaries
of the Will

Many Christian travelers have had the experience of crossing the
threshold of a particular country, province, city or neighborhood
only to find that the prevailing atmosphere has suddenly turned
oppressive.

Several years ago, my family and I encountered this type of
clinging unease as we navigated our way through the streets of
Titograd, Yugoslavia. We had arrived in town after an adrenaline-
rich day of driving through the mountains of Kosovo and Montene-
gro, and were anxious to find a place to put in for the night. As we
proceeded to investigate local lodging options, however, the sense
of oppression became so pronounced that we decided to press our
search for accommodations elsewhere.

What was gnawing at us? The gremlins of fatigue? The bewil-
derment of novel surroundings? It was not until we checked our
map the next morning that we stumbled across another possibility.
It seemed that during our brief sojourn in Titograd we had been
situated under the dark shadows of the North Albanian Alps—a
mere fifteen miles from the border of the world's most virulent
atheistic state. It also dawned on us that Titograd, as the birthplace of Yugoslavia's revered Communist leader Josip Broz Tito,
was likely one of the country's last remaining bastions of Communist true believers, a fact we were later able to confirm.

Nor was our experience in the southern Balkans an isolated
incident. This same inexplicable eeriness has been a periodic
traveling companion during journeys through the Welsh and Scottish highlands, New Mexico's northern plateau, and Andalusian
Spain, including a side trip to the famed monolith of Gibraltar.
While cherishing the natural evocative power of each of these
dramatic landscapes, at a deeper level our spiritual senses sug-

gested we were in the presence of something besides esoteric beauty.

As we learned from Titograd, subsequent research can often yield intriguing clues as to the forces behind spiritual disquiet. In the above cases these clues involved such things as our proximity to Celtic and native American ritual sites, the lingering effects of the Moorish occupation of Spain and Gibraltar's long-standing reputation as a center of witchcraft and occult practices. As we were told repeatedly by Christians throughout Andalusia, "The Muslims themselves may be long gone, but the spirit of Islam remains."

Spiritual Territoriality and Human Systems

While it is true that factors such as repressive political institutions, brooding topography and general dinginess can dampen our emotional reaction to a place, an oppressive atmosphere can also pervade settings where democracy, beauty and material affluence are in full bloom. In some instances, no outward clues at all can account for our inner restlessness. While some individuals elect to shrug off these negative feelings as subjective mood swings, more and more Christians are coming to the realization that what they are experiencing is related directly to the presence and influence of unseen territorial spirits.

According to Fuller Seminary professor C. Peter Wagner, the reason so little is known about this widespread and ancient phenomenon is simply that "spiritual territoriality has not been a prominent issue for theologians and biblical scholars through the years." Obviously hoping to reverse this trend, Wagner has written a book on the subject suggesting that Satan delegates high-ranking evil spirits to control nations, regions, cities, tribes, people groups, neighborhoods and other significant social networks. The major assignment of these demonic powers, Wagner believes, "is to prevent God from being glorified in their territory."[4]

Assuming the basic validity of spiritual territoriality, the next glaring question is, *How* does Satan gain control over an area or, more importantly, a people? The Bible tells us in Psalm 24:1 that the earth and all who dwell in it are the Lord's. At the same time, John 14:30 refers to Satan as the "ruler of this world." Are we caught in a paradox?

To answer these questions, we must begin by noting an important distinction. While God is the rightful head of human *families* (*ethnos*—tribes and people groups), Satan is in general control over human *systems* (*kosmos*—kingdoms and structures).[5] Whereas God's authority is derived through *fatherhood*, Satan's rule, in the latter instance, is achieved through the *volition of men.*

Because all human peoples belong to God initially by right of fatherhood, Satan has no automatic control over them. Unless individuals give themselves over to the rulership of Satan willingly, they will remain under the tender influence of the Holy Spirit.[6] Satan's objective, then, is to gain control over the lives of human beings by dominating the systems—political, economic and religious—that they have created. And as real and meaningful as these systems appear to men, Satan knows they are no more authentic than that conjured by the Wizard of Oz. His sole intent— achieved through deceptive, behind-the-scenes manipulation—is to make the fantasy credible. Thus, when the ancient Greeks sought wisdom through the Oracles of Delphi, he accommodated them. When the Germans began dreaming of the Third Reich, he dazzled them through "anointed" speeches of Joseph Goebbels and Adolf Hitler. As millions of Africans, Tibetans, Arabs and Haitians searched for supernatural power to help them cope with life's problems, he provided it in a potent array of shamans, marabouts and gurus.

Today the paramount goal of many citizens, particularly in the affluent West, is to forge a "New World Order" crowned with peace and prosperity. To the chief architects of this new utopia—many of whom have become infatuated with the high-tech pursuit of leisure—the ultimate keys to success are philosophical tolerance and human initiative, precisely the kind of "racing stripes" Satan likes to add to human systems in order to abet their continued worship.

Sparkling as they do with promise, today's prevailing systems are reminiscent of Celtic lore in which unsuspecting travelers were tempted into bright fairy banquets only to find themselves trapped by the enchanted domain. In the Old Testament, God was acutely aware of the dangers inherent in human kingdoms, and for this very reason labored to persuade the Israelites to forgo an earthly king in favor of His direct supernatural leadership. At the heart of His concern was the knowledge that man-inspired initiatives turn quickly into manmade substitutes—idolatrous doorways through which demonic agents access societies and inflict spiritual bondage. Oblivious to these infiltrations, modern man has become prey to the dark side of his own house: the capitalist to his materialism, the Communist to his totalitarianism and the Muslim to either fundamentalism or spiritism.

Establishing Beachheads and Renewing Allegiances

There is no evidence that satanic powers have any natural predilection for particular geographical areas or ethnic groupings. That demonic activity is more pronounced in certain regions and among certain peoples today is due to the fact that spiritual "beachheads" have been established there by previous generations. At some time, in one fashion or another, human beings welcomed evil spirits to dwell among them.

In most of these enemy strongholds, the scope and intensity of demonic control seem to exist in direct proportion to the explicitness of the original welcome, and to the care taken to sustain the spiritual allegiance through various festivals, rites and pilgrimages.

The fact that mountainous areas manifest a high degree of demonic activity is no arbitrary phenomenon. As Asian studies scholar Edwin Bernbaum observes: "People have traditionally revered mountains as places of sacred power and spiritual atonement." Among the numerous examples cited by Bernbaum are the isolated Qollahuaya people of northeastern Bolivia who treat nearby Mount Kaata very much like a human being. "Rather than pray to it," Bernbaum reveals, "they feed it, stuffing llama fat into holes and caves and pouring sacrificial blood onto earth shrines."[7]

In midsummer months, Japanese artists and "divine-possession clubs" climb Mount Ontake—the Mountain of Trance—in order to be incarnated by Shinto gods."[8] Elsewhere, in remote Tibet, Hindus and Buddhists trek dangerous mountain passes to bathe in the icy waters of Manasarovar—the Lake of the Mind—before gazing on holy Mount Kailas, the realm of the highest gods.

The Himalayan Mountain range may represent the world's densest concentration of spiritism. In all of the nations skirting these icy behemoths—Nepal, India, Bhutan, China, Pakistan and Tibet—overt demonic manifestations are commonplace. According to eyewitness accounts from long-term resident missionaries in Nepal, Christian workers have been bitten (with resultant puncture wounds) and had food supplies eaten by evil spirits. On other occasions, mysterious lights perched atop high mountain peaks have come hurtling down toward their residences only to be driven off by urgent rebukes in the name of Christ.[9]

In his outstanding book *Eternity in Their Hearts*, Christian anthropologist Don Richardson retells a revealing story about how some of the region's earlier human inhabitants may have established a beachhead for much of this spiritual activity.

> A branch of mankind which we shall call "proto-Santal" migrated eastward "from forest to forest" until high mountains blocked their way. Desperately they sought a way through the mountains, but every route proved impassable, at least to their women and children. . . .
>
> Facing this crisis . . . they lost their faith in God and took their first step into spiritism. "The spirits of these great mountains have blocked our way," they decided. "Come, let us bind ourselves to them by an oath, so that they will let us pass." Then they covenanted with the *Maran Buru* (spirits of the great mountains), saying, "O, Maran Buru, if you release the pathways for us, we will practice spirit appeasement when we reach the other side."

Centuries later, in 1867, Richardson relays that a Norwegian missionary by the name of Lars Skrefsrud, along with a Danish colleague, discovered the 2.5 million-strong Santal people living in a region north of Calcutta, India, not far from the foothills of the

Himalayas. But as the great mountains were not in the immediate Santal homeland, Skrefsrud puzzled as to why the Santal word for *demons* translated as "spirits of the mountains." The mystery was solved when an esteemed Santal elder named Kolean proceeded with the narrative about his ancestors' eastward migration.

> "Very shortly," Kolean continued, "they came upon a passage [the Khyber Pass?] in the direction of the rising sun." They named that passage Bain, which means "day gate." Thus the proto-Santal burst through onto the plains of what is now called India. Subsequent migrations brought them still further east to the border regions between India and Bangladesh, where they became the modern Santal people. . . . Under bondage to [their] oath . . . the Santal began to practice spirit appeasement, sorcery, and even sun worship. [10]

On the opposite side of the planet, in the Caribbean nation of Haiti, demonic forces are also much in evidence. Although voodoo has been sensationalized in such movies as *The Serpent and the Rainbow* and *The Mighty Quinn,* its role as the primary junction between thousands of Haitians and the spirit world should not be discounted.

Inherited from West Africa, voodoo is essentially a cult of the spirits. Its Creole name, *vodou,* derives from *vodun,* which means "spirit" in the language of the Fon people of Benin and Nigeria. From the voodooist perspective, the Almighty Master of the universe is too remote to involve Himself with the daily problems of mankind, and has therefore delegated spirits to serve as intermediaries. From the mid-1600s African slaves transported to Haiti were forced to convert to Roman Catholicism and forbidden to practice their ancestral religion. Instead of deserting their spirits, however, the slaves worshiped them secretly in the guise of Catholic saints.

One of the primary haunts of Haitian spirits, or *loa,* are waterfalls. Each year thousands of islanders, including many Catholics, make their way on pilgrimages to several sites. The most popular of these are the falls of Saut d'Eau near Ville Bonheur.

On a promontory overlooking the sacred waterfall a woman

stands with her palms outstretched before her and implores the benevolence of the loa: "My baby is dead. Give me another! If you answer my prayer, I will be like butter in your frying pan—you may fry me, sauté me, do whatever you wish." Underneath the falls, another woman suddenly screams and staggers. "Trembling from head to toe, she collapses like a rag doll. The loa has answered her call. People crowd around to prevent her from harming herself on the rocks. Others touch her to share in the divine presence as she crawls down the falls like a snake. 'Danbala ap monte l!—Danbala is riding her!' A leading voodoo spirit, symbolized by the snake, *Danbala Wedo* has chosen to reside in this grandiose setting. With him dwells his wife, *Aida Wedo;* their rainbow symbol gleams through iridescent droplets. The woman possessed by Danbala now becomes the 'horse,' losing her own personality to take on that of the spirit who rides her."[11]

Evil spirits will generally remain entrenched in an area like Haiti or the Himalayas until their original invitation is revoked—an action that, unfortunately, is rarely taken. Whatever their education or outlook, people are almost universally reluctant to renounce events and systems that they perceive to be legitimate—if unflattering—elements of their own heritage. Consequently, rather than dispense with their old beliefs and customs, many societies make an effort to adapt them to contemporary attitudes and lifestyles.

While Muslims exchange their pre-Islamic heathen rituals for the Hajj, Hindus wade into the holy Ganges every twelve years for the Kumbh Mela Festival. As Europeans and Americans celebrate Druid paganism through Halloween, Brazilians lose their inhibitions to the frenzied and colorful beat of Carnivale. By repackaging ancient rites of spirit welcome and appeasement as popular, and seemingly more benign, festivals and pilgrimages, the tenant rights of demonic powers are thereby reaffirmed by successive generations.

In Japan, long considered to be one of the world's more resistant mission fields, Emperor Akihito reaffirmed his country's ties with the spirit world during a recent coronation ceremony on the grounds of the Imperial Palace. Wearing the white silk robes of a

high Shinto priest, Japan's new emperor communed with his myth-
ical ancestor the Sun Goddess in a torchlight enthronement ritual
(the Daijosai) that continued until dawn. In addition to offering the
goddess specially grown rice and an array of other foods from the
land and the sea, Akihito also recited a prayer beseeching her to
promote the welfare of the Japanese people.

To some Japanese, those rites symbolized Emperor Akihito's
final transformation into a divine being—receiving the soul of the
Sun Goddess as he joined with her in symbolic sexual union.[12] In
actuality, the ceremony was a detailed adaptation of the annual
Babylonian ritual known as "The Sacred Marriage," a rite in which
the king (an incarnate god) engaged in sexual intercourse with the
goddess Inanna prior to her "fixing the destiny" of the land. Ironically, a major part of the attendant festival was held in a specially
prepared facility called the *Akitu*-house.[13]

Spiritual Capitals: Identifying the Real Centers of Power

While we might be tempted to conclude that the power centers
of today's modern society are found in cities like London, Moscow,
Tokyo and Washington, D.C., these choices make sense only if we
also assume that genuine power is associated with material wealth
and/or weaponry. In reality, however, we know that such things
are of little consequence. Real power, spiritual power, is of a
different order.

The trick is determining precisely where this real power is concentrated. For Christians the focal point is nothing less than satanic command and control centers: evil principalities that are
responsible for deploying demonic legions throughout the world.
In scriptural parlance, the act of pinpointing—and then neutral-
izing—these strategic enemy command posts is known as "binding
the strongman."[14]

Spiritual capitals, or strongholds, are related to both location
and personalities. In the former sense they are specific centers of
demonic control operating within borders defined by the will of

local societies; in the latter, they are associated with spiritual strongmen and their entourages of unclean spirits.

Today, a hierarchy of evil powers radiates out over the earth to administrate areas and peoples already under satanic dominion (strongholds), and to wage war against those that are not.[15] In Scripture, certain "spiritual strongmen" (high-ranking spirits) are actually referred to by the territories they control. These include as the prince of Persia (Daniel 10:13), the prince of Greece (Daniel 10:20), the king of Tyre (Ezekiel 28:12) and the spirit of Babylon (Revelation 17:3–5). In other cases, leading satanic powers have assumed the identity of territorial deities, such as Bel in Babylon (Jeremiah 51:44), Baal-Zebub of Ekron (2 Kings 1:2–3) and Apollyon of the underworld (Revelation 9:11).

Although it is easy to do so, spiritual strongholds should not be confused with the thousands of *sacred sites*—such as Australia's Mt. Uluru and Sweden's Gotland—that lie scattered across the global landscape. While such sites are often located within strongholds, the two are not synonymous. Sacred sites (which are visible) represent *meeting points* between the material and spiritual domains, while strongholds (which are invisible) represent the *dwelling places*, *command centers* and *workshops* of unclean spirits.

Viewed strategically, there appear to be at least two categories of spiritual strongholds. The first of these, which we might call *captive* strongholds, is found in areas where human partnerships with evil spirits have resulted in dense demonic populations and the domination of surrounding societies. The other, which we might call *frontier* strongholds, is essentially a demonic beachhead operation in areas that are not fully under satanic control.

To lift this discussion out of the abstract, I have included the following list of examples.

Spiritual Capitals

Captive Strongholds
- Lhasa, Tibet
- Peshawar, Pakistan

Frontier Strongholds
- San Francisco, California, U.S.A.
- New Orleans, Louisiana, U.S.A.

- Karbala and Najaf, Iraq
- Beijing, China
- Allahabad, India
- Marrakech, Morocco
- Baalbeck, Lebanon
- Tripoli, Libya
- Konya, Turkey
- Mecca and Medina, Saudi Arabia
- Benares, India
- Cairo and the Lower Nile, Egypt
- Baku, U.S.S.R.

- Beirut, Lebanon
- The Horn of Africa
- Khartoum, Sudan
- Bali, Indonesia
- Tirana, Albania
- Sinjar Hills, Iraq
- Pagan, Burma
- The Himalayas
- Outer Mongolia
- Teheran, Iran
- Qom, Iran

- Babylon, Iraq

- Hollywood, California, U.S.A.
- Amsterdam, Holland
- Medellin, Colombia
- Gibraltar
- Andalusia, Spain
- Ville Bonheur, Haiti
- Czestochowa, Poland
- Rio de Janeiro, Brazil
- Athens and Delphi, Greece
- Dalmatian Coast, Yugoslavia
- Monte Carlo and the French Riviera
- Central Honshu, Japan
- Utah, U.S.A.
- Vienna, Austria
- Northern New Mexico, U.S.A.
- Lake Titicaca and environs, Peru
- Welsh and Scottish highlands
- Las Vegas, Nevada, U.S.A.
- Bahia, Brazil
- Havana, Cuba
- Serbia, Yugoslavia
- Mayan-Toltec areas, Central America

While the above list is obviously incomplete—and space unfortunately does not permit inclusion of rationales for each entry—it does at least provide a starting place for prayer.[16] From here it is up to each of us to research and establish our own assignments. By doing our homework, not only do we acknowledge the incomparable power of prayer to demolish strongholds,[17] but we also avoid wasting valuable spiritual ammunition on inconsequential or phantom targets.

This said, those with the passion and capacity to do battle will also want to train their intercessory sights on the following cities, each of which represents locations where fierce spiritual warfare is currently underway.

——————————— **Cities Under Siege** ———————————

- London, England
- New York, New York, U.S.A.
- Berlin, Germany
- Hong Kong
- Manila, Philippines
- Johannesburg, South Africa
- Stockholm, Sweden

- Kathmandu, Nepal
- Singapore
- Addis Ababa, Ethiopia
- Moscow, U.S.S.R.
- Guatemala City, Guatemala
- Belfast, Northern Ireland
- Jerusalem, Israel

Spiritual Fronts: The 10/40 Window

Since our primary mission as Christians—reaching the lost—involves us directly in spiritual warfare, the component of the "reality" mapping process involving spiritual fronts is of particular importance. Now that we have learned something about the enemy's methods of gaining and maintaining territorial control, our next step is to determine where we will most likely engage his forces. While *all* satanic strongholds represent legitimate targets for concerted intercession and evangelism, a specific order of battle strategies is necessary if Christian warriors are to operate cohesively.

While we should not establish our target priorities by location alone, neither can we ignore the location intelligence we have on enemy troop concentrations.[18] If our mandate is to "demolish strongholds" and "proclaim liberty to the captives" (2 Corinthians 10:4, NIV, and Isaiah 61:1), then we will have to confront the enemy where he is found in strength. Fortunately, we have an excellent idea of those boundaries.

In the spring of 1990 I visited one of the Church's best target analysts, Dr. David Barrett, at the headquarters of the Southern Baptist Foreign Mission Board in Richmond, Virginia. As editor of the *World Christian Encyclopedia* and a leading expert on missions and church growth statistics, Dr. Barrett has become a repository for annual progress reports generated by most Protestant denominations and mission agencies. Upon receipt, these reports, along with numerous other pieces of missions intelligence, are loaded by

Dr. Barrett and his staff into a Vax computer for cataloging and analysis.

At one point in my conversation with Dr. Barrett, he took me into an office where a large world map covered with a piece of clear acetate hung on the wall. In the middle of this overlay I could see a crude oval drawn with a grease pencil. Using his computer data on unreached people groups as a guide, Dr. Barrett explained that he had carefully traced the current frontiers of world evangelization. The result was a discriminate border that, on its eastern trajectory, engulfed all of North Africa and the Near East before knifing across the midsections of India and Burma. In the Orient, the boundary undulated around Southeast Asia, China's outlying provinces, Japan and North Korea before finally darting westward through the spiritually parched expanses of Mongolia, Soviet Central Asia, Turkey and Albania.

Pointing at the oval, Dr. Barrett declared matter-of-factly: "That is our remaining task. Within these frontiers reside at least ninety-five percent of the world's unreached peoples—including all un-evangelized megapeoples."[19]

More recently, Argentine-born mission executive Luis Bush has labeled roughly this same area as the *10/40 Window*—so named because of its geographic position between the tenth and fortieth latitudes.[20]

As the Church prepares to confront the 10/40 Window, she is faced with a challenge of enormous proportion. For lying within the frame of this strategic territory are the central headquarters of virtually every major non-Christian religious system on earth: Buddhism, Communism,[21] Confucianism, Hinduism, Islam, Shintoism and Taoism. Only the corporate offices of materialism lie outside its borders, and they are absorbed with the task of subtly impeding Christian mobilization for battle.

By playing host to these religious nerve centers—and some 95 percent of the world's unreached peoples—the lands and societies of the 10/40 Window can hardly avoid becoming the primary spiritual battleground of the 1990s and beyond. And when the epic conflict finally unfolds, enemy operations will in all likelihood be managed from two powerful strongholds—Iran and Iraq—situated

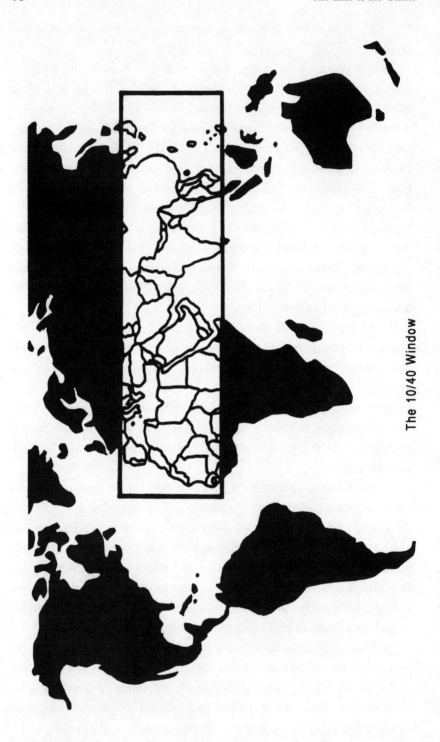

The 10/40 Window

at the epicenter of the Window. The scene could not be more dramatic: a latter-day scenario in the vicinity of ancient Persia and Babylon. After a pause of nearly 7,000 years, the world is once again focused on the very cradle of civilization, the poignant dreamland where God's first dealings with man took place.

The Garden of Dreams

The archives of Scripture reveal that, following Satan's initial defeat in the Great Heavenly War, there were two crucial moments in history that involved particularly venomous counterattacks against the designs of God. One of these, recorded in Revelation 12:3, was the dragon's determined attempt to devour the Christ Child—an operation, happily, that failed. The other well-known episode, registered in the book of Genesis, met with some success.

Eden, which means "Delight," was the site where God first set up camp on this earth. It was, in many respects, His Garden of Dreams—a magical place, devoid of sin, where He walked with man and shared His heart and ways. Here God handed out man's first mandate, or commission: *to be representatives of His Kingdom order in the earth.* Out of this place called Delight, through Adam and Eve and their offspring, the knowledge and blessing of God was to flow into all the earth.[22]

Sadly, Genesis 3 reveals that Eden was also home to a crafty serpent who, energized by cruel spite, was determined to transform God's Garden of Dreams into the equivalent of a spiritual toxic waste dump.

Launching his campaign with a masterful deception, Satan succeeded in facilitating the entrance of sin into the world. And while Adam and Eve's moral breakdown led to their banishment from Eden, there is no indication in Scripture that the serpent went with them.

Instead, there is striking evidence that the serpent of Eden has established a global command and control center atop the oily residue of the Garden's once flourishing vegetation and animal life. The Bible alludes to such concentrations of demonic authority as "seats," and they are not places friendly to the purposes of God. At the same time, as we proceed to examine more closely the historical and operational intricacies of this stronghold, readers should bear in mind that while God expects us to be vigilant and sober-minded about such things, He does not want us to be fearful or unduly impressed. While the Bible does not whitewash the fact that there is evil in the world, neither does it speak of it in triumphal terms. In the end, all malign spiritual forces will be subject to the awesome power and righteous judgment of the Almighty. Even now, as we shall discover in chapter 7, the victorious strategies of God are unfolding apace in and around the seat of Satan.

Notes

1 Quoted in *Distilled Wisdom*, ed, Alfred Armand Montapert (Englewood Cliffs, N.J.: Prentice-Hall, 1964), p. 20.

2 Quoted in *Overcoming the Dominion of Darkness* (Tarrytown, N.Y.: Chosen Books, 1990), p. 24.

3 Chuck Kraft, *Christianity with Power* (Ann Arbor, Mich.: Vine Books, 1989), p. 15.

4 C. Peter Wagner, "Territorial Spirits," *Wrestling with Dark Angels*, C. Peter Wagner & F. Douglas Pennoyer, eds. (Ventura, Calif.: Regal Books, 1990), p. 77.

5 This theory was first proposed to me by missiologist Steven Hawthorne following a 1990 missions conference in Houston, Texas.

Buttressing the fact of God's universal fatherhood, the prophet Malachi asks rhetorically: "Do we not all have one father? Has not one God created us?" (2:10). In Matthew's Gospel Jesus warns: "And do not call anyone on earth your father; for One is your father, He who is in heaven" (23:9). Later on, the apostle Paul speaks to the Ephesian Christians about "One God and Father of all who is over all" (4:6).

Satan's authority over human systems is affirmed in John 14:30 where Jesus refers to him as the "prince of this world (kosmos)." It is also evidenced in both Matthew 4:8–9 and Luke 4:6 where the devil shows Christ "the kingdoms of the world" and offers to exchange them in return for illicit worship. The good news is that, eventually, "The kingdoms of this world [will] become the kingdoms of our Lord, and of his Christ; and he shall reign for ever and ever" (Revelation 11:15).

6 See Acts 17:26–28 (NASB).

7 Edwin Bernbaum, *Sacred Mountains of the World* (San Francisco: Sierra Club Books, 1990), pp. 183–184.

8 Percival Lowell, *Occult Japan* (Rochester, V.T.: Inner Traditions International 1894/ 1990), pp. 223–229; see also Bernbaum p. 58.

9 Conversation in the early 1970s with a veteran missionary to Nepal whose eleven-year ministry in the country involved outreach to Tibetan-Buddhist monks; corrob-

orating evidence was provided in conversations with a Nepali monk, Lobsang-la Dorje, and an indigenous Nepali Christian.

Light phenomena are also reported to occur with some regularity in Britain, the United States, India and Scandinavia. In Britain and the U.S., the phenomena have been widely observed by scientists, and even captured on video tape. Primary activity sites include the Smoky Mountains of North Carolina, central Wales (between Llanidloes and Devil's Bridge), and the Peak District of Derbyshire in Britain. In 1987 a dramatic upsurge in the incidence of light phenomena attracted wide public attention—some people thinking it had something to do with a research unit of British Aerospace. According to a description given by British scientist Paul Devereux, "The lights emerge from the summits of the hills and mountains in the form of purple-white flashes and as globes of blue light. These same summits are extensively punctuated with prehistoric cairns (pagan stone piles often used as altars)."

Light phenomena associated with spirits have also been reported among such diverse and far-removed peoples as arctic Eskimos and native Hawaiians, African Ewe and Scandinavian Lapps. In North America, encounters with spiritual lights have been recorded by Mexico's Tzeltal people, as well as by the Yakima, Snohomish, Penobscot and various California Indian tribes in the United States. See Paul Devereux, *Places of Power* (1990), *Earth Lights* (1982), *Earth Lights Revelation* (1989).

10 Don Richardson, *Eternity in Their Hearts* (Ventura, Calif.: Regal Books, 1981), pp. 34–40.

11 Carole Devillers, "Of Spirits and Saints," *National Geographic* magazine, March 1985.

12 "Secret Rite Climaxes Akhito's Coronation," *The Seattle Times*, November 23, 1990.

13 See H.W.F. Saggs, *The Greatness that Was Babylon* (London: Sidgwick & Jackson, 1962/1988), pp. 330–337.
Note: It is not known if the similarities between the Daijosai and the Sacred Marriage arise from specific historical contact between ancient Japan and Babylonian culture, or were simply choreographed by related, spiritual powers.

14 Matthew 12:29 and Mark 3:27.

15 An example of this spiritual hierarchy is found in Haiti, where Legba is always the first loa to be invoked in voodoo rites. To do otherwise could mean that the other spirits, which he dominates, might not respond.

16 For more information on this subject see the author's forthcoming book, *Faces of the Dragon* (address inquiries to The Sentinel Institute, P.O. Box 6334, Lynnwood, WA 98036).

17 2 Corinthians 10:4.

18 While it must be reaffirmed that our true enemy is never flesh and blood, those disturbed by the use of any military analogy will ultimately have to reconcile their sensitivities with Scripture. See 1 Samuel 17:45; Psalm 144:1; Ephesians, 6:10–18; 2 Corinthians 10:4; 1 Thessalonians 5:8; 1 Timothy 1:18; 2 Timothy 2:4; Revelation 19:11–21.

19 Conversation with Dr. David Barrett, Richmond, Virginia, April 1990.

20 It is important to note that while this term is a helpful label, it is also an inexact one. In Asia, for instance, several concentrations of unreached peoples living in areas

such as Northern China, Mongolia, Indonesia and Soviet Central Asia, are left
outside the borders of the 10/40 Window.

21 Communism's place on the list is based on the assumption that Moscow has abdi-
cated its leading revolutionary role to China—and, perhaps to a lesser extent, North
Korea.

22 See Genesis 1:26–28; also, Psalm 36:8 declares: "They feast on the abundance of
your house; you give them drink from your river of delights" (NIV).

5

By the Rivers of Babylon

By the rivers of Babylon, there we sat down, yea, we
wept when we remembered Zion.

Psalm 137:1

And he cried out with a mighty voice, saying, "Fallen,
fallen is Babylon the great! And she has become a
dwelling place of demons and a prison of every unclean
spirit, and a prison of every unclean and hateful bird."

Revelation 18:2 (NASB)

For at least the past seven millennia, the land of Mesopotamia has served as a dwelling place of demons, spiritual van-
dals whose idea of a good time is trashing the handiwork of a
superior Craftsman. In league with the region's human civilizations—Assyria, Babylon and, now, Iraq—they have forged a
remarkable legacy of arrogance, violence and debauchery.

These dark princes have remained in the land because they have
found a welcome haven. From the days of the first family's willingness to entertain the serpent in Eden, virtually every generation
to populate this strategic area has kept the sheets turned down in
their spiritual guestrooms. As a consequence, perhaps no other
address on earth today can boast so formidable a congregation of
evil spirits.

The Peacock Angel

A modern example of this is found in the Sinjar Hills of north-western Iraq. Here, around the towns of Mosul and Lalish, live the Yezidi people—known in the area as the "devil worshipers." A tribe of some 150,000, the Yezidis are a mixture of Arabs and Kurds. Like Christians, they believe Satan to be a powerful angel; but unlike Christians, they accord him great respect and, in fact, worship.

Among other things, Yezidis believe that the chief of the angelic hosts, whom they call *Azaziel* rather than Lucifer, played a major role in creation. They contend that Azaziel, far from being respon-sible for man's fall, merely provided Adam and Eve with practical counsel on the biological functions of the body.[1]

Actually, the name *Azaziel* is seldom used among modern Yez-idis, and the name *Satan* is strictly forbidden. Instead, he is called *Melek Taus,* or the Peacock Angel. Every October the bronze im-age of the Peacock Angel—called the *Anzal,* or Ancient Pea-cock—is paraded through Lalish followed by torches and incense. Along the procession route, the hymn-singing faithful prostrate themselves before the sacred symbol.[2]

At the annual Feast of the Assembly, an event that combines "the mystic experience of a revival with the joy of a carnival," children are baptized at a shrine where the hallowed White Spring wells up into tanks inhabited by sacred newts. Later, as darkness creeps over the Lalish Valley, pilgrims pass their hands through the flames of oil lamps carried by Yezidi faqirs, while the leading sheikhs seek the guidance of Melek Taus before his bronze image. Around midnight the secret ceremony is closed with Arabic chants in the inner court of the sanctuary.[3]

The great prophet of the Yezidi religion is Sheikh Adi Musa-fir. Yezidi traditions record that some eight hundred years ago Musafir, at the age of twenty, was riding by moonlight across a plain. In front of an old tomb an apparition rose out of the ground: two camels with eight-foot legs, heads like water buffaloes, long bristly hair, big, round, ox-like eyes glowing green and jet-black skin. Meanwhile, the tomb grew larger until it touched the clouds, taking the shape of a minaret, which began to shake. Suddenly the apparition turned into a handsome boy with a peacock's tail who said to him:

> "Fear not; the minaret may well fall and destroy the world, but you and those that hearken to you will be unharmed and will rule over the ruins. I am Melek Taus and have chosen you to proclaim the religion of truth to the world."[4]

Even more revealing are the following excerpts taken from the two Yezidi sacred books, *The Book of Revelation* and *The Black Book*. Quotations from *Kitab el-Jelwa* (*The Book of Revelation*):

> √ "Every age has a Regent, and this by my counsel. Every generation changes with the Chief of this World. . . ."
> √ "I guide without a scripture; I point the way by unseen means unto my friends. . . ."
> √ "Three there are opposed to me, and three names do I hate."

Quotations from *Meshaf Resh* (*The Black Book*):

> √ "Neither is it permitted to us to pronounce the name of Satan (because it is the name of our God).
> √ "King Ahab and Amran were of us, so that they used to call the God of Ahab Beelzebub. . . . We had a king in Babel whose name was Nebuchadnezzar. . . . And Ahasuerus in Persia. . . ."[5]

Omens, Ghosts and Ziggurats:
A Tale of Four Cities

"Baghdad," as one writer has observed, "is an old city, but not half as old as Mesopotamian time." In this part of the world the dust sweeps in from more ancient places—from Ur of the Chaldees, from the Assyrian capitals of Nineveh and Nimrud and, of course, from Babylon.

Cities, perhaps more than any other spotlight, reveal best the story of demonic entrenchment in this time-worn land. Of the four we have chosen to profile, Ur and Nineveh-Nimrud (considered one metropolis in the manner of Minneapolis-St. Paul) have succumbed to the ravages of nature; Babylon has been ceremoniously rebuilt; and Karbala stands firm as a metaphor of the Islamic struggle.

Ur of the Chaldees

In Genesis 12:1 God spoke to Abraham, apparently with some urgency, saying: "Get thee out of thy country, and from thy kindred, and from thy father's house, unto a land that I will show thee" (KJV). The question is, Why? What did God see that persuaded Him He could not carry out His covenantal plan through Abraham right where he was?

The answer may have to do with the fact that, as powerful city-states emerged in ancient Mesopotamia, virtually all of them were built around temple organizations and patron deities. This was certainly the case with Ur of the Chaldees, Abraham's famed hometown.

In fact, the spiritual ruler of Ur—a moon god that would ultimately become the supreme deity of the entire Babylonian empire[6]—was nicknamed "The Controller of the Night." This suggestive title is surpassed only by the literal name of this idol: *Sin!* *Sin*'s emblem, the crescent moon, was later adopted, along with the lunar-based calendar, as primary religious symbols of Islam.[7]

Nimrud and Nineveh of the Assyrians

Another of the most powerful deities of the day—*Ishtar*, the goddess of love and war—was associated with Assyria's imperial capitals of Nineveh and Nimrud. While these great cities have since been demoted to archaeological mounds bookending the modern Iraqi town of Mosul, they were in their heyday impressive metropolises dominated by temple complexes honoring the pagan Ishtar.

In his book *The Treasures of Darkness*, Thorkild Jacobsen lists several Sumero-Babylonian texts and hymns celebrating Ishtar as the divine harlot, a goddess whose prolific sexuality allowed for 120 men without tiring. Associated with the cult of Ishtar were transvestite dancers (*kurgarru* and *assinnu*) and a high priestess known as the *Entu,* whose role it was to please the gods on a sumptuous couch atop the ziggurat.[8]

In fact, Ishtar's legacy of temple prostitution extended well beyond the Entu. In the fifth century B.C., the Greek traveler Herodotus reported that in Babylon, "every woman must once in her life go and sit in the temple of Aphrodite and there have intercourse with a stranger." (The process required the woman to wait until a stranger cast a coin into her lap and solicited her, 'in the name of the goddess Mylitta' [a title of Ishtar].) "When she has surrendered herself," Herodotus continued, "her duty to the goddess has been rendered and she may return home."[9]

Babylon the Great

With an estimated 4,000 gods associated with its polytheistic culture, Babylon—*Bab-ili,* or "Gateway of the Gods"—was clearly well-named. For the most part, those gods that elected to enter the city did so via a celestial passage, which only the king and certain temple attendants could visualize.

The temple complex in Babylon and most other cities within the empire included the *ziggurat*—a great stepped tower of three to seven stages, at the top of which stood a small temple. Many viewed the high temple as being an intermediate dwelling place for the gods on their way down from heaven to earth. The most famous of the ziggurats, the Tower of Babel, was thus a kind of ladder "connecting" heaven and earth.[10]

Once on earth, the gods' primary point of contact with human beings was through graven images, or idols, that remained in a state of honored repose within the temple. To ensure that the deity took up his or her dwelling within the idol, the Babylonians practiced a fascinating ritual called "The Opening of the Mouth." Once the image left the hands of its human craftsmen, its next stop was a preliminary "gargle" with holy water, after which

> the god was led at night by torchlight to the river bank, where he was seated on a reed-mat facing east, with incantations and "washing of the mouth" continuing all night. In the morning, after the sacrifice of a ram, came the crucial point of the ritual, when the idol

became a sentient thing. To the accompaniment of an incantation, "Holy image that is perfected by a great ritual," the priest "opened the eyes" of the god by touching them with a twig of the magical tamarisk. The statue, now alive with the deity immanent within it, was led by the hand to his temple and, after further offerings, placed on his throne.[11]

Omens and divination were also an integral part of Babylonian society. At the start of every new year, the king (believed to be an incarnate god) and a temple priestess (in the role of the goddess Ishtar) engaged in "Sacred Marriage" (ritual intercourse) as a prelude to the "fixing of destinies" for the coming year. On a less exalted level, messages from the spirit world were also conveyed through such things as liver divination, dreams, astrology and even the movements of certain animals. Astrology and liver divination were apparently the preferred tools for forecasting matters of state. (Private citizens generally relied upon other means.)

To the Babylonians, the supernatural world was fully alive. Gods, ghosts and demons were everywhere. The latter, equal in power with the gods but far less rational, were especially feared. In addition to *Rabisu,* the Croucher, a ubiquitous demon who lurked in doorways and dark corners, other dreaded spirits were associated with such things as childbirth, plague, night, ruins and open spaces—connections that remain to this day.

There were also the ghosts of dead humans to be reckoned with. Especially terrifying were "wandering ghosts"—the restless and vengeful wraiths of those who had died as a consequence of violence or encroachment upon some taboo. Those haunted by such spirits endeavored through prayers, incantations and professional exorcists to send them to Cuthah—a city considered to be the "assembly place of the ghosts."[12] Cuthah is mentioned in 2 Kings 17:24, 30 as the city of Nergal, god of the underworld.

Babylonian exorcist-priests were called *ashipu*—a word used by the prophet Daniel for "enchanter."[13] Akin to modern-day witch doctors, their procedures were recorded in collected magical texts called *Shurpu* and *Maqlu*—titles that mean "burning" (owing to the prescribed ritual destruction by fire of wood, clay and waxen images).

Karbala of the Shiites

Another important site in Iraq is that of Karbala. It is significant not for its history of demons and divination, but as the shrine that instills Shi'ite Muslims with their fervor for martyrdom. Here, in A.D. 680, Muhammad's grandson Hussein was massacred with his 72 followers in an attempt to regain from the ruling Sunni caliph, Yazid, the reins of the Islamic succession. In his failed attempt, Hussein became the Shi'ites' patron saint of martyrdom. Each year on Ashura, the anniversary of Hussein's death, Shi'ites around the world conduct a bloody passion play in which they attempt, through self-inflicted wounds, to participate in the sacrifice of their hero.

The late Ayatollah Khomeini often rallied his frenzied followers with the cry "Every day is Ashura and every place is Karbala!" By repeatedly referencing the sacrifice of Hussein, the Imam made it clear that good Shi'ites prefer a bloody death to a life of shame. "We are ready to be killed," he declared with frightening determination, "and we have made a covenant with God to follow the path of our leader, the Lord of the Martyrs."[14]

Karbala and nearby Kufa are also significant in Shi'ite eschatology. Tradition dictates that after the Islamic messiah—known as the *Mahdi*—makes his initial appearance in Mecca, he will return to Iraq to establish his capital in Kufa (the city of Muhammad's son-in-law, Ali). "On that day," according to one scholar, "all the believers will be assembled in that city and the surrounding areas, which will expand immeasurably to the neighborhood of Karbala to accommodate all the Shi'ites. Karbala that day will be the frequenting place of the angels and the believers."[15]

Reviving the Spirit of Babylon

In his 1957 lectures on the book of Revelation entitled "The Apocalypse," theologian J. A. Seiss stated that "there seems to be reason for the belief that the literal Babylon will be restored, and that we are to look to the coming up again of that primal city."[16]

For nearly three decades after Mr. Seiss' prediction, there was little visible support of his interpretation of Scripture. In the late

1980s, however, the skepticism of many Christians was disturbed by the busy sounds of construction. Eyes soon followed ears to a remarkable sight about an hour's drive southwest of Baghdad. There on the banks of the Euphrates River, visible through the shimmering heat and ancient dust, the great forty-foot-high yellow brick walls of Babylon were indeed rising again.

Working with plans drawn up by Robert Kolderwey, a German scholar who excavated the Babylon site early in the century, thousands of Iraqi, Egyptian and Sudanese laborers carefully restored many of the once-great city's most prominent features. Using a combination of original and specially made new materials, the architects and builders managed to recreate the 300-foot-high ziggurat dedicated to the Babylonian god Marduk, the coronation hall of Nebuchadnezzar, and the blue-tiled Ishtar Gate. To date, the architecture of the famous Hanging Gardens remains a mystery, although the government has announced a $2 million reward to the engineer who first unlocks its secret.

While some dismiss the new Babylon as little more than an ancient-world Disneyland, it is clear that there is more to this undertaking than first meets the eye. For all intents and purposes, a *spirit*, not just a city, has been reborn—Babylonian excess characterized by delusions of grandeur and the intoxication of violence (see Revelation 18:7; 17:4–6).

As the most recent incarnation of this spirit, Saddam Hussein has also been among its greatest champions. In his calculating mind, the original rationale behind the restoration of Babylon was, no doubt, to allow modern Iraqis to bathe in the reflected glory of Mesopotamian civilization. "We want to be the great Arab country we were in the past," declares Jabra Ibrahim Jabra, an influential Iraqi writer and academic. "Saddam Hussein, he focuses this enthusiasm . . . as we see through his eyes and image." At the same time, states Jabra, "a great king is only great if he builds a city or rebuilds one."[17]

No fewer than a dozen empires were ruled from what is now Iraq and throughout the 1980s, Saddam's propaganda machine was hard at work identifying him with those empires' greatest rulers. (Myth, it has been said, is more potent than history.)[18] Thus,

Saddam has often been referred to as *Al Mansour*, a conquering Abbasid caliph whose name means "the one whom God made victorious." In early 1990 at a birthday celebration held in his hometown of Takrit, Saddam was toasted as the modern embodiment of Sargon the Great. In other settings he has been associated with the ancient Babylonian kings Hammurabi and, perhaps most notably, Nebuchadnezzar.

Time-warp portraits of Saddam shaking hands with that infamous biblical monarch adorn select Baghdad street corners. A tile fresco in a small museum near Babylon's Ishtar Gate depicts the two leaders in even more dramatic fashion. On the left, Saddam smiles with satisfaction over his modern capital (*sans* recent Allied bomb damage), while on the right Nebuchadnezzar casts a steely-eyed glance at his new palace.

At the entrance of every Iraqi village, towering cut-out figures of Saddam can be seen at great distances. In the daytime they hover over rural commerce like malevolent guardians; after dark they emit what dissident author Samir al-Khalil calls "a lurid fluorescent glow." In many respects Saddam Hussein has himself taken on the aura of Babylon and its most fearsome and megalomaniacal leader. While Nebuchadnezzar boasted he had "no rivals from horizon to sky," Saddam emerged in the 1980s with a bevy of honorific titles including "the standard bearer," "the father leader" and "the knight of the Arab nation."[19]

What does the association mean? Nebuchadnezzar's dream, of course, was nothing short of immortality. He believed the serpent's original lie to Adam and Eve—a lie that echoes to this day throughout the Mesopotamian basin. And his arrogance, violence and debauchery rose to unprecedented heights. In recent days, this spirit of Babylon has manifested itself in a remarkably similar fashion.

Not only has a dark personality cult around Saddam raised him to near-immortal status,[20] but he has shrewdly exercised the power of life and death. Those who bow down receive the king's favor. Those who do not become kindling for the fiery furnace. As al-Khalil observes:

. . . the Leader's omnipotence is acted out dramatically, as though performed on a stage. Favors are bestowed on people in such a way as to break the very rules the Leader's state enforces; he opens a hot line to the citizens at a fixed hour in order to listen to complaints, and follows this up by releasing someone's husband or son from a life sentence that his police had originally imposed; he hands out television sets and wads of freshly minted notes while touring villages in the south; and he drops in on apparently unsuspecting humble citizens to have breakfast and listen to their complaints.[21]

Fear is employed with equal flair. Like Nebuchadnezzar's courtiers (with the delightful exception of the Jews who feared Yahweh more), the men who have surrounded Saddam offer a portrait of groveling obeisance. Former Iranian U.N. Ambassador Mansour Farhang tells of seeing "two Iraqis walking backward and sideways when they left the room—in an effort to avoid turning their backs to the exalted leader."[22] Their caution was advised. In the past, high-level officials who have ignored or crossed Saddam have been cut up in pieces and delivered to their families in black canvas bags.[23]

Arabian Nights of Terror

A primary manifestation of the spirit of Babylon is a preoccupation with fear, violence, death and the destruction of the human spirit—choice sacrifices to the invisible rulers of darkness. Perhaps nowhere else on earth have people suffered so ferociously for so long. In earlier centuries, the unfortunates of Mesopotamian society were liable not only to be pitched into Nebuchadnezzar's infamous fiery furnace, but also to have their "lying tongues" pulled out by the Assyrians—a race of studied executioners who also burned, flayed, impaled and buried their victims alive.[24]

During the Abbasid dynasty in the seventh century, the governor of Mesopotamia's Iraq province, al-Hadjadj, launched a reign that one historian has termed "frank terror." Upon assuming his governorship, he promptly executed all dissident rivals—an act that would later be emulated by Saddam Hussein. In full view of their severed heads, al-Hadjadj then delivered a public address that

captured the spirit of Babylon. It contained these immortal lines
that have been passed on to generations of Iraqi schoolchildren:

> "I see heads before me that are ripe and ready for the plucking,
> and I am the one to pluck them, and I see blood glistening between
> the turbans and the beards."[25]

If anything, the advent of "modern civilization" has served only
to make state-sponsored slaughter more efficient. From the early
1970s, Saddam Hussein and his immediate predecessors razed
more than 4,000 villages, evicted at least 1.5 million people and
killed upward of a quarter-million individuals.[26] In the past
decade, an estimated 35,000 people were executed for their religious beliefs alone.[27] Thousands of others—primarily Kurds and
Kuwaitis—were disposed of for other reasons.

In this unimaginably brutal land, it is possible to be arrested,
tortured, even executed for such things as telling political jokes,
failing to display the president's portrait, taking a picture of the
Tigris River at sunset and accidentally spilling coffee on a newspaper photo of Saddam.[28] In the northern town of Sulaymaniyah,
the bodies of victims were returned to relatives along with a bill for
the bullets used in their executions. Others have been killed by rat
poison, beatings, poison gas and hanging. In one particularly grisly
episode, the government hung the mutilated bodies of several
victims on Liberation Square while Radio Baghdad summoned
people to "come and enjoy the feast."[29]

The footsoldiers of this terror are the members of Iraq's massive
secret police apparatus. This four-headed monster includes the
Amn al-Khass (State Internal Security), the *Estikhbarat* (Military
Intelligence), the *Mukhabarat* (Baathist Party Intelligence) and
the *Presidential Affairs Department* (Direct Presidential Intelligence). The largest and most dangerous of these is the Mukhabarat, an agency that watches over the other police institutions and
was active in the atrocities perpetrated in Kuwait. When the ranks
of the secret police are added to those of the Border Guards, the
Mobile Police Strike Force, the General Department of National-
ity, the General Department of Police and the Armed Forces, an

astonishing twenty percent of the Iraqi labor force is charged, according to al-Khalil, "with one form or another of violence."[30]

In Stalinesque fashion, the Iraqi secret police have managed to place an effective mental straitjacket on much of the citizenry. Nearly everyone is afraid to speak for fear their words will be recorded by one of Saddam's ubiquitous hidden videocameras, a block watch informer or, worse yet, a member of their own family. In a 1977 publication, the Iraqi president wrote:

> To prevent the father and mother dominating the household with backwardness, we must make the small one radiate internally to expel it. Some fathers have slipped away from us for various reasons, but the small boy is still in our hands and we must transform him into an interactive radiating center inside the family. . . . You must place in every corner a son of the revolution, with a trustworthy eye and a firm mind that receives its instructions from the responsible center of the revolution.[31]

Nadhim Kzar, the first chief of Internal State Security under Saddam, reportedly ordered the torture and execution of several thousand people. In 1971, more than four hundred rivals were liquidated in the aptly named *Qasr al-Nihayyah,* or "Palace of the End." Famous for his habit of extinguishing cigarettes in the eyeballs of his victims, Kzar did much to nurture the widespread and sadistic forms of torture practiced today. A sampling of these methods have included roasting victims over flames, amputating noses, limbs and sexual organs, and hammering nails into joints. Children are tortured in front of parents, and suckling infants are held in cells next to mothers and denied food so that their cries will induce confessions. One survivor even reported that the entrance to his torture chamber was cynically marked with a mat that read *Welcome.*[32]

It is also worth pointing out that the Iraqi regime has not reserved these horrors solely for its own domestic population. In occupied Kuwait, for instance, Iraqi soldiers and secret police tortured and summarily executed thousands of citizens before being driven back by advancing Allied troops. In oblique reference to the demonic nature of the carnage, General Norman Schwarzkopf could describe the participating Iraqi forces only as "not of the same human race."

Reflecting on the days of horror, Dr. Khalid Shalawi, head physician at Kuwait City's Mubarak Hospital, said he often wept over what had happened. According to eyewitness accounts from insiders like trauma nurse Basma Yusef, Iraqi torture victims were brought in with cigarette and acid burns, fingernails and facial hair torn out, holes drilled through their kneecaps and intestines inflated with air. Others were kicked in the stomach, electro-shocked on the genitals and suspended upside-down. One man had his ears cut off, while another was burned so badly "he had no skin." Scores were murdered with ax blows. "The head is open and the brains are out," Yusef recounted. "Some, their eyes have been taken out."[33]

Nor were women exempt from the nightmare. *Newsweek* reported that the Iraqis paraded one nursing mother before captured Kuwaiti resistance fighters. "Here is the milk of Kuwait," they taunted. "Drink it." Others, including countless rape victims, fared worse. Some were gang-raped and killed, their nude bodies stuffed into trash bins. Rasha Kabundi, a young mother of three, was shot four times in the chest and jaw before the top of her skull was removed with an electric saw. Her body, too, was found in a rubbish heap.[34]

While it is hard to imagine, Kuwaitis are actually second-echelon targets when it comes to Iraqi Baathist cruelty and racism. At the top of the list are Persians and Jews. In 1981, the Iraqi government printing house issued a widely circulated pamphlet by the former governor of Baghdad and father-in-law of Saddam Hussein, Khairallah Tulfah. In the booklet, entitled *Three Whom God Should Not Have Created: Persians, Jews and Flies*, Tulfah calls Persians "animals God created in the shape of humans." Jews are a "mixture of dirt and leftovers of diverse peoples," while flies are a trifling creation "whom we do not understand God's purpose in creating."[35]

Insofar as the Jews are concerned, Saddam Hussein has been visited in his dreams, just as the spirits came to Nebuchadnezzar's successor, Nabuna'id, in similar fashion directing him to render supreme honor to the moon god Sin. Visited first by an unnamed messenger urging the resurrection of Babylon's glory, Saddam subsequently claimed to have received dreamtime instructions concerning the recent targeting of Iraq's Scud missiles from no less than the Prophet Muhammad.

Easier to get at but no less hated are the Persians. During the war with Iran, fighting was particularly bitter in the southern marches that the Iraqis call *Majnoon,* or "madness." One American reporter visiting the front was astounded when an Iraqi officer told him with a broad grin, "You wait until nighttime, and you will see how we are killing these Iranian dogs. We are frying them like eggplants." Each night hundreds of Iranians would be lured into the marshes and electrocuted by an elaborate system of underwater cables attached to generators. The next day their bodies would be piled on top of one another in head-to-toe stacks, sprinkled with lime and dirt and used as a road for military vehicles.[36]

In what could almost pass for a tribute to the heathen god Moloch, a frequently appearing phrase in Assyrian royal annals declares, "Their corpses I formed into pillars; their young men and maidens I burned in the fire."[37] While Moloch and the Assyrian Empire have retreated into history, the spirits that once animated them have not.

The Aftermath of War

An anecdote illustrative of street-level thinking in Iraq was provided recently by *Los Angeles Times* reporter Mark Fineman and a German student named Thomas. Looking for a slice of "the real Iraq," the two wandered into a bookstore on Baghdad's Rashid Street where they found, much to their surprise, a copy of Adolf Hitler's *Mein Kampf.* The owner of the store walked over to the shelf and picked up the book reverently. "You Americans will never understand us," he said. *"Mein Kampf* is one of my best sellers. It's a brilliant work by a powerful man. Here in Iraq, we like Hitler. Hitler sells. . . ."[38]

Interestingly, researchers during the Gulf War uncovered Saddam's own version of Hitler's famous work. Entitled *Unser Kampf,* or "Our Struggle," the book outlines Iraqi aims to unite the Arabs and split the West. In it, the Iraqi dictator declares: "We believe in a policy of tension, in the preparation of war."[39] Perhaps surprisingly, the words *we* and *our* as employed here by Saddam are genuine. As one low-level civil servant put it recently: "Even if Saddam is killed, a thousand more will spring up to take his place."

Those who believe that traditional weapons of warfare will put an end to the brutality that is Iraq are sadly mistaken. For the battle cannot be directed against a single individual—even one as despicable as Saddam Hussein—any more than it can be against flesh and blood in general. Like a spiritual hydra, so long as the demonic principalities at the root of the land flourish, the spirit of Saddam and his vision of Babylon will live on.

It is often acknowledged that Iraq's history is the bloodiest and most unstable in a bloody and unstable neighborhood. "There are a lot of theories as to why that is," notes Laurie Mylroie of Harvard University's Center for Middle Eastern Studies. "But none of [them] really explains it very well."[40]

None, that is, short of the prodigious blood lust and destructive urges of resident unclean spirits.

Notes

1 John S. Guest, *The Yezidis* (London: Routledge & Kegan Paul, Ltd., 1987), p. 30.
2 K. Jansel, "They Worship the Satan," *Depthnews*, January 7, 1989.
3 Guest, pp. 37, 96–97.
4 *Ibid.*, p. 31.
5 *Ibid.*, pp. 200–204.
6 *Sin* was elevated to the top of the Babylonian pantheon by *Nabu-na'id* (Nabonidus) in an effort to make Babylonian religion more acceptable to subjects like the Arabians and Aramaeans. For while the latter esteemed the moon god, they had more difficulty identifying with *Marduk*, the supreme Babylonian deity associated primarily with the city of Babylon.
7 See chapter 3, "Revelations & Bewitchments: The Mystical World Of Islam."
8 H. W. F. Saggs, *The Greatness that Was Babylon* (London: Sidgwick & Jackson, 1962/1988), pp. 302–305.
9 Quoted in Saggs, p. 303.
10 *Ibid.*, p. 308.
11 *Ibid.*, p. 309.
12 From a Babylonian incantation recited by Saggs, p. 266.

13 See Daniel 2:10.

14 From a speech given by Ayatollah Khomeini in Teheran on September 12, 1980; quoted in *Islam and Revolution*, ed. Hamid Algar (Berkeley: Mizan Press, 1981), p. 305.

15 Muhammad Baqir Majlisi (Bihar 2), quoted in *Islamic Messianism*, Abdulaziz Abdulhussein Sachedina (Albany, N.Y.: State University of New York Press, 1981), p. 165.

16 J. A. Seiss, *The Apocalypse, Lectures on the Book of Revelation* (Grand Rapids: Zondervan, 1957), p. 397.

17 "Saddam's Dream: Babylon Reborn," *The Seattle Times*, October 7, 1990.

18 The most dramatic fabrication allowed Saddam to produce a family tree that traced his ancestry back to the royal Arabian line and through them to the Prophet Muhammad.

19 Samir al-Khalil, *Republic of Fear: The Politics of Modern Iraq* (London: Hutchinson Radius, 1989), p. 110.

20 The extent of Saddam's personality cult has been rivaled in recent years only by those surrounding the U.S.S.R.'s Joseph Stalin and North Korea's Kim Il Sung. Prior to the Gulf War, Iraqi evening television opened with a song of devotion to the dictator, and in a typical radio broadcast his name was mentioned from thirty to fifty times an hour. Schoolchildren throughout the nation could be heard reciting his praises regularly, and a phalanx of poets wrote bushels of flowery tributes. His face adorned everything from watches to radios to huge billboards, and his hands—including fingerprints— were reproduced in exacting detail for the dramatic crossed sabre Victory Arch monument in downtown Baghdad.

In one particularly cultic ritual, *Newsweek* magazine reported in 1990 that some Iraqis have used their own blood to write pledges of allegiance or paint portraits of their "leader-struggler." Even those who choose not to go this far must be careful, however, as the Baathist cult is reinforced by the death penalty: Public insult of the president or the top party institutions has been a capital offense since 1986.

21 Al-Khalil, p. 116.

Note: Those who argue that the Iraqi dictator represents an aberration and that Islam has forever changed the mentality of the region might consider the words of Jordanian Supreme Court judge Sheikh Abdullah Ghoshah, who once remarked: "Allah, the Almighty, loves the Muslim to be arrogant when he is fighting, as it manifests that he is indifferent to his enemy and that he determines to vanquish him." Quoted by John Laffin in *The Challenge of Islam*—"Islam's Clandestine Operations" (Souldern, England: Institute for Demographic Studies, 1988).

22 Special to the *Los Angeles Times*; reprinted in *The Seattle Times*, September 16, 1990.

23 Mesopotamian leaders especially have felt the need to keep their military commanders off-balance. Thus the caliph Mu'tasim, who invaded the Byzantine Empire and developed a Muslim precursor to the Inquisition, once accused his top general of heresy and starved him to death in a locked room in his palace. In the late 1980s, in Saddam's Iraq, at least four leading generals and more than a dozen colonels met their end under mysterious circumstances. Many others have reportedly been purged before and since. Finally, as al-Khalil points out, "The mere fact of a soldier's membership in what might be construed as a political organization, irrespective of

actual engagement in political activity, has been a capital offense for many years now."

24 Saggs, p. 217.

25 Al-Khalil, p. 123. On p. 59 al-Khalil describes another macabre link in the continuum of violent intrigue that has typified Mesopotamian political life from the early days of the Babylonians and Assyrians. In 1963, some sixteen years before Saddam Hussein would assume power in Iraq, his Baathist Party executed President Abd al-Karim Qassem in a coup. In an effort to demoralize Qassem's lingering supporters, the victorious conspirators televised the president's bullet-ridden corpse propped up in a chair in the studio. As al-Khalil details the clip, "A soldier sauntered around, handling its parts. The camera would cut to scenes of devastation at the Ministry of Defense where Qassem had made his last stand. There, on location, it lingered on the mutilated corpses of Qassem's entourage. . . . Back to the studio, and close-ups now of the entry and exit points of each bullet hole. The whole macabre sequence [then] closes with a scene that must forever remain etched on the memory of all those who saw it: the soldier grabbed the lolling head by the hair, came right up close, and spat full face into it."

26 Estimates by the Society for Threatened Peoples (a German human rights organization). "Iraq Disregards Human Rights," Christian NewsWorld, June 1990.

27 Based on a CBS "60 Minutes" interview with Dr. Abo Ali, a physician, a survivor of Iraqi torture and the head of the London-based Islamic Daawa Party, October 7, 1990.

28 In occupied Kuwait, one's head could be lost merely by using currency bearing the image of the emir.

29 Al-Khalil, p. 52.

30 Ibid., p. 38.

31 "Saddam Harks Back to a Glorious Past," The Independent, August 11, 1990.

32 From an Amnesty International report on torture in Iraq. "Thousands Killed in a Reign of Terror," The Independent, March 16, 1990.

33 "Kuwaitis Weep for Countrymen After Senseless Acts by Iraqi Forces," The Seattle Times, March 1, 1991; Steven Strasser, "Kuwait: The Rape of a Nation," Newsweek, March 11, 1991; report by Amnesty International fact-finding team, reprinted in The International Journalist, January 18–24, 1991.

34 Ibid.

35 Al-Khalil, p. 17.

36 Mark Fineman, "In '84, Iraq Displayed Electrifying Brutality," The Seattle Times, August 15, 1990.

37 Saggs, p. 217.

38 Mark Fineman, "Searching for the Heart and Soul of Iraq," The Seattle Times, November 18, 1990.

39 "Saddam Watch: His 'Unser Kampf,'" Los Angeles Times, February 23, 1991.

40 Doyle McManus, "In Unforgiving Iraq, Hussein's Job—and His Life—On the Line," Ibid., February 26, 1991.

6

The Reemergence of the Prince of Persia

"The prince of the kingdom of Persia withstood me twenty-one days; and behold, Michael, one of the chief princes, came to help me."

Daniel 10:13

We are at war. And our battle has only just begun. Our first victory will be one tract of land somewhere in the world that is under the complete rule of Islam. Nothing can stop Islam from spreading.

Abd al-Qadir[1]

On this blessed day, the day the Islamic community assumes leadership, the day of victory and triumph of our people, I declare the Islamic Republic of Iran—the first day of God's government.

Ayatollah Ruhollah Khomeini (on the occasion of the formal proclamation of the Islamic Republic of Iran on April 1, 1979)[2]

It is a curious and tragic irony that the very regime that bestowed upon its enemies the epithet of "The Great Satan" should itself be controlled by him. Today, spiritual Persia stands alongside Babylon as one of the foremost obstacles in the path of advancing ambassadors of Christ.

There is mounting evidence to suggest that the powerful demonic prince of Persia has recently been loosed from his cosmic struggle with the archangel Michael and is once again prowling the neighborhoods of the Middle East.[3] If indeed this is so, the reemergence of this spiritual strongman may well have coincided with the advent of Iran's violent and far-reaching Islamic revolution.

If Iraq (Babylon) has become the favorite dwelling place of demonic hosts, Iran (Persia) has become their workshop. Fundamentalism has become their caustic raw material, and the Ayatollah Khomeini, who died June 3, 1989, their seemingly immortal master craftsman.

No mere political burp, the transformative events in Iran sent lasting shock waves throughout the entire world community. In the aftermath of the revolution, one stunned observer, Dr. Marvin Zonis, director of the University of Chicago's prestigious Middle East Institute, told colleagues at a high-level State Department seminar:

> The message from Iran—no matter how bizarre or trivial it sounds on first, second, fourth or thirty-ninth hearing—is in my opinion the single most impressive political ideology which has been proposed in the twentieth century since the Bolshevik Revolution."[4]

The story began—and, in a sense, concluded—on a frigid January day in 1979. For nearly twelve hours, Iranians of all ages waited in the cold along the major traffic artery between Teheran's Mehrabad Airport and the capital. Stirred with a sense of historic anticipation, they had come to catch a glimpse of their Imam. After spending years in exile in both Iraq and France, the revolution's symbol, eighty-year-old Ayatollah Khomeini, was returning home.

When the elderly cleric's Air France jumbo jet finally landed, the delirious crowd had grown to more than three million. Many, including Khomeini himself, passed out from the emotional exhaustion generated by the moment. Alongside her riveting description of the event, journalist Robin Wright pointed out that few observers at the time seemed capable of fully fathoming the portent of Khomeini's return. Instead of championing the traditional revolutionary theme of progress, the Iranian revolution took its people deep into the past for answers.

Establishing God's Government

If we are to understand what Khomeini had in mind when he proclaimed April 1, 1979, as "the first day of God's government," we must begin with a brief but important lesson in Islamic history. For while the Ayatollah's deeds will be remembered as part of our modern times, the impetus for his actions was derived from an era long gone.

The lesson begins shortly after Muhammad's death in A.D. 632 when his followers argued over who had the right to pick up the Prophet's political and spiritual mantle. On one side of the argument were the wealthy Umayyads, chief among the old ruling families of Mecca. On the other side were purists who asserted that rightful leadership of the Muslim community belonged to Muhammad's family.

Since the Prophet had no surviving sons, the latter faction had championed Ali, his first cousin and son-in-law, as the logical heir. Known as the *Shi'at Ali*, or party of Ali, they would eventually form the more militant Shi'a branch of Islam. The split between the two groups became permanent when the Umayyad caliphs[5] (precursors of the majority Sunnis) assassinated Ali and his sons, Hassan and Hussein (the latter at the famous battle of Karbala).

While the Umayyads managed to retain political power, the Shi'a viewed them as merely *de facto* rulers, unworthy usurpers who lacked spiritual legitimacy. "The rightful leadership of Islam," according to the partisans of Ali, instead "passed through a kind of apostolic succession of Imams."[6] Though not equal in stature with the Prophet, these Imams nevertheless served as important vessels of divine guidance and mediation and were, in fact, known as the "speaking Qur'an."[7]

Beginning with Ali in A.D. 650, most Shi'ite Muslims believe there was a total of twelve such Imams, the last of whom went into hiding around A.D. 940. Widely considered to be a messianic figure, the twelfth Imam was hidden from vengeful rulers some five years after the death of his father, Hasan al-Askari, and for the next approximately seventy years retained contact with his followers through four vice-regents who conveyed messages and collected taxes.[8] When the last of these vice-regents died, contact with the Imam was severed and the Shi'a community entered a period known as the Greater Occultation. Now called the "Hidden Imam," Shi'ites consider him *al-Qa'im al-Mahdi*—the "Savior who will rise" or "The Expected One."

Until the reappearance of the Mahdi, Shi'ites believe Allah's will, as expressed through Islamic faith and practice, is interpreted by the clergy, or *ulama*. Taking this doctrine a step further, the Ayatollah Khomeini bestowed upon himself the title *Vilayat-e-Faqih*, a dual politico-spiritual distinction that means the "Guardianship of the Supreme Religious Leader." While the role fell short of claiming the kind of spiritual horsepower possessed by the twelve Imams—who, according to Khomeini, "existed before the creation of the world in the form of lights situated beneath the divine throne, [and] were superior to other men"[9]—it nevertheless allowed him to speak as Islam's chief authority until the unveiling of the Expected One.

More than most clerics, Khomeini understood the importance of political power. Sir Muhammad Iqbal's maxim that "religion without power is only philosophy"[10] made perfect sense to him. Having finally established that "one tract of land under the complete rule of Islam," the Ayatollah set out to organize his government as a regency for the Mahdi. "Prepare yourselves to be of use to Islam," he told his fellow Iranians. "Act as the army of the Imam of the Age, in order to be able to serve him in spreading the rule of justice."[11] The preamble to the revised Iranian constitution later referred to the "ideological mission" of the Revolutionary Guard as one of "extend[ing] the sovereignty of God's law throughout the world."[12]

Shortly after returning to Iran in 1979, the Ayatollah and his

austere entourage shifted their base of operations from the holy
city of Qom to the northern Teheran suburb of Jamaran—a neighborhood that literally (and perhaps suggestively) means "haven of
snakes." Nearly a decade later, Robin Wright reported that "a
huge white banner was stretched across Jamaran's high entrance
gates. 'God, God,' it beseeched rather plaintively, 'keep Khomeini
alive until the Mahdi's revolution.' "[13]

While this prayer was not answered in the way its petitioners
intended, in another sense the spiritual path set forth by the vengeful Ayatollah continues to be pursued with great fervor throughout
the Muslim world. In Iran itself, which presently boasts the
second-highest population growth rate in the world—and is expected to reach the one billion mark in eighty years—former Prime
Minister Mussavi happily told a state TV audience after the 1986
census: "Some eleven million Iranians have been born since the
revolution, and [all these] have been brought up with the cries of
'Death to America and *Allahu akbar* (God is great).' "[14]

Revisiting the Valley of the Assassins

Perhaps nowhere else in the world is the concept of martyrdom
rooted more firmly than among the Shi'ites of Iran. While the
original impetus for this can be traced back to Hussein's massacre
at Karbala, Khomeini and his Islamic Republic have done much to
reenergize the doctrine among the masses. This has been accomplished by such means as Friday sermons and martyrs memorials,
as well as through numerous military campaigns and exercises
with names like "Karbala" and "Martyrdom."

Yet another source of inspiration on the subject for many pious
Shi'ites is found in the legacy of the mysterious Cult of the As-
sassins, which flourished in and around Iran from about A.D. 1090
until 1256. The group was led by the shrewd and charismatic
Hasan-i-Sabbah—an almost literal prototype of the Ayatollah
Khomeini. Dubbed "the Old Man of the Mountain" because of his
mountaintop fortress of Alamut situated in Iran's rugged Elburz
Mountains, Sabbah was born in the middle of the eleventh cen-

tury. Nearly a millennium later, his birthplace, the holy city of Qom, would become Khomeini's primary residence and seat of government.

The Old Man's followers, properly known as Nizari Ismailis, were on the right wing fringes of the Shi'ite movement and, according to researcher Peter Willey, "were fervent supporters of Ali and two of his descendants, Ismail and Nizar."[15] They were fully prepared to die for their faith or their master. Many did. But before their sect was largely extinguished by the invading Mongols in the mid-thirteenth century, the Ismailis managed to strike terror in the hearts of their enemies[16] through artful and widely talked-about assassinations.

Shortly after Sabbah's death, the intrepid Venetian traveler Marco Polo wrote about the inner workings of the Assassin strongholds. In fact, it was he who reportedly first gave them their name—mistakenly thinking it was a corruption of the word *hashishin*, or eater of hashish. (The drug was reported to have been mixed into a potion that the Old Man administered to his devotees prior to their murderous missions.) In actuality, the Assassins derived their name from the word *assas*, or "mission," a designation intended to emphasize Sabbah's general philosophy rather than specific clandestine hit operations.

Polo reports that Sabbah's "troops" were actually boys between the ages of twelve and twenty who hailed from simple hill families in the vicinity of his fortress. Once they were inside his domain, the charismatic Sabbah would expound to his young devotees on the virtues of paradise. At an appropriate time, the Old Man would arrange for his initiates to enter into a drug-induced sleep and then be carried into a garden "so charming," Polo writes, "they deemed it was Paradise." When he wished to send any of these on missions, he would say to them:

> Go thou and slay so and so; and when thou returnest my angels shall bear thee into Paradise. And should'st thou die, nevertheless even so will I send my angels to carry thee back into Paradise.[17]

Khomeini, too, spoke often of paradise and martyrdom. He, too, assembled young boys—some not ten years old—for suicide missions. With the Imam's photo pinned over their hearts and his taped messages plugged into their ears, these *basiji* (volunteers) primed themselves for the moment when they would either take, or give up, life. "Our nation is no longer ready to submit to humiliation and abjection," Khomeini challenged them. "It prefers a bloody death to a life of shame. We are ready to be killed and we have made a covenant with God to follow the path of our leader, the Lord of the Martyrs [Hussein]."[18]

During the war with Iraq, after months of religious indoctrination in at least three separate camps throughout Iran, thousands of *basiji* graduated to the moment of truth. Around their foreheads they tightened red bandannas painted with Qur'anic scriptures; around their necks they hung plastic keys that they hoped fit the gates of paradise. Soon they would be sent to the front to clear the enemy's minefields with their feet.[19]

Before his death in the war, Mohsen Naeemi left one final note lest anyone doubt his commitment to the cause at hand. "My wedding is at the front and my bride is martyrdom," he wrote. "The sermon will be uttered by the roar of guns. I shall attire myself in my blood for this ceremony. My bride, martyrdom, shall give birth to my son, freedom. I leave this son in your safekeeping. Keep him well."[20]

Other graduates of Khomeini's martyrdom training camps headed West, or else into select areas of the Middle East, to take out targets offensive to Islam. Many were members of the Imam Hussein Suicide Brigade established by one of the Ayatollah's prime pupils—Ali Akbar Mohtashemi. Deeply influenced by Khomeini's teaching, Mohtashemi had served at age sixteen as a courier between the Islamic leader and his underground followers in Iran. By the late 1970s, he was a trusted member of the Imam's inner circle and, along with two others, was tabbed to supervise the formation of revolutionary Islamic terrorist operations abroad.[21]

Mohtashemi's prime recruiting grounds—and battlefield—was Lebanon. Among the country's large, disaffected Shi'ite population, many youth found Iran's message of martyrdom as salvation highly attractive. Hatred for Israel and the West was fierce, and

Mohtashemi's suicide squads offered an opportunity to obtain both revenge and paradise in one explosive moment. "When we attack the Israelis," one teenage fighter explained, "we don't talk of worldly matters. We dream of martyrdom and *hoor al-ain* [virgins of paradise]." In the 1980s Islamic suicide attacks against hated foreign nationals in Lebanon were videotaped and, with spliced-in testimonials, made available through shops as inspirational material.[22]

Despite his demanding and manipulative ways, and the obvious blood on his hands, Hassan-i-Sabbah was regarded as a folk hero and inspiration after his death. Here again, the parallels between the Assassin leader and Ayatollah Khomeini are profound. Even after ordering the deaths of hundreds of innocent foreigners abroad[23] and sending multiplied thousands of his own people into bloody oblivion or lifetime deformity ("We should sacrifice all our loved ones for the sake of Islam," he declared),[24] the Imam was still venerated to a degree that can be explained only in spiritual terms.

This supernatural hold was perhaps evidenced most dramatically during the hours of wild anguish surrounding Khomeini's 1989 funeral procession and burial. As the Imam's coffin wound its way through the streets of Teheran enroute to the Behesht-i-Zahra Cemetery, frenzied zealots attempted to rip off a piece of the burial shroud (which they deemed holy), instead causing the dead leader's corpse to spill unceremoniously to the dusty ground where it was nearly trampled. For more than nine hours, an estimated ten million chanting and breast-beating mourners were hosed down by firetrucks to keep them from succumbing to heat prostration, while police struggled to evict another group of distraught followers who had occupied Khomeini's freshly dug grave and refused to move. When the Ayatollah's coffin was finally laid to rest, an overcome media correspondent summed up the nation's raw emotions when he blurted out over live TV: "O stars, stop shining! O rivers, stop flowing!"[25]

Five months later, as the crowds finally thinned and darkness fell across the southern fringes of Teheran, 30-year-old war cripple Hassan Samabati hobbled painfully to his master's tomb in the

Martyrs Cemetery. For Samabati, it had become a ritual of inspiration, but one strewn with powerful emotional landmines.

Once inside the cemetery, Samabati later explained, "Things
flash before my eyes. I see my friends being torn to pieces in
battle. I see the faces of the dead." Not far away, a fountain
spurting red water—the symbolic blood of the young martyrs who
fell for the Ayatollah's revolution—recycled the memories. At the
tomb itself, Samabati murmured prayers quietly through the alu-
minum grill surrounding the late Iranian leader's sarcophagus.
After an hour or so, the Old Man's spirit became palpable. "The
Imam appears before me," testified the man with shattered legs. "I
talk with him. I'm like a person reborn when I leave here."[26]

"This was Khomeini's century," eulogized Hamze Jalali, a young
Iranian teacher. "He was unique. He was a superman."[27] Echoing
this theme, former Algerian president Ahmed Ben Bella declared,
"A brilliant light appeared in Iran which illuminated the whole
Muslim world."[28] Indeed, the global rise of Islamic fundamentalism throughout the late '70s and '80s can be tied almost directly to
the Ayatollah's neon leadership during this period.[29]

The Association of Militant Clerics: Exporting the Politics of Hate

1991

The Luciferian objectives of the prince of Persia—theft, murder
and destruction—are essentially the same as those pursued by his
neighbor in Babylon. In Iran, however, this powerful strongman is
able to work with the added advantage of an almost perfect spiritual control point—fundamentalist Islam. Although his subjects
are harnessed to a system of extreme malice, its demonic characteristics are virtually undetectable to them. Indeed the epic and
visceral hatred of many Persian-linked fundamentalists is often
couched in terms of God's will, with violence seen as an inevitable
attendant.[30]

The biggest offense to Khomeini's religious sensibilities were
the superpowers. In a memo directed at Iran's so-called pragma-
tists, he declared: "I am confident that the Iranian people, par-

ticularly our youth, will keep alive in their hearts anger and hatred for the criminal Soviet Union and the warmongering United States. This must be until the banner of Islam flies over every house in the world."[31]

Analysts around the world were both disturbed and dumfounded by such statements. How was it possible for a head of state living in the 1980s to employ such inflammatory rhetoric? Writing on the roots of Muslim rage in *The Atlantic Monthly*, Islamic scholar Bernard Lewis emphasized that "it should by now be clear that we are facing a mood and a movement far transcending the level of issues and policies and the governments that pursue them."

While hatred and violence continue to represent the driving force and chief exports of the Iranian revolution, the Islamic clergy are its preeminent salesmen. In the spring of 1982, an initial marketing meeting of sorts was held in Teheran. Sponsored by the bizarrely named (to Western ears) Association of Militant Clerics, the meeting's main goal was to lay the groundwork for a spiritually cleansing worldwide Islamic "crusade." Though dominated by Iranian fundamentalist clergymen, the event also drew religious radicals from more than two dozen other Islamic states. In December of the same year, Iranian president Ali Khamenei poured fuel on the fire when he called on Friday prayer leaders (Islamic pastors) from forty countries to turn their mosques into "prayer, political, cultural and military bases" and to "prepare the ground for the creation of Islamic governments in all countries."[32]

In between prayers, Iran's 75,000 mosques provide everything from militant ideological indoctrination classes to martial arts and weapons training. Each mosque is considered not only a place of worship and instruction, but also a garrison for local *komitehs* (religious police) and "block watch" units known as the *Bassij Mostazafin* (Mobilization of the Impoverished).[33]

Not one to minimize the power of the pulpit, the Ayatollah Khomeini once wrote:

> "The first Muslims . . . used to accomplish important business
> on the occasion of the hajj or at their Friday gatherings. The Friday
> sermon was more than a sura from the Qur'an and a prayer followed

by a few brief words. Entire armies used to be mobilized by the
Friday sermon and proceed directly from the mosque to the
battlefield—and a man who sets out from the mosque to go into
battle will fear only God, not poverty or hardship, and his army will
be victorious and triumphant."[34]

Feeding Iran's fundamentalist pulpits are its seminaries. Fourteen of these are located in the city of Qom, which many experts
believe is the real seedbed of Islamic radicalism. Interest in Islamic study has increased dramatically in recent years, with student enrollment in Qom alone rising from about 6,400 in 1975 to
more than 18,000 in 1991. Six thousand of these are on full
scholarships from "target" countries such as Lebanon, Iraq, Pakistan, Kuwait, Afghanistan and Tunisia. Students from Iran and
other Islamic countries are also used to further fundamentalist
aims while studying in the West.[35]

One report indicated that in 1982 a close associate of Khomeini,
Ayatollah Hosein Ali Montazeri, spent millions of dollars recruiting Muslim students and immigrant guest workers in France, Britain and West Germany. At least one hundred full-time recruiters
were alleged to have operated under the cover of mosques and
Islamic student centers in Europe. The same report also described
an Islamic missionary terror network in the United States where
some 60,000 students from Islamic nations pursue various studies.
"Khomeini's followers have been building in the U.S. for fifteen
years," according to former Iranian Prime Minister Ali Amini, and
"they are very well hidden and financed."[36]

Several educational institutions inside Iran itself are actually
fundamentalist-run terror training centers.[37] Notable among these
are Melli University northwest of Teheran and Shiraz University.
In addition to native Iranians, the student bodies of these "schools"
are made up of Iraqi, Lebanese, Saudi and Kuwaiti Shi'ites, as
well as aspiring revolutionaries from such diverse locations as
Ireland, Paraguay, Turkey, Sri Lanka and the Philippines.

At these and other facilities throughout Iran, thousands of pupils
complete courses ranging from Islamic law and sabotage to advanced computer hacking.[38] Guest lecturers from Europe, Asia

and the Middle East provide further insights into such exotic subjects as exploiting priests and journalists and the use of psychology in *jihad*. In addition to employing resident ayatollahs and Revolutionary Guards, instructors are brought in from Libya, Pakistan, North Korea and various P.L.O. centers.[39]

During the 1980s, most of these training programs, along with international covert operations, were coordinated out of a four-story building in downtown Teheran known as Taleghani Center. From here the numerous tentacles of Islamic mission work and terrorism (including suicide squads) spread out under the general auspices of the Council for the Islamic Revolution. According to Wright, "the council reportedly received more than $1 billion annually" in the form of contributions from hundreds of Friday gatherings around the world and state allocations from Iran's revolutionary treasury. Outside of Europe, specific incidents of Iranian-inspired subversion have been recorded in Egypt, Turkey, Kuwait, Bahrain, Saudi Arabia, Yemen, Pakistan, Afghanistan, Ethiopia, Malaysia, Iraq, Lebanon, Israel, Sudan and the Philippines.[40]

One major beneficiary of these funds has been the shadowy terrorist network of Islamic Jihad. Reportedly consisting of more than thirty separate entities, the group is said to be governed out of Iran by a Supreme Coordinating Council with five regional and various local commands. After several years of operation, the organization's bloody handiwork has become all too familiar throughout Europe and the Middle East.

Under the Temples of Baalbek: Little Teheran and the Hizballah

Considering all of this from the perspective of the spiritual dimension, it comes as no real surprise that of all the flaming ideological arrows launched out of Iran in the past decade, the first to ignite locally was in the city the ancient Greeks called Heliopolis, or the City of the Sun. Also known as Baalbek,[41] the city is located in the central Biq'ah (or Bekaa) Valley of eastern Lebanon, a region sometimes referred to as "Hollow Syria." The site may also be synonymous with Baal-gad, which the book of Joshua describes as being "in the valley of Lebanon below Mt. Hermon."[42]

In the early 1980s, Baalbek found itself on the receiving end of the first substantial deployment of Revolutionary Guards outside of Iran. Arriving initially by the dozens, the Guards (or *Pasdaran*) may now number as many as 5,000. Hard counts are difficult to come by, however, as the Iranians tend to keep a low profile and their Lebanese "disciples" are among the most radical in the world. With some of the British and American hostages believed to have been held in the nearby Sheikh Abdullah Barracks, Westerners venture into this largely Shi'ite city at their own peril.

Shortly after their arrival in Baalbek, the Iranians went about the business of giving their new quarters a proper revolutionary facelift. In a matter of months, the city was dubbed "Little Teheran" by its Lebanese inhabitants. Bars closed, veils came down and posters bearing Khomeini's brooding visage were plastered throughout the downtown area. Two blocks from the main intersection—which they renamed Ayatollah Khomeini Square— the Revolutionary Guards set up an Islamic propaganda office under an Iranian flag and a large banner reading *Lovers of Martyrdom*. Out of these quarters, as well as in local mosques and over the radio, the Pasdaran offered instruction in Islamic revolutionary thought to the local population.

Though they are less than 35 miles from front-line Israeli positions, the Guards have not yet engaged their mortal enemies in direct combat.[43] Instead, they sow and nurture patiently the seeds of hatred that they trust will one day erupt in a violent anti-Zionist conflagration. While heroic signs exhort the faithful to "March on Jerusalem!", most of Baalbek's militants seem momentarily content to grind the soles of their shoes over a Star of David etched into the sidewalk near the Revolutionary Guard center.[44]

During a recent visit to Lebanon, ABC News correspondent Charles Glass recalls looking down on the sweep of the Bekaa Valley and longing to revisit Baalbek, a stop he had known in the mid-'70s. Not daring to descend into this city that one barely escaped British journalist had described as "not a place of compromise," Glass instead pondered a series of questions. Foremost among these: "Why did Iran bring its ideology to Baalbek rather than some other town?" and "Why did the Revolutionary Guards go to Baalbek in 1982 and make it one of Hizballah's headquarters?"[45]

These questions are not inspired only by curiosity; they are crucial to our understanding of spiritual tactics in the unseen world. The surface answer that there are (were) Shi'ites in Baalbek is of no major consequence—not when one considers that more than a million Shi'ites today populate scores of other towns up and down the length of Lebanon. The question, again is, Why Baalbek?

If we pause to recall that the real power in Iran these past years has not been the revolutionary regime of the Ayatollah Khomeini, but rather an established spiritual principality under the dominion of the prince of Persia, we are suddenly presented with new possibilities in relation to the question of Baalbek.[46] Among these is the fact that, for thousands of years, Baalbek has been a center of pagan cult worship. This activity, which attracts demonic spirits like flies to raw meat, reached its apex during the Greco-Roman periods when a number of major temple complexes were erected in and around the city.

Among the impressive ruins still visible in the ancient metropolis are those of the massive Temple of Jupiter, the well-preserved Temple of Bacchus and the rounded Temple of Venus. Traces of a temple honoring the popular Greek god Hermes also remain along with the Sacrificial Lakes. The existence of these facilities, and especially the prevalence of bacchic symbols in their interior, suggest strongly the earlier presence of secret Greco-Roman mystery religions.[47]

The symmetry between extremist Shi'ite fundamentalist organizations and these secret religious societies is striking. Both emphasize the mystical meaning of revelation; both revere their leaders as semi-divine; both retain a doctrine of the elite; both promote the concept of brotherhood; both promote "passion plays" during which frenzied action can involve self-laceration; and both carry expectations that members will commit crimes for the sake of the group.

On at least two occasions, Greco-Roman secret societies actually pursued clandestine political action. The first of these occurred in 415 B.C. when several groups pledged to overthrow the Athenian democracy. In order to pledge, all members had to participate in a common crime. Later on, in 63 B.C., Catiline led a conspiracy out of a secret religious society to overthrow the Roman government.[48] In both practice and principle, there is little to distinguish these episodes from those involving Hassan Sabbah and, later, the Islamic Jihad.

While *Bacchanalia* (the Latin word for the mystery religions) sometimes included certain elements not found in covert Shi'ite circles—such as alcohol and sexual excess—there are enough similarities in structure and mode of operation here to give any good investigator ample cause to look for a single perpetrator or mastermind. Thus, the reason the prince of Persia directed his Iranian subjects into Baalbek to form their secret societies (as opposed to some other Lebanese Shi'ite town) is simple: *He already had pre-positioned assets and a long-lasting welcome there.*

Perhaps the ultimate expression of Iranian-fueled hatred and conspiracy is the shadowy and violent Hizballah, or Party of God. Born out of the union between satanic agents and willing human partners, this hideous offspring bears the terrifying image of a serpent. In between its vicious strikes, this dragon curls up under the temples of Baalbek and in the warren-like slums of southern Beirut. Though not often seen in the daylight—a time when it is busy digesting its prey (hostages, which are viewed as the limbs of the Great Satan)—a tour of its lair nevertheless reveals chilling evidence of its existence. Spray-painted slogans of death. Dark and furtive glances. Posters and murals of the Islamic Devourer. The latter, which adorn dank buildings and crumbling alley walls, feature a being with glowing red eyes staring out from beneath a dark shroud. Fangs drip with the blood of Christians, infidels or Zionists. Some are disemboweled, others decapitated. The images are conceived in hell.

According to *Time*, their Persian masters "spend anywhere from

$15 million to $50 million a year to finance Hizballah activities."[49] In return, the serpent gives its allegiance to the mullahs of Teheran. In a manifesto issued in February 1985, the leaders of the newly formed Party of God declared:

> "We the sons of Hizballah's nation—whose vanguard God has given victory in Iran and which has established the nucleus of the world's central Islamic state—abide by the orders of a single wise and just command currently embodied in the supreme Ayatollah Khomeini."[50]

Additional funds are derived from lucrative cannabis and opium crops in the Bekaa Valley. While personal use of narcotics is strictly forbidden to Shi'ites, the Ayatollah Khomeini encouraged the production and export of drugs—to the U.S. in particular—as "an agent of social destruction."[51] Profits are used, among other things, to supplement the costs of international expansion into places like the U.S.S.R. (Hizballah is reportedly operating out of the Soviet Armenian capital of Yerevan)[52] and the Sudan. (According to a respected Sudanese politician now in exile, the current Islamic regime has set up four military training centers for members of its own Muslim brotherhood. These, in turn, are operated by Iranian and Arab instructors who have been trained by the Hizballah in Lebanon.)[53]

The Dangers of the Ungodly Path

The Islamic Devourer does not hesitate, when it cannot find foreigners to feed on, to turn on its own. In Iran, its eyes are the police, state intelligence services, Revolutionary Guards and, most of all, the ever-vigilant komitehs. The komitehs are composed of sold-out purists who patrol schools, offices and neighborhoods looking out for any who deviate from the "godly path." When they find them, the komitehs are authorized to dispense stern warnings, or even drag offenders into the dragon's lair. "The komiteh come by," explained one woman. "If you're in the yard, they tell you to put on a scarf." You do what you are told. For those caught flirting with inappropriate music, dress and relationships, the consequences can be severe.

Since public courting is a risky proposition (unmarried couples traveling in the same car after dark are liable to be arrested by the *komitehs*), the only alternative most Iranian young people have—other than waiting for an arranged marriage—is to date over the telephone. In a 1989 interview with *Newsweek,* the headmistress at the Fatima Girls High School in downtown Teheran, Tehereh Shoraka, announced proudly that "not one girl among 1,400 students [has] a boyfriend. The last case of dating was more than a year ago."[54] During "Public Morality Week" in the fall of 1990, "women letting the faintest wisp of hair peep from their chadors were sternly reprimanded."[55]

A few months earlier, two BBC journalists and a female reporter were looking through some clips in their editing room in the Laleh Hotel. At seven o'clock in the evening one of the men took a phone call from the hotel security man. "It is after six o'clock. You have a woman in the room. It is not permitted."[56] Shaul Bakhash related that before his death "Khomeini noted with satisfaction that if the Shah had to rely on a secret police, the Islamic Republic could call on a nation of thirty-six million informers."[57]

Among the primary targets of these informers: religious minorities. In his book on Islamic government, the Ayatollah wrote: "In our own city of Teheran now there are centers of evil propaganda run by the churches, the Zionists, and the Baha'is in order to lead our people astray and make them abandon the ordinances and teachings of Islam. Do we not have a duty to destroy these centers that are damaging to Islam?"[58]

Throughout 1990, Christian churches in Iran came under a fresh attack by the fundamentalists. Several pastors and Bible teachers were arrested by Muslim authorities, and in December an Assemblies of God pastor, who had converted from Islam thirty years before and was actively involved in the translation of the *Living Bible* into the Farsi language, was publicly hanged by the Iranian government.[59]

The Persian Gulag is presently said to hold at least 5,000 political prisoners in more than 650 prisons and torture centers.[60]

Many of these prisoners are held on charges unheard of in Western judicial systems—*Moharebeh* (enmity to God) and *Mofsed fil Arz* (corruption on earth). Thousands have been executed in the past decade and, as in neighboring Iraq, the use of torture is widespread.[61]

According to survivors of Gohar Dasht, one of Iran's most notorious prisons, torture sessions were (and quite possibly still are) routinely conducted under loudspeakers that broadcast Islamic prayers and religious speeches. Hovering over their suffering victims, mullahs would snarl, "Are you wretched? Do you repent?"

One young man held in Tabriz Prison recounted:

> "They laid me prone on a bed and fastened me to it and started flogging me. After several lashes, they starting hitting the soles of my feet with something like a metal bar. I felt as if my bones were melting and then they flogged my back again . . . [and] with every lash they chanted: 'Allah-o-Akbar' (God is great). They were laughing at my pain. . . . During the flogging, when I said: 'I have a backache,' one of them stepped on my back and twisted the heel of his boot on my backbone. I fainted."[62]

Finally, in documents and testimonies still coming out of Iran, there is mounting evidence that the Khomeini regime has conceived a particularly ghoulish practice. When the father of Ali Niaz Baz was granted permission to see his son shortly before his scheduled execution, he was shocked at what he saw—and heard. Unable to walk, his son was supported into the meeting room on the shoulders of two Revolutionary Guards. His complexion was astonishingly pale, his lips severely cracked. With his remaining strength, the young man whispered to his father, "They have taken my blood." With that he was taken away and shot.[63]

In the manner of all bloodsucking gods, the prince of Persia will, in the short term, grow even stronger and more formidable. His rallying point will be the ensign of Islamic fundamentalism; and as it is lifted ever higher in the years ahead, the hatred of millions of terminally sentenced demons will give way to a level of violence the world has not yet known.

Notes

1 Extracted from *Jihad—A Ground Plan* (London, 1978); quoted in *The Challenge of Islam*, "The Many Faces of Islam," John Laffin.

2 Quoted in *Islam & Revolution*, ed. Hamid Algar (Berkeley: Mizan Press, 1981), pp. 265–266.

3 See Daniel 10 for background.

4 Quoted in *Sacred Rage*, Robin Wright (New York: Simon & Schuster, 1985), p. 31.

5 The first appointed successor to Muhammad was actually a wise and learned man by the name of Abu Bakr. He was called a *khalifa*, or "deputy of the prophet." Out of this decision, the great institution of the Caliphate was born.

6 Edward Mortimer, *Faith and Power—The Politics of Islam* (New York: Vintage Books, 1982), p. 44.

7 Abdulaziz Sachedina, *Islamic Messianism* (Albany, N.Y.: State University of New York Press, 1981), p. 15.

8 Called *safir*, these vice-regents or ambassadors had the difficult dual task of drawing a protective darkness over the name and whereabouts of the Imam, while at the same time proving his existence to his reliable adherents. See *The Occultation of the Twelfth Imam* by Jassim Hussein (London: Muhammadi Trust, 1982).

9 Ayatollah Khomeini; from the book *Islamic Government*, which originated from a series of lectures given at Najaf, Iraq, while he was in exile between January 21 and February 8, 1970. Contained in *Islam & Revolution*.

10 Quoted in *In the Path of God*, Daniel Pipes (New York: Basic Books, 1983).

11 Ayatollah Khomeini in *Islam & Revolution*, p. 146.

12 Reported in *The Reign of the Ayatollahs: Iran and the Islamic Revolution*, Shaul Bakhash (New York: Basic Books, 1984), p. 233.

13 Wright, *In the Name of God*, pp. 188–189.

14 Scheherazade Daneshkhu, "Iran's Growing Population Problem," *MEI*, February 16, 1990.

15 Peter Willey, "The Assassins," *The Traveller*, date unknown.

16 Mostly Arab (Abbasid) and Turkish rulers, along with European Crusaders.

17 From the writings of Marco Polo, quoted in *Sacred Rage*, pp. 39–40.

18 Ayatollah Khomeini in a message delivered in Teheran on September 13, 1980; *Islam & Revolution*, p. 305.

19 Nathan Adams, "Iran's Ayatollahs of Terror," *Reader's Digest*, January 1985.

20 Quoted in Wright, *Sacred Rage*, p. 36.

21 Nathan Adams, "Iran's Mastermind of World Terrorism," *Reader's Digest*, September 1990.

22 One such testimonial was left behind by Sana'a al-Muhaidli, a 19-year-old Muslim girl who drove her explosive-laden car into an Israeli military convoy in south Lebanon.

"My beloved ones! . . . Now I am planted in the soil of the South, which I irrigate with my blood and love for it. How I wish you knew how happy I am!

"Oh mother!. . . I am not dead. This is only the first step. There will follow a second, even greater, and then a third, a fourth, then hundreds of equally courageous and daring operations. . . . Do not be angry with me because I left home without telling you. . . . I have not left to get married, or to live with anyone. I have gone to meet the courageous, honourable and happy martyrdom. My last will is to be called, 'The Bride of the South!' " Reprinted in Gairdner Ministries (now People International) newsletter, "Islam in Britain."

23 Including people like Malcolm Kerr (president of The American University) and the 241 members of the U.S. Marine peacekeeping force in Beirut; victims of Iranian death squads operating in Britain in 1988; and scores of French shoppers and worshipers bombed by terrorists under the guidance of Iranian "diplomat" Wahid Gordji.

24 Quoted in *In the Name of God*, p. 87.

25 *Ibid.*, p. 204.

26 Ray Wilkinson, "Seeking Iran's Soul," *Newsweek*, November 13, 1989.

27 *The Independent*, June 7, 1989.

28 Pipes, p. 325.

29 In the Gaza Strip a carpenter who named his shop "Khomeini" explained that the name is fashionable and appealing to Muslims. In the Soviet Union, Khomeini's influence was seen in the proliferation of his portrait and green Islamic flags. In Indonesia, the governor of Jakarta was dubbed "Mr. Khomeini No. 2" when he closed down nighttime amusement houses. In Egypt police found a summary of Khomeini's book on Islamic government stashed among the possessions of Sadat's assassins. See Pipes, pp. 325–327.

30 In a speech before his disappearance in Libya in 1978, the pro-Iranian Lebanese cleric Musa as-Sadr shrieked: "What does the government expect? What does it expect except rage and revolutions? Arms are man's beauty. . . . Brothers, line up in a row of your choice: that of tyranny or that of Husain. I am certain that you will not choose anything but the row of revolution and martyrdom. . . ." Reported in Shireen Hunter, *The Politics of Islamic Revivalism* (Bloomington, Ind.: Indiana University Press, 1988), p. 62. The Ayatollah himself proclaimed in early 1982, "Weapons in our hands are used to realize divine and Islamic aspirations." A prime target for these weapons, Khomeini believed, were hypocritical Gulf emirs who, if they did not surrender fully to Islam, would be "put to the sword and dispatched to hell, where they shall roast forever." Reported in Wright, *Sacred Rage*, p. 27.

31 Quoted in *In the Name of God*, p. 196.

32 *Iran Times*, January 7, 1983; see also Bakhash, p. 235.

33 The institution of the Bassij was established by Khomeini in the aftermath of the failed U.S. effort to rescue its embassy hostages. Subordinate to the Revolutionary Guard, the original goal was to involve at least twenty million people in the Bassij network.

34 Ayatollah Khomeini; from the book *Islamic Government*, excerpted in *Islam & Revolution*, p. 131.

35 In a June 1988 message to the twentieth annual meeting of the American and Canadian Islamic Students Societies, Iran's Ayatollah Jannati admonished students to "do everything in [their] power . . . to spread the message of Islam and the Iranian revolution" and to "never relent" in their fight against the "agents of corruption."

Reported in "Jannati's Message to U.S. & Canadian Islamic Students Societies," from Ettela'at, in *Joint Publications Research Service*, August 8, 1988.

36 Nathan Adams, "Iran's Ayatollahs of Terror," *Reader's Digest*, January 1985. (Note: While increased vigilance is needed in regard to Islamic infiltration strategies, the vast majority of the Islamic students in North America have no connection whatsoever with terrorism or other subversive activities. It would, therefore, be a great mistake for Christians to withhold love and hospitality in the name of fear.)

37 A September 12, 1989, edition of *The Economist* reported that, in a wrenching twist of fate, the former U.S. embassy in Teheran is now a school for Revolutionary Guards and the home of a glass boutique that sells glued-together shredded documents from the "den of spies."

38 A 1990 *Reader's Digest Special Report* (see footnote 21) revealed that Iranian operatives have managed to penetrate the reservations computers of major Western airlines enabling them to access passenger manifests.

39 See Wright, *Sacred Rage*, pp. 34–35, and Laffin, "Islam's Clandestine Operations."

40 See Pipes, pp. 328–333 for more detail.

41 From Baal-Biq'ah, a local deity known as the "Lord of the Plain."

42 Joshua 11:17; *Unger's Bible Dictionary* (Chicago: Moody Press, 1966), p. 113.

43 In her book *The Politics of Islamic Revivalism*, author Shireen Hunter observes that "Iran's Revolutionary Guards were missionaries more than fighters in Lebanon" (p. 68).

44 Robert Fisk, "Iranian Ambitions Beneath Black Flags of Baalbek," *The Independent*, June 26, 1989; William Barrett, " 'We are here at the order of Khomeini,' " *The Seattle Times*, August 9, 1983; Wright in *In the Name of God*, p. 114.

45 Charles Glass, *Tribes with Flags* (New York: Atlantic Monthly Press, 1990), pp. 398–399.

46 Using this paradigm we are reminded of the importance of spiritual alliances that often lurk behind systemic (politico-religious) ones.

47 *Encyclopædia Britannica (Micropædia)*, Vol. 1, 15th Edition, p. 704.
    Note: The Greco-Roman mystery religions were actually secret cults/societies that involved special initiation rites as well as common meals, dances and ceremonies. Depending on the particular society, sexual promiscuity and/or political intrigue could also be involved.

48 *Encyclopædia Britannica (Macropædia)*, Vol. 12, 15th Edition, p. 779.

49 John Greenwald, "At War On All Fronts," *Time*, August 17, 1987.

50 Quoted in Hunter, p. 66.

51 Laffin.

52 Based on a conversation with Marie Broxup, Director of the Society for Central Asian Studies, in London, July 1990.

53 "Islam Marches toward the Heart of Africa," *The Independent*, June 15, 1990.

54 Ray Wilkinson, "Seeking Iran's Soul," *Newsweek*, November 13, 1989.

55 "Perplexed," *The Economist*, September 12, 1990.

56 "Walking in Fear under the Imam's Gaze," *The London Times*, July 2, 1990.

57 Bakhash, p. 226.
    Note: To further assist the government in keeping track of its citizenry, the Iranian parliament enacted a compulsory plan in 1988 for public fingerprinting.

58 Ayatollah Khomeini; from the book *Islamic Government*, excerpted in *Islam & Revolution*, p. 128.
    Note: Those who wanted to believe that Iran had moderated in recent years must have been bitterly disappointed when, in January 1990, demonstrators gathered outside of the home of the "moderate" Grand Ayatollah Montazeri chanting, "Death to liberals!"

59 Media release, Office of Information, Assemblies of God, February 5, 1991.

60 Gordon Martin, "Khomeini Enemies Were 'Baked Alive,' " *London Daily Telegraph*, January 11, 1990.

61 Recent comprehensive reports prepared by the U.N. Human Rights Commission and Amnesty International leave no doubt that Iran's penal system is administered by hell itself. The author of the U.N. report, Señor Reynaldo Galindo Pohl, describes the torture of a ten-year-old girl in a wheelchair, the burning alive of a woman and two teenagers in a baker's oven, and the practice of pre-execution rape. Reported in *The Daily Telegraph*, January 11, 1990 (see footnote 60); and Leonard Doyle, "Iran Defends Torture of Terrorists," *The Independent*, November 17, 1989.
    According to author Suroosh Irfani, top Islamic judge Ayatollah Mohammadi Gillani declared in an official interview that the execution of a nine-year-old girl was justifiable in Islam because this was the age of puberty for girls. Accordingly, stated Gillani, "there is no difference for us between a nine-year-old girl and a forty-year-old man." (Reported in *Revolutionary Islam in Iran: Popular Liberation or Religious Dictatorship* (London: Zed Press, 1983), p. 264.
    Other reports out of Iran indicate that prisoners have been subject to mock executions, flogged, electro-shocked and forced to drink urine. A punishment not yet applied (so far as is known) is Ayatollah Ardebeli's suggestion of amputating criminals' "right hands and left legs" and then "leaving them to die." Reported in "Iran: Violations of Human Rights," an Amnesty International Report, 1987, p. 28.
    To pacify the consciences of Islamic judges who deemed it "un-Islamic" to carry out the death sentence on virgin females, one Islamic authority ruled that such girls could be married off to Revolutionary Guards for as long as it took to deflorate them. Once they had essentially been raped, they could then be executed "Islamically." Khomeini took the whole matter a step further when he decreed that women and girls arrested on charges of "waging war against God" are automatically regarded as "spoils of war," thereby making it religiously acceptable for them to be raped by their guards and torturers. Hojatalislam Hadi Ghaffari, a leading member of the radical Islamic Republic Party—who once threatened, "We will murder any member [of Parliament] opposed to Imam Khomeini's line of thought"—is also known as the "professional rapist of the Islamic regime." Reported in Irfani, pp. 266–267.

62 Amnesty International Report, 1989, p. 91.

63 Irfani, pp. 265–266.
    Note: Documents issued by the chief prosecutor's office in 1981 indicate that Khomeini himself sanctioned the practice of draining the blood plasma from those prisoners sentenced to death prior to their executions.

7

Closing on Eden

"Ask of me, and I will make the nations your inheritance, and the ends of the earth your possession."

Psalm 2:8, NIV

It is not a question of territorial termination of the mission cause, but a matter of fulfilling the Genesis mandate—to be a blessing to all the peoples of the earth.

Dr. Ralph Winter[1]

"Woe to the inhabitants of the earth and the sea! For the devil has come down to you, having great wrath, because he knows that he has a short time."

Revelation 12:12

In the summer of 1945, at a secluded desert location known only as "site Y" near Los Alamos, New Mexico, a group of top government scientists squinted off into the distance through shielded glasses. Among them was Dr. Robert Oppenheimer, one of the chief architects of the Manhattan Project. Tension was pervasive. Years of hard work—and the fate of nations—hung in the balance. As the countdown finally expired in a blinding flash of light, Oppenheimer watched as the world's inaugural mushroom cloud rose like a malevolent genie escaped from his lamp. Overwhelmed by the awesome spectacle unfolding before him, Oppenheimer silently recited two lines from the Bagavadgita:

> I am become death, the shatterer of worlds;
> Waiting that hour that ripens to their doom.

In many respects, the devil's unremitting fury as expressed in and through the fiendish networks of modern-day Persia and Babylon is kindred to this ancient oath. The words were once his inspiration; the deeds are now his handiwork.

Satan is enraged by the sure knowledge of his own impending doom, and his countenance and demeanor reflect increasingly the loathsome bile of spite. It is seen in Beirut's macabre posters of the Islamic Devourer. It is heard in the bitter rhetoric of the Friday imams. It is acted out in the beating of an Algerian mission worker, the hanging of an Iranian pastor, the torture of Egyptian teenage converts.

Such paroxysms of anger and violence, while undeniably destructive, are also demonstrations of satanic futility. They are the cheap shots inflicted by a frustrated player in the waning moments of a lost contest, the gratuitous massacre ordered from the *fürherbunker* as the Allies close in on Berlin. The truth is, as Satan scans intelligence reports on his battlefield operations, he has plenty of cause for concern.

The Shrinking Frontier

In the days of the early Church, mission strategy was relatively simple. *All* lands were unevangelized, *all* peoples were unreached. No matter which direction they set out in, the first missionaries were assured of one thing—when they eventually reached their ministry destination, they would have an exclusive franchise.

Ignited by heaven's eternal flame, these pioneer torchsticks of the faith left the Land of Promise and launched out toward the dusky horizons of Asia, Africa and Europe. God, as promised, went with them; and by the end of the first century, their efforts had paid off in the form of a modest necklace of churches around the Mediterranean basin.

For the next 1,800 years, the fortunes of their successors would ebb and flow with the prevailing tides of obedience and intercession. By A.D. 500, vigorous expansion had given way to dissipation, and over the next 450 years, Christianity lost many of its early Mediterranean beachheads to the encroachments of Islam. Happily, splendid resurgences took place in central and northern Europe, and in the years between A.D. 1500 and 1800, the first waves of the Gospel reached the shores of Australia and the Americas.

Up until this point, from a satanic perspective, things had not gone altogether badly. Occasional disappointments such as the Reformation and the arrival of the Gospel in the Americas were to be expected. The important thing was that, from the standpoint of global geography and momentum, Christianity was still fairly contained.

What was *not* expected, and certainly much less welcomed, was the disastrous eruption of global evangelization in the twentieth century. Of the 788 known global plans for world evangelization conceived by the Church since the issuance of the Great Commission, 540, or nearly seventy percent of them, were birthed subsequent to 1900. In the thirty-year span from 1961 to 1991 alone, the tally of new worldwide plans more than tripled the number launched during the first 1,500 years of Church history.[2]

And what has been the net result of all of these new plans? Much to the dismay of the enemy, the borders of the unevangelized world have been heaved backward so forcefully that 75 percent of the world's population now have a reasonable opportunity to hear the Gospel.[3] In geographic terms, this means virtually all people living outside of the 10/40 Window (4.5 of the world's six inhabited continents), and an increasing percentage of those who dwell *within* this important frontier.

In short, the soldiers of the Lord of hosts have now encircled the final strongholds of the serpent—the nations and spiritual principalities of the 10/40 Window. While the remaining task is admittedly the most challenging phase of the battle, the armies of Lucifer are faced presently with a community of believers whose spiritual resources—if properly motivated, submitted and unified—are truly awesome.

According to Dr. David Barrett, possibly as many as 260 current global outreach initiatives are making progress. Taken together, these efforts are responsible for mobilizing a significant percentage of today's overall force of 285,000[4] foreign missionaries—38,000 of whom hail from emerging-world countries.

In addition to these impressive numbers, Barrett further reckons that there are now some 21,000 parachurch agencies supplementing the endeavors of nearly 4,000 foreign mission boards or societies. In conjunction with local churches, these groups are responsible for distributing nearly 1.5 billion Scriptures[5] and holding 2,500 mass evangelistic campaigns (in some 1,300 cities and towns) each year. As of 1990, there were also 2,160 Christian radio and TV stations flooding the airwaves with the Gospel.[6]

As data on these and other ministry activities are gathered and analyzed by Satan's worldwide networks, the preliminary damage assessments must be numbing. Consider, for example, the following:

Global Evangelism Overview[7]

√ Every day of the year approximately 364,000[8] people around the world hear the Gospel for the first time. Of these, about 70,000 determine to give their lives to Christ.

√ At the end of the first century, the ratio of nonbelievers to Christians was 360 to 1. Today the ratio is 7 to 1.

√ Every year Christianity realizes a net gain of about 44,000 new churches.

√ In A.D. 100, there were 12 unreached people groups per every congregation of believers. Today, with 5 million churches worldwide, there is one unreached people group per every 416 congregations.

Select Regional Profiles[9]

√ The Church in Africa is increasing by an average of 20,000 members per day: A continent that was 3 percent Christian in 1900 is more than 40 percent Christian today.

√ In 1900 Korea had no Protestant church. Today, Korea is 30 percent Christian with more than 4,000 churches in Seoul alone.

√ In Islamic Indonesia, the percentage of Christians is so high the government will not print the statistic—which is probably nearing 25 percent of the population.

√ After 70 years of oppression in the Soviet Union, people who consider themselves Christian number over 80 million.

√ The Chinese Church Research Center concludes that there are at least 50 million Christians today in China, compared to fewer than one million in 1949.

√ In the midst of all the trouble in Nicaragua, the evangelical population has jumped from about 7 percent to 50 percent.

If these statistics could be superimposed on a map of the world and viewed in time-lapse fashion, the impact of the past hundred years would be that of a spiritual blitzkrieg. In fact, so overwhelming has this progress been to date that a growing number of Church and mission leaders are talking seriously about a final push to victory. Many are praying, planning and working toward a fulfillment of the Great Commission by the year A.D. 2000.

David Barrett calls this phenomenon *convergence* and adds that "in the last 30 years the major Christian confessions have converged startlingly on the subject of world evangelization."[10] His observation is bolstered by many of the "decade themes" posted by these various confessions at the beginning of the 1990s:[11]

- Worldwide Decade of Evangelization (Catholic Church)
- Decade of Harvest (Assemblies of God)
- Decade of Evangelism (World Methodist Church)
- Decade of Decisions (Presbyterian)
- Decade of Evangelism (Anglican Communion)
- Decade of Destiny (Church of God)
- Decade of Bold Mission (Southern Baptist Convention)
- Decade of World Evangelization (charismatic renewal)

As the church's decision-makers acquire ever more accurate intelligence on the status of today's evangelistic campaign, many of them are proceeding to redeploy resources along the front lines of the 10/40 Window. Even traditional mission fields such as black Africa, Latin America and India are being rapidly transformed into valuable launching platforms aimed at the heart of the unreached world. The word today is that the frontier is shrinking—and Satan knows it.

Open Doors and Windows of Opportunity

As we contemplate the millions of unreached souls that continue to languish within the 10/40 Window, we must also consider the fact that today's spiritual battlefield is not solely related to location, but increasingly to strategic timeliness as well. In addition to geographical windows of need, we must also pay attention to windows of opportunity.

What suddenly makes this issue all the more important is the fact that in recent days God has sovereignly punched holes in the ramparts of several prominent enemy strongholds. Some of these are so gaping, and so inviting, that Christian workers have been seen pinching themselves to confirm they are still stationed in reality. While the more obvious of these breaches are situated in Eastern Europe, equally dramatic openings have been encountered in such far-flung places as Outer Mongolia, Nepal and the Arabian Peninsula—all locations with proven anti-Gospel credentials.

That so many exceptional opportunities should manifest themselves at the very hour in which the Church is engaged in an unprecedented global mobilization is surely more than raw coincidence. Indeed, in theological parlance, the relevant term is *providential*. With the critical ratio of Gospel supply and demand finally looking reasonable, God may have fired the first shots of the final battle for the liberation of planet earth.

At this historic juncture, the Church is faced with at least three salient questions:

1) Where, specifically, are these *kairos* breaches located?

2) What are the best ways of exploiting these unique opportunities?

3) How long will these openings last?

While subsequent chapters will address questions two and three, God's recent breaching handiwork may be seen today at sites along

each of the three major fronts of the 10/40 Window: Asia; Eastern
Europe and the U.S.S.R.; and the Middle East and North Africa.

Asia

Despite setbacks in China, the years 1989 and 1990 brought
marvelous news out of several other Asian strongholds. Notable
among these were the Hindu kingdom of Nepal, the Killing Fields
of Cambodia and the ancient Mongolian homeland of Ghengis
Khan.

The kingdom of Nepal witnessed, in order of occurrence, bloody
political upheaval, the installation of a democratic interim government and the drafting of a new constitution.[12] After 35 years of
repression, the Christians of Nepal were free in 1990 to celebrate
Christmas for the first time without fear. In fact, the Nepal Christian Fellowship organized a Christmas service at the Royal Acad-
emy Auditorium in Kathmandu and invited a government minister
as the guest of honor. Even the prime minister, Dr. Krishna Prasad
Bhattarai, sent a warm message of felicitation.[13]

Although there were no known Christians in Nepal in 1950, the
Christian Church in this exotic mountain kingdom presently has
more than 50,000 believers worshiping in several hundred house
churches—a tenfold leap over the past decade alone.[14]

In Cambodia, fifteen years after Pol Pot's Khmer Rouge ram-
paged through the land murdering from twenty to thirty percent of
the country's seven million people, the Phnom Penh government,
as of April 1990, granted official recognition to the Christian
Church as a legal entity. The nation's 4,000 believers are now
permitted to worship publicly and, in an amazing twist of events,
have even conducted recent evangelistic crusades in government-
owned buildings.[15]

A third divine breach was opened recently in the north Asian
land of Mongolia—long considered the world's most spiritually
destitute setting. After conquering much of the known world between the thirteenth and fourteenth centuries, the enigmatic Mongol hordes retreated into a long season of isolation. Despite the
efforts of Nestorian and, later, British and Scandinavian mission-

aries, Mongolia was unable to claim any national Christian church until the 1980s.[16]

Creating an interesting piece of trivia, Mongolia in 1924 became the world's second Communist state and the first in Asia. Since Mongolia was a close fellow traveler with the Soviet Union for nearly three-quarters of a century, when Mikhail Gorbachev introduced *glasnost* and *perestroika* in the late '80s, the experiment inevitably spilled over into Mongolian social politics. Unlike their northern mentors, however, the Mongols have apparently decided to stick with the results. As a consequence, the once xenophobic Mongols have opened up for the first time in centuries to the Western world.[17]

Perhaps not surprisingly, a significant move of God is now unfolding in this ancient land. In August and December 1990, for instance, ministry teams distributed more than one thousand pounds of Christian literature on the streets of the Mongolian capital of Ulan Bator. On each occasion, the materials were gobbled up within thirty minutes. At the same time, an open worship service was held with newly converted Mongol believers in the restaurant of the main tourist hotel. The leaders of this fledgling national church—which include a government tour guide in his early thirties and a man whose name translates as "Iron Hero"—have shared a genuine vision to carry the Gospel to unreached peoples within the country, including 80,000 Muslim Kazakhs in the western provinces.[18]

Like all windows of opportunity, these new openings in Asia will one day close. While no one knows precisely when that day will come, it certainly behooves the Church—in Asia and elsewhere—to behave as if she were facing a deadline. In Mongolia the threat is the potential return of government hard-liners; in Cambodia it is the prospect of a reprise with the Khmer Rouge. Even in Nepal, one formerly jailed American missionary believes Nepalese Christians "need to step on the gas." Citing what he sees as excessive tentativeness in taking full advantage of the new political climate, Operation Mobilization's Dave McBride told *Pulse* magazine in December 1990: "We [have] just experienced the most open period of all time in Nepal, and the bulk of the churches missed it." Quickly adding that the country is "still open," McBride nevertheless warned that "if they're going to sit around, waiting to see what happens next, then they're really going to miss great opportunities for evangelism."

Eastern Europe and the Soviet Union

In the second half of March 1990, a group of new Eastern European leaders met at Northwestern University's Medill School of Journalism to discuss where the recent democratic revolution in Europe is headed. Not unexpectedly, the Europeans spoke of the need for even more free enterprise, civil liberty and political diversity. At the same time, however, the speakers also wanted to talk about a more basic need in their homelands: *morality*. Said Romania's new U.N. ambassador, Dragos Munteanu: "When you live in a moral void for 45 years, the basic need is a society based on morality."[19]

Much the same could be said of the Soviets. According to Anatoli Koliada, a priest at the Alexander Newski Russian Orthodox Church: "The Russians are becoming insecure as a result of the collapse of Communism." And having lost their beliefs, he says, "people are coming back to the churches. They are looking for something."[20]

An even more poignant example of today's search for truth and meaning in the Soviet Union is offered in the following excerpt from a letter published recently in a popular secular Russian magazine (the writer is *not* a believer):

> I just turned over the last page of a great book, and I am overcome by feelings of gratitude and happiness. But there are some bitter questions which remain unanswered. Why only now? Why so late? Half of my life is gone. Oh, if it could only have been ten years earlier! At the age of thirty I was able to read the Gospel for the very first time.
>
> It was entirely by chance that this small book fell into my hands, and I approached it with purely literary curiosity. I was gripped by what I read and it became clear that the value of this book is not to be underestimated. Gradually I began to boil with indignation. To

> think that such a treasure had been hidden from me! Who decided,
> and on what grounds, that this book was harmful to me?
>
> In our time of unrest and brokenness, when crystal palaces turn
> out to be cardboard shacks, when once majestic kings are now
> covered with shame, when under the granite edifices are unstable
> foundations of clay, then I know that there is a book to which I can
> always return, and it will help, comfort and support me in the
> darkest hour.[21]

Rarely in history has the Church faced a more welcome opportunity than it does in today's U.S.S.R. Not only is spiritual hunger
at near-starvation levels, but according to the British-based Keston
College, two mid-1990 opinion surveys indicate that "religious
organizations enjoy more trust from the Soviet public than any
other institution."[22] Even the state is cooperating. In September
1990, on the strength of a 341-to-2 vote, the Soviet legislature
brought an abrupt end to decades of state-sponsored atheism by,
among other things, extinguishing a long-time ban on Sunday
schools, home prayer meetings and overt evangelism. In reference
to the latter, newly worded legislation states explicitly that the
government cannot "restrict the study, financing or propagandiz-
ing" of any of the U.S.S.R.'s various religious faiths.[23]

To date, the combined impact of this unprecedented spiritual
hunger and liberty has been nothing short of a religious stampede.
One exhausted priest who has been baptizing crowds regularly of
up to one hundred at a time, groaned: "I feel like a squashed
lemon afterwards."[24] Sunday schools are also booming. After visiting a new program in Moscow, a flabbergasted correspondent for
Komsomolskaya Pravda wrote: "An unthinkable amount of children were crammed in there." Another journalist who attended
religious lessons at a church in Vilnius, Lithuania, observed that
they attracted "ten times more children and adults than expected."[25]

Besides coping with the crowds, another challenge for the
Church is to extend a hand to her former oppressors—especially
secret police, atheist propagandists and Marxist professors. According to some, like Lutheran church superintendent Gunther
Krusche, they are starting to ask for help. "They are totally dis-

oriented about the future," notes Krusche. "Theirs was not a hope in heaven, but a hope for a future in this society, and now it is lost."[26]

When a group of international humanists visited Moscow's Institute for Scientific Atheism in July 1989, one of the delegates, agnostic philosophy professor Paul Kurtz, asked an Institute member how many truly committed atheists there were in the U.S.S.R. The member laughed nervously and said: "There are only a thousand—and most of these are connected with the Institute for Scientific Atheism!"[27]

For the majority of those other Soviet thinkers who are suddenly feeling like intellectual orphans, help is on the way. In Moscow, former imprisoned Orthodox lay activist Alexander Ogorodnikov has recently received government permission to organize the Free University of Christian Democracy, which will offer open training courses taught by both Soviet and Western personalities.[28]

Similarly, the International Institute for Christian Studies (IICS) has recently signed contracts with Moscow State and Novosibirsk State Universities to provide resident Christian professors. At the former school, which boasts Mikhail Gorbachev as an alumnus and is considered the most prestigious institution of higher learning in the Soviet Union, IICS professors will teach in the Departments of Philosophy and of Religion and Freethinking (formerly the Department of Atheism). In Novosibirsk (where earlier talks by a British mathematician reconciling science and the Bible were packed), IICS has been granted permission to establish a Chair of Christian Studies, which will operate within the newly formed Department of Secular and Theological Philosophy.[29]

Another dramatic step was taken in late October 1990, when more than one thousand Soviet pastors, evangelists and lay leaders from every corner of the U.S.S.R. gathered in Moscow's Ismailovo Complex for a historic four-day Congress on Evangelism. Joining their brethren in common cause were 152 international Christian leaders representing 58 mission agencies and 20 nations. In all, 97 separate workshops imparted strategies on topics ranging from pastoral leadership to evangelizing intellectuals.[30]

With their newfound support from abroad, Soviet Christians

today are tackling a dazzling array of ministry challenges. On the social end of the spectrum this includes volunteer work by members of the Moscow Baptist Church at the large Kashchenko mental hospital,[31] counseling with suicidal residents in Leningrad's massive urban housing complexes, and ministry inside various prisons, pre-schools, orphanages and retirement homes.

In a different, but equally creative, approach to ministry, believers in the southern city of Krasnodar have set up evangelistic street lending libraries on main boulevards near the center of town. Consisting mainly of wooden tables displaying a range of Christian literature, the libraries permit interested passersby to check out and review the reading materials for one week at a time. The ministry has attracted both significant interest and quality converts—the latter coming primarily via stage-two "reader fellowships."[32]

Other indigenous churches and mission societies are actively conducting pioneer evangelism among peoples living in the Soviet hinterlands. One Ukraine-based group, the Light of the Gospel founded in 1989, has already sent out five fully supported missionaries—three of them to do pioneer evangelism in the Yakutsk region of central Siberia. Other teams have traveled to such exotic locations as the Black Sea coast, the Tien Shan Mountains separating China and the U.S.S.R., and Sakhalin Island situated in the Soviet Far East.[33]

Outside of the Soviet Union itself, perhaps the most rigorously patrolled stronghold in Eastern Europe in recent years has been the tiny nation of Albania. With its dramatic 1967 proclamation that it would henceforth assume the role of the world's first atheist state, Albania in a spiritual sense became the storied "mouse that roared."

For more than twenty years, Albania guarded her distinction jealously, not even hesitating to break ranks with the likes of the Soviets and Chinese over alleged ideological impurities. Proving there was a method to their madness, the Albanians used their isolation to cloak a brutal and systematic obliteration of all national religious institutions.

In early November 1990, however, the results of years of Chris-

tian intercessory prayer manifested themselves in a big way when
Albania's president, Ramiz Alia, delivered a landmark speech
calling for sweeping constitutional reforms and a lifting of the
infamous 1967 ban on religion. Three months later, massive street
demonstrations in the Albanian capital of Tirana resulted in the
toppling of a prominent statue of former Communist leader Enver
Hoxha, as well as the careers of several hard-line politicians.

Even more startling evidence of the transformation underway in
Albania came in March 1991, when television audiences were
treated to live footage of the nation's Communist Party leader
walking arm in arm with Mother Teresa. The happy occasion, it
turned out, was the announcement of the first formally recognized
religious charity in Albania since the Communist crackdown in
1967.

As with Asia, the threat in Eastern Europe today is that these
dramatic spiritual and political gains will be reversed. In addition
to the obvious concerns over a possible crackdown—especially in
the U.S.S.R. and Albania where a strong hand has traditionally
been welcomed in times of acute instability—there are the equally
serious prospects for ethnic civil war and moral poisoning through
materialist imports from the West.[34]

The Middle East and North Africa

If the ministry openings in Eastern Europe and the Soviet Union
managed to catch most of the Christian headlines in the late '80s
and early '90s, the recent Gulf War diverted some of this attention.
Properly so. For in the view of Egyptian journalist Mohammed Sid
Ahmed, no other event in modern times, not even the defeat of the
Arabs by Israel in 1967, "has shaken the region as profoundly as
this crisis has."[35]

In Iraq, citizens who were traumatized by the Gulf War and
continued internecine strife are being ministered to by Christian
relief and reconstruction workers from throughout the Middle East
and elsewhere. Stories are still emerging from the one hundred or
so members of the Baghdad Presbyterian Church who were con-
scripted into Saddam's army and sent to the front in the days

before the war. Many Iraqis are reportedly open as never before to
the Gospel message. Is this the hour of fulfillment for Jeremiah's
ancient prophecy?

> "Babylon's warriors have stopped fighting;
> they remain in their strongholds.
> Their strength is exhausted;
> they have become like women.
> Her dwellings are set on fire;
> the bars of her gates are broken.
> One courier follows another
> and messenger follows messenger
> to announce to the king of Babylon
> that his entire city is captured,
> the river crossings seized,
> the marshes set on fire,
> and the soldiers terrified."
> This is what the Lord Almighty, the God of Israel, says:
> "The Daughter of Babylon is like a threshing floor
> at the time it is trampled;
> the time to harvest her will soon come."[36]

In liberated Kuwait, massive reconstruction requirements[37] and
gratitude toward the West have afforded the Church of Jesus Christ
her first substantial foothold on the highly controlled Arabian Peninsula. With fewer than a million people to start with, and many of
those having been killed, kidnaped or wounded during the recent
fighting, the emirate has had no choice but to import large numbers of foreign nationals. If expatriate Christian workers from such
places as the United States, Canada, Europe, India, Egypt and the
Philippines comprise even five percent of this evolving post-war
foreign labor force, it will place more than 60,000 Christians in
the heart of the Islamic motherland (not including those stationed
in Saudi Arabia and other Gulf countries).

At this time when Westerners—and Americans in particular—
are hailed by ordinary Kuwaitis as liberators, the opportunity to
share the love of Jesus in both word and deed has never been
greater. In the aftermath of a savage attack by fellow Muslims,
many locals are reexamining their Islamic roots and values. Some

like Ali Salaam, a young Kuwaiti interviewed by CNN (via radio) during the latter stages of the occupation, appear to have lost their spiritual underpinnings altogether: "After five-and-a-half months, we don't pray anymore. Prayer doesn't help."

While Kuwait and Iraq remain the prime focal points of God's redemptive initiatives in the region, *Los Angeles Times* reporter Kim Murphy points out that "a growing number of Saudis are becoming convinced that long after the Americans have gone home, the guns are put away and the Kuwaiti issue [is] settled," their own country will emerge from the crisis "a remarkably different place." Murphy goes on to confirm that "a number of re-form-minded Saudi businessmen, government officials and acade-micians are using the invasion of Kuwait as an opportunity to open the secretive kingdom's doors permanently to the West. 'Of course there will be change,' says a young Foreign Ministry official. 'We are in a crisis, and crisis breeds opportunity.' "[38]

Kairos, Muslims and the Supernatural

Another development that has undoubtedly caused great alarm in Satan's camp of late relates to the recent dramatic rise in su-pernatural power encounters among Muslims. First evidenced in the early 1980s, many observers report detecting a significant surge in both the frequency and scope of these occurrences around 1987. Accounts from Muslim converts and missionaries in the field tend to fall into three basic categories: dreams and visita-tions, miraculous healings and special deliverances (both physical and spiritual).[39]

Such is the magnitude of this phenomena that a number of Christian agencies and missionaries are taking time to reexamine doctrinal positions relative to divine healing and demonization. After multiple head-on collisions with reality, many of these work-ers have grown weary of fishing for elusive explanations and have decided instead to ask the Lord for increased power in their min-istries. From the sound of things, God seems to be obliging.

Although space and prudence serve here as rigorous constraints when it comes to sharing many of the stirring vignettes from God's current passage through the Muslim world—a supernatural journey that many believers see as another prayer-inspired *kairos* response—the stories that follow offer valuable insights into divine power, character and ways.

Divine Visitations in Algeria

In the early 1980s, a truly remarkable incident took place in a North African village located some 125 miles east of the city of Algiers. According to testimony, on one unforgettable night in 1983—with no prior warning and for no immediately discernible reason—God sovereignly descended upon this coastal township with gracious bounty. Moving from house to house, and communicating through a combination of dreams, visions and angelic visitations, He did not rest until every member of this Muslim community was properly introduced to His only begotten Son, Jesus.[40] As might be expected, come daybreak, nearly every villager had a story to tell.

As the Holy Spirit lingered and these simple citizens managed to piece together the magnitude of what had happened to them, a sense of spiritual awe settled over the entire village. In the weeks that followed, their conclusions led to a dramatic wholesale conversion involving some 400 to 450 Muslim villagers—a nearly eighteenfold increase in the size of the Algerian national church!

When amazed mission workers, who had had no direct involvement in this extraordinary development, began to investigate possible reasons for this sovereign visitation, they came across a stunning piece of information. It was at virtually this very site that, in June 1315, Raymond Lull, a Spanish missionary from Majorca, had been stoned to death by frenzied Muslims after preaching in the open market.[41]

The blood of martyrs, it has often been said, represents the seed of the Church. Lull, who is generally considered to be the first missionary to the Muslims, certainly believed this. In his book, *The Tree of Life*, he wrote that Islamic strongholds are best conquered "by love and prayers, and the pouring out of tears and

blood."[42] In retrospect, it appears that it was precisely this formula that summoned the recent supernatural events in Algeria.
Falling into the ground on that summer day in the fourteenth
century, the seed of Raymond Lull's poured-out life was subsequently watered by the tears of generations of pious intercessors.
Faithfully tending their cause, these saints waited patiently until,
sometime in the late twentieth century, the golden vials of heaven
overflowed and God was released to summon forth fruit in its due
season. (See "The Role of Prayer," chapter 10.)

Adding even more luster to this marvelous story is the fact that
it has apparently triggered a book of Acts–style revival throughout
other parts of Algeria, which continues to this day. During the
summer of 1990, I had the high privilege of meeting with several
dozen former Muslims who had come to faith in Christ within the
previous eighteen months. Nearly all reported some type of supernatural intervention. Churches are spreading like wildfire, particularly among the Kabyle Berber people living in and around the
Atlas Mountains. One recent Arabic-speaking visitor described as
many as several thousand new believers meeting for Bible studies
and marathon prayer sessions in homes and on mountaintops.[43]

Deliverance and Church Growth in Afghanistan

A similar chronicle has been recorded in recent years inside the
war-torn nation of Afghanistan. Like the account in Algeria, it too
begins with prayer and the faithfulness of pioneer evangelists.
After being prayed into the country as tentmaker missionaries in
1951,[44] Dr. and Mrs. J. Christy Wilson worked with vision-
impaired Afghans until an increasing number of Muslim conversions at their eye institute prompted the government to expel them
in March 1973. Heartbroken, the Wilsons did the only thing they
could think of—they prayed for the friends they were forced to
leave behind.

In a retrospective account of those days, Dr. Wilson writes:
"God gave us a wonderful promise concerning them [the blind]"
from Isaiah 42:16 (NIV):

> "I will lead the blind by ways they have not known, along un
> familiar paths I will guide them; I will turn the darkness into light

before them and make the rough places smooth. These are the things I will do; I will not forsake them."[45]

Seventeen years later that promise was kept in dramatic fashion when a leader of the Afghan Church, a blind man, was captured by fanatical Muslim guerillas. Taken deep into rebel-held territory, Ahmed[46] was tossed into a basement and subjected to cruel electro-shock torture. In the middle of a discussion about how they would kill him, however, a nearby explosion sent his tormentors scurrying outside to see what had occurred. During these moments, Ahmed was able to escape from his captors and launch out on an incredible return journey to Kabul. Days later, after crossing miles of tortuous terrain and multiple rebel checkpoints, Ahmed returned, like the apostles in the book of Acts, to the marketplace. Since resuming his witness for Christ, this unique blind man has helped many Afghan Muslims to see for the first time.[47]

Miracles and Salvation Among Turks

In his current foray into the heart of Islam, God has repeatedly left His calling card with members of the world's huge Turkish community.[48] At least 35 percent of all recent Turkish converts describe having had spiritual dreams and visions in which Jesus has appeared to them as the Son of God.[49] In Soviet Central Asia, several Turkish Uzbeks and Kirghiz have also reported physical healings, while workers among Bulgaria's Turkish minority have shared extraordinary tales of the dead being raised to life.[50]

Even the 125,000-member Turkish guest worker community in Germany has been brushed by the power of God. For one woman lying in a Berlin hospital in 1988, the timing could not have been better. Paralyzed from the waist down, Shengul had sustained her injuries by jumping out of a second-story window to avoid being stabbed by her alcoholic husband. She had little to live for when, one night, Jesus appeared to her in a dream. "Who are You?" she asked at first. "I am the Jesus who has the power to heal you," He replied. With that He reached out and touched her. Then, before turning to leave, He set something on her nightstand.

Upon waking the next morning, Shengul wondered if what she

had experienced was real, or merely a vivid dream brought on by her medication. As a test, she decided to swing her legs out of bed and try to walk. Having made it halfway down the hospital corridor before startled nurses rushed her back to bed and called her doctor, Shengul was delirious with joy. When her physician, a fine Christian man, finished his examination, he pronounced her completely healed! Suddenly remembering the gift Jesus had left her on her nightstand, she turned to find a Turkish Bible (which the Lord had prompted her doctor to place there while she was asleep) shining like a golden jewel. In the months that have followed, Shengul has become a radiant witness to the power of the living Christ.[51]

Praise God!

An International Bouquet

In a recent article, folk Islam specialist Bill Musk recounts the story of Gulshan Esther, a former Pakistani Muslim who, like Shengul, was approached by Jesus in a vision in which He healed her crippled limbs and soul. After her healing, Gulshan, too, was directed to the Word of God. Only instead of finding it lying on an adjacent nightstand, she was given a vision of a man ten miles to the north who would provide her with a copy of the Scriptures. Needless to say, she found him.[52]

Additional stories, some of which are not yet possible to share, come from such far-flung places as Soviet Central Asia, the Comoro Islands and Tunisia, and corroborate the fact that God is clearly moving in a new way among truth-seeking Muslims. The recipients of this amazing grace, as in the days of the Bible, range from the lowliest waif to the most exalted leader. Unimpressed by manmade barriers, this grace has flowed into the dark abyssal realms of Iraq, Saudi Arabia and, notably, the Islamic Republic of Iran (where, in an impressive tribute to the Hound of Heaven, more Muslims have come to Christ since 1980 than were recorded in all the previous 1,000 years).[53]

Facing the Last of the Giants

As we consider the facts before us, it is apparent that something extraordinary is happening in the earth. While no man can comprehend the complex maneuvers of the Almighty with absolute certainty, there are nevertheless increasing signs that God may be leading His people deep into the autumn season—a time of final harvest before the onset of winter darkness. Among the more striking of these signs are several that we have alluded to earlier: 1) a dramatic realignment of spiritual and political forces in the earth; 2) an unprecedented mobilization of missionary plans and personnel; and 3) a noteworthy increase in supernatural signs and wonders.

Of the many ideas on the subject of how God might intend to wind down the historical process and bring closure to world evangelization, one of the more interesting is the theory that the armies of the Lord are currently being vectored toward Eden. That the territory of ancient Mesopotamia currently represents the geographical bull's eye of the 10/40 Window affords the theory a measure of credibility. In fact, the only thing necessary for this theory to become reality is for the evangelistic forces currently surrounding the Window to continue their inward advance at a more or less uniform pace. If they do, Christian soldiers from around the world will reenact the celebrated Allied link-up at the Elbe at the end of World War II; only this time their boots will be moistened by the great tributaries of Eden—the Tigris and Euphrates.[54]

That God would in the end lead His Church full-circle back to Eden is more than just poetic; it is also logical. For it is from this site that Satan's original lie has resonated throughout the earth for thousands of years. Having usurped the paradise originally intended for mankind, it makes sense that the serpent will eventually be defeated on that selfsame soil by the offspring of God's banished children—back to fulfill, in inverse fashion, their original mandate to extend God's Kingdom throughout the earth.[55]

Returning to Eden, however, will be no cakewalk. As we have documented, within the 10/40 Window are rooted many of the most formidable spiritual strongholds on the planet. At their center, Persia and Babylon stand like the twin pillars of Hercules. As the Church closes in on the last of these giants, she should not expect them to cede any territory without a fight—a lesson

Christians in many areas are learning the hard way. When a Saudi woman was delivered from demonic possession in Colorado Springs, for instance, she revealed that virtually the entire population of her family village on the outskirts of the Islamic holy city of Mecca was "mad." Greatly desiring to see others among her people set free through the power of God, she contacted a male cousin about coming to the U.S. for deliverance. Shortly after the arrangements were made, however, the man wandered out into the wilderness and was never seen again.[56]

It is Christians themselves, however, who are often the primary targets of the enemy's wrath. In Nigeria, India and the southern Philippines, Christian homes and places of worship have been firebombed. In the Sudan, China, Turkey, Vietnam and scores of other nations, believers are being routinely arrested and imprisoned for their faith. At a February 1990 meeting of the Evangelical Christian Baptist Union in Moscow, delegates representing Soviet republics with Muslim majorities brought the sobering report that "Muslim mullahs were [now] threatening to cut out the tongues of the Christians."[57] In Afghanistan, a mullah who was converted in the late 1980s after reading the Scriptures was shot dead by the *mujahedin.* Another Afghan believer by the name of Zia was tortured to death in western Pakistan.

In March 1990, villagers in Bahn, Liberia, found the bodies of the Reverend Tom Jackson and his wife, June—murdered after forty years on the field translating the Bible into the local Gio and Mano languages.[58] The same month, masked gunmen entered the house of William Robinson while the missionary and his wife were singing their young children to sleep. Forced into a bathroom, Mr. Robinson was subsequently killed with a silencer-tipped pistol. The couple had been administering a home for handicapped children in the southern Lebanese village of Rashaya el Foukhar since 1983.[59] In 1990, Father Alexander Mein, a beloved Soviet Orthodox priest, was brutally murdered by an ax-wielding assailant on his way to conduct church services.[60]

Knowing their time is short, the creatures of the night are in a foul mood. Though they cannot resist the worldwide campaign of love currently being prosecuted by the Church of Jesus Christ, they can inflict temporal casualties. There should be no illusion about the nature of global spiritual warfare in the 1990s—the enemy's claws are out. In the end, the believers' garden of victory will be laced with the blood-seed of many new martyrs of the faith, each one planted victoriously in the grand tradition of Raymond Lull, Father Mein, William Robinson, Zia and the Jacksons.

"At the very moment of our suffering in this world," writes pastor Don Williams, "we are also to know the touch of glory because we live in a kingdom both come and coming. Thus, God's Spirit is upon us. We have been sealed, anointed, and filled by him. . . . Knowing a joy unspeakable, we rejoice in our tribulations, for in them we share in the very sufferings of Christ himself."[61]

Notes

1 Quoted in *Mission Frontiers*, Vol. 9, No. 9, September 1987.

2 Extrapolated from *Seven Hundred Plans to Evangelize the World*, ed. David Barrett and James Reapsome (Birmingham, Ala.: New Hope, 1988), pp. 8–9.

3 Luis Bush in *Countdown to A.D. 2000*, ed. Thomas Wang (Pasadena, Cal.: A.D. 2000 Movement and William Carey Library, 1989), p. 40.

4 Including Roman Catholics.

5 Including whole Bibles and Scripture portions.

6 David B. Barrett and Todd Johnson, *Our Globe and How to Reach It* (Birmingham, Al.: New Hope, 1990), Global Diagram No. 14, p. 27.

7 Barrett and Johnson, Global Diagram No. 12, p. 25; also, *A.D. 2000 and Beyond*, Vol. 1, No. 5, November–December 1990.

8 Over the course of a year, this translates into 133 million people—or the equivalent of the entire population of Brazil—touched by the Gospel.

9 *A.D. 2000 and Beyond*, volume cited above.

10 Barrett and Johnson, p. 72.

11 Barrett and Johnson, Global Diagram No. 22, p. 35.

12 While parliamentary elections in April 1991 and the legislation that follows will have a big impact on how the new constitution is interpreted and applied, one positive omen is that, in the meantime, all religious prisoners have been freed and pending religious cases dismissed.

13 Letter from Nicanor Tamang, Nepalese Christian worker, Dehradun, India.

14 Stan Guthrie in *Pulse*, December 28, 1990.

15 Correspondence with Cambodia specialist at CAMA Services, Thailand, and Radha Manickam, director of Cambodia Ministries, Seattle.

16 It should be noted that Mongolia proper is presently divided into three geographic

tiers: the northernmost, consisting of two autonomous republics in Soviet Siberia; the sovereign middle, known as Outer Mongolia (or, under the Communist regime, the Mongolian People's Republic); and the southern reaches (Inner Mongolia) ruled as a province of the People's Republic of China. While mission work into Outer Mongolia evidenced no tangible fruit at all, efforts by European and American missionaries on the Chinese side continued into the 1930s and resulted in numerous churches.

17 "Democracy Gets a Chance," *Time*, August 13, 1990.

Note: Highlighting new diplomatic relations with the United States, the Mongolian government, in August 1990, signed an agreement with Secretary of State James Baker that, among other things, welcomes up to fifteen Peace Corps volunteers a year, mostly to teach English. (About this same time, a distinctly Christian organization also inked an agreement to bring in nearly two dozen English teachers.) Still other ministry opportunities surfaced when Baker announced an aid package providing scholarships, exchange opportunities and assistance in business management, banking, law, computers, bio-technology and agriculture.

18 Conversation with individual involved in direct ministry activities in Mongolia, September 1990.

19 "East Europe Is Trying to Rediscover, Re-establish Basic Morality," *The Seattle Times*, March 26, 1990.

20 "Idea of Going Home to Failing Economy Fills Troops with Fear," *Ibid.*, November 17, 1990.

21 Excerpted from a translation appearing in the November 1989 "USSR Prayer & Information Letter" distributed by Pirkko Poysti of Russian Christian Radio.

22 Keston College news report, June 5, 1990.

23 "Soviet Legislators OK Home Prayer and Sunday Schools," *Los Angeles Times*, September 27, 1990.

24 *The Daily Telegraph*, November 21, 1989.

25 Reported by Oxana Antic, Radio Liberty Research, March 2, 1990.

26 "The People Involved in East Germany's Revolution," *The Seattle Times*, November 11, 1990.

27 Paul Kurtz, *Free Inquiry*, Fall 1989.

Note: One recent visitor to the Soviet Union who did not find this issue amusing is arch-atheist Madalyn Murray O'Hair. Having reserved time and space at the 1989 Moscow Book Fair to peddle her atheistic merchandise, *Pulse* reporter Art Moore writes that instead Ms. O'Hair "sat conspicuously alone," her visage obscured by a wall of Muscovites lined up to receive free New Testaments distributed by the Evangelical Christian Publishers Association. (In a December 1989 phone conversation with Doug Ross, it was learned that after the ECPA's on-hand stock of 10,000 New Testaments was dispensed, an addition 17,000 Soviets had to be promised "rainchecks.") Upon returning to the United States, Ms. O'Hair declared: "I am completely stunned to find out that the U.S.S.R. is completely indifferent to atheism."

28 Guthrie, *Pulse*, October 26, 1990.

29 From *IICS Update*, "Eastern Europe Welcomes IICS" (summer 1990), and an IICS fax communique received March 22, 1991.

Note: IICS has also been asked to help establish Christian lectures for a new Department of Christian Studies at Charles University in Prague.

Also, in a News Network International feature, "Christian Values Making Inroads in Soviet Education" (December 11, 1990), Susan Isaacs reports that the U.S.-based Christian College Coalition and other evangelical groups like IVCF, Wheaton College and CSI have recently initiated various exchanges with Soviet universities. Radio Liberty's Oxana Antic cites a *Moscow News* report in late 1989 indicating that students from Moscow University's journalism department would henceforth study the Bible as a formal component of their academic pursuit.

30 Report by Kathy Giske in *Strategic Times Journal*, Vol. 4, No. 4, October–December 1990.

31 Dr. Kent Hill, *The Puzzle of the Soviet Church* (Portland: Multnomah Press, 1989), pp. 282–283.
Note: According to Hill, this ministry of love has been praised openly by the hospital's chief physician, Dr. Valentin Kozyrev, and the Soviet press.

32 George Otis, Jr., "The Soviet Union in Transition," *Strategic Times Journal*, Vol. 4, No. 1, January–March 1990.

33 *Ibid.*

34 In a December 1989 article, "The Cross and the Kremlin II," published in the *World Monitor*, theologian Harvey Cox shares a revealing story about Ana, a serious young Soviet woman in her late twenties who, according to Cox, is also a committed Orthodox Christian. Cox writes: "She said . . . that some weeks earlier she had spent a hundred rubles for a ticket to a . . . rock concert by the British rock group Pink Floyd. I was surprised. She had told me during my last visit how much she despised both rock music and the cultic attitude toward it of many of her young friends. Now she shrugged. 'There is nothing else to spend rubles on,' she said."

35 From a *Los Angeles Times* article by Michael Ross, "Turmoil in Region Just Beginning, Say Many Analysts," carried in *The Seattle Times*, September 14, 1990.

36 Jeremiah 51:30–33 (NIV).

37 According to David Snow, an analyst with Derby Securities in New York, the postwar situation in Kuwait "is shaping up as one of the most massive construction projects of all time."

38 From a *Los Angeles Times* article by Kim Murphy, "U.S. Presence Brings Glasnost to Soviet Society," carried in *The Seattle Times*, September 6, 1990.

39 There is evidence that God has moved in a supernatural fashion among Muslims for many centuries. The point being stressed here is simply that, in recent years, this activity has apparently surged.

One fascinating account from the past comes from the writings of Marco Polo and concerns a miraculous event alleged to have occurred during the reigns of the last Abbasid caliph, al-Musta'sim. According to Polo, from the time of his accession to power, al-Musta'sim's "daily thoughts were employed on the means of converting to his religion [Islam] those who resided within his dominions, or, upon their refusal, in forming pretenses for putting them to death." Christians within the empire—primarily Nestorians and Jacobites—were particularly abhorred by the caliph, so he devised with the help of his wise consorts what he deemed to be a perfect "Catch-22" situation for them.

Ordering the Baghdad Christian community to appear before him, al-Musta'sim recited the text of Matthew 17:20: "If ye have faith as a grain of mustard seed, ye shall say unto this mountain, Remove hence to yonder place, and it shall remove." After he had finished reciting he said: "If it be true, let us see which of you will give the proof of his faith; for certainly if there is not to be found one amongst you who possesses even so small a portion of faith in his Lord, as to be equal to a grain of mustard, I shall be justified in regarding you, henceforth, as a wicked, reprobate, and faithless people." The caliph then granted the Christians ten days to consider whether to move the mountain he pointed out, convert to Islam or die "the most cruel deaths."

After brief consultation, the Christian community committed themselves to a period of 'round-the-clock prayer and fasting, beseeching the Lord to deliver them from their predicament. On the eighth day, a godly bishop dreamed that he was instructed by God to search for a particular shoemaker who would lead them in prayer for the removal of the mountain. After importuning the humble man, who considered himself unworthy of such a task, he relented and sought the Lord for His gracious favor.

When the appointed day finally arrived, the Christians marched in solemn procession to the mountain. Viewing all this as a vain spectacle, the caliph and his guards stood nearby, waiting like vultures to descend upon their already-dying prey. At the front of the gathering, the shoemaker knelt down and, lifting up his hands toward heaven, worshiped the Lord. At the end of his prayer, he suddenly cried out in a loud voice: "In the name of the Father, Son, and Holy Ghost, I command thee, O mountain, to remove thyself." In fine form, the mountain obeyed and, as Polo recounts, "The earth at the same time trembled in a wonderful and alarming manner."

Many onlookers, not surprisingly, were reportedly converted that day. Among their number, albeit secretly, was the caliph himself. From that day forward, al-Musta'sim was said to have worn a cross concealed under his garments. Its discovery upon his death has been given as the reason he was not buried in the shrine of his predecessors. (*The Travels of Marco Polo*, ed. W. Marsden, ann. John Masefield [New York: Dorset Press, 1987/First published by Everyman's Library, 1908], pp. 44–47.)

40 See Revelation 14:6.

41 See Ruth Tucker, *From Jerusalem to Irian Jaya* (Grand Rapids: Zondervan, 1983), pp. 52–57.

42 Excerpt from Lull's book *The Tree of Love*, quoted in Tucker, p. 54; originally cited in Samuel Zwemer, *Raymond Lull: First Missionary to the Moslems* (Funk & Wagnalls, 1902), pp. 52–53.

43 From a firsthand account shared by the teacher-evangelist involved, spring 1990.

44 A "tentmaker" missionary is one who uses his or her professional skills to both accommodate and support ministry abroad. The term is taken from Acts 18:3 where the apostle Paul is mentioned as a tentmaker by trade. Dr. Wilson is widely considered to be the father of the modern tentmaking movement, which today mobilizes hundreds of bi-vocational missionaries throughout the world.

45 J. Christy Wilson, "The Experience of Praying for Muslims," *Muslims and Christians*

on the Emmaus Road, ed. J. Dudley Woodberry (Monrovia, Cal.: MARC, 1989), pp. 329–330.

46 Not his real name.

47 From a September 1990 conversation with an individual involved currently in a direct discipleship role with Ahmed.

48 With a heartland that stretches from China to Europe, ethnic Turks make up one of the largest components of the Muslim empire.

49 From a 1989 report by Craig Meyer, associated with veteran missionary work to Turkish peoples.

50 From an extremely reliable source who wishes to remain anonymous.

51 Meyer report, 1989.

52 Bill Musk, "Dreams and the Ordinary Muslim," *Missiology: An International Review*, Vol. XVI, No. 2, April 1988.

53 One Interserve executive met an Iranian working on a Bible translation in a neighboring country who assured him that "Khomeini has been our best missionary—his 'religion' has turned many to seek truth elsewhere, including the Bible" (*GO*, September–October 1988).

54 According to Saggs, the late scholar E. A. Speiser argued persuasively before his death that "the geographical details given in Genesis 2:6–14 require it to be conceived of as a part of the Near East closely connected with Mesopotamia" (p. 441). Elsewhere Saggs writes: "Anyone who visits south Iraq today may judge it an improbable region for the beginning of civilization. . . . But there are other sides to south Iraq. Through it run the Euphrates and the Tigris, making the land along their banks luxuriant with lush vegetation. . . . By the time human beings first arrived, the whole area must have been criss-crossed by an intricate network of former water channels great and small, with a variety of dry levees (raised banks), wet patches, natural ditches, ponds, lagoons, fens, swamps and oases. The greater distribution of water away from the rivers would have resulted in far more permanent vegetation cover than exists today. Areas of poplars and willows would have been much more extensive, and individual trees would have been much bigger than any found today . . ." (pp. 2–4).

55 Seiss notes, "It is also distinctly prophesied that Babylon shall be the very last of the powers of the earth compelled to drink of the cup of the divine wrath in the great day of the Lord." He cites the passage in Jeremiah 25:17–26 concluding that "the king of Sheshack shall drink after them." He explains that "all the Jewish interpreters agree that *Sheshack* is another name for Babylon. In another place Babylon is called "the hindermost of the nations"—a reference to her belated judgment (p. 899).

56 Reported by the same source, an indigenous Arab, mentioned in footnote 47.

57 Cited by Herbert Schlossberg in *A Fragrance of Oppression*.

58 "U.S. Missionary Is Slain in Southern Lebanon," *International Herald Tribune*, March 29, 1990.

59 *Ibid.*

60 Giske.

61 Don Williams, *Signs, Wonders, and the Kingdom of God* (Ann Arbor, Mich.: Vine Books, 1989), p. 151.

Note: After one Iranian Christian was arrested a few years ago, Islamic authorities added insult to injury when they talked his wife into becoming a Muslim, and one subsequently married her. Condemned to death and cut off from his former wife and four children, this man of God pressed on in the faith by establishing Bible studies for prison guards and fellow inmates. "Don't pray for my release," he instructed his fellow believers. "God has called me here to minister."

8

The Transformation
of Magog

I think it is quite possible to imagine the separation of
the [Soviet] Central Asian republics from the rest of the
country.

> Vyacheslav Ivanov, member of the
> U.S.S.R. Congress of People's Deputies[1]

Long live the last Congress of the Communist Party!

> Message on placards outside July 1990
> Communist Party Congress[2]

"Son of man, set your face toward Gog of the land of
Magog, the prince of Rosh, Meshech, and Tubal, and
prophesy against him, and say, 'Thus says the Lord
God, "Behold, I am against you." ' "

> Ezekiel 38:2–3 (NASB)

One of the few advantages of the rapid acceleration of
history is that we are increasingly able to decipher the mysteries of
prophetic players and events that have lain shrouded in the mists
of time. Some of these new insights are already vivid enough to
shatter long-standing preconceptions; and even those whose precise meanings remain elusive at least have us looking in the right
direction.

Nowhere is this seen more clearly than in the prophetic confederation alluded to by the prophet Ezekiel.[3] For years Christians have puzzled over the role of an atheist superpower—the Soviet Union, or biblical Magog—in what is essentially an Islamic alliance. Today, however, the world's most significant (and, until recently, the most under-reported) story concerns the inexorable Islamization of the U.S.S.R.

The fact is, the land of Magog[4] is currently undergoing a politico-religious transformation of epic proportions. When this development is viewed in tandem with the recent Gulf War and the earlier Islamic revolution in Iran, it is clear that the prophetic future is now being determined along a north-south axis (rather than via the east-west line so familiar to most North Americans and Europeans).[5]

With the long-term survivability of the Soviet empire now being challenged on every front, many people are beginning to question just what a breakup might mean. One recent article observed pointedly that "American Cold Warriors who . . . fervently hoped for the collapse of 'the evil empire' now find themselves without a clear guide to steer them through difficult questions." (Historian John Gaddis likens this situation to that of a dog who spends a good deal of time chasing cars, but who gives little thought to what happens if he actually catches one.)[6] The possibilities can be mind-boggling.

While at first glance it may appear that the impending breakup of the U.S.S.R. is merely an extension of the recent parting of the Iron Curtain, history will record these two events as exact opposites. For whereas the former occasion served to *open* an important window of ministry opportunity, the latter will almost surely *close* one. And from a strategic standpoint, preparing for closures is every bit as important as readying for openings.

Perestroika in Peril: The Dissolution of the Soviet Empire

There can no longer be any doubt that, as far as the vast majority of Soviet citizens is concerned, the once-vaunted Communist system has been weighed in the balance and found wanting. Disillusionment is especially high among its former patrons. One elderly pensioner, beribboned with medals, confided to a Western reporter: "As soon as the [1990 Party] Congress is over, I am leaving the Party, and so are many of my colleagues. Our ideal does not work."[7] Another deserter, S. K. Chapaev, lamented in almost dirge-like tones: "What I believed in all my life has become dust. . . . My entire life has been crossed out and has turned out to have been for nothing."[8]

At street level, however, the operative word is *anger*. Venting their frustration with the government's failure to provide either adequate political freedoms or basic consumer goods, some 1990 May Day marchers carried the Soviet flag with the hammer and sickle cut out. Others defiantly hoisted signs reading: *Down with the empire of Red fascism, Communism is a universal shame* and *I'll trade you the entire government for a kilogram of macaroni.*

More than forty million Soviet citizens now live below the official poverty line[9] and for just about everyone else, life is getting worse. In this illusory workers' paradise, a rash of state bankruptcies has sent unemployment soaring. Housing is so scarce that families are forced to pile up on one another in dilapidated shoebox apartments. The cost of meat and bread has quadrupled, and prices on many other goods have shot up by as much as sixty percent.[10] In order to obtain valuable hard currency, some desperate Soviet troops pulling out of East Germany sold Kalashnikov rifles, surface-to-air missiles and anti-tank grenades illegally to reporters for the German magazine *Tempo*.[11]

Clearly the Soviet economy is sliding into chaos.[12] Even the government admits that, of 1,000 consumer items monitored in state stores, more than 900 of them are no longer available on a regular basis.[13] In the Moscow region, by the end of 1990, 28 out of 30 bakeries were either producing below quota or out of commission entirely; soldiers were digging for potatoes, and jars of cigarette butts were being sold by street vendors for $16.

Yet the biggest shortage in the country is not meat, tobacco or macaroni—it is confidence in the government. "The only thing we believe in now," said one frazzled woman shopper, "is God."[14] During a July 1990 broadcast from the Kremlin Palace of Congresses,

Soviet correspondent Sergei Lomakin reported that "even the polls
show that a mere eighteen percent of those polled currently trust the
Party."[15] The results of a survey reported in October 1990 on the
ABC News program "Nightline" indicated that thirty percent of all
Soviet citizens said they would emigrate if they could.[16]

But they cannot, and frustration is running high. On a recent
Sunday evening, eight hoodlums burst into Voskhod, one of Moscow's expensive, new, privately owned restaurants. As diners dove
for cover, the assailants opened fire with sawed-off hunting rifles,
then came running after them with sticks and knives. After ten
minutes of terror, three people were dead and five wounded, including an Australian tourist. Last year, according to official figures, overall crime in the U.S.S.R. rose by 32 percent.[17]

The government's worst problem, however, is with its restive
nationalities. In the words of senior Party official Igor Mal-
aschenko: "We have succeeded almost too well in removing ideology from the country. And when all other 'isms' disappear, the
one people turn to, most easily, is nationalism."[18] Lending credence to these remarks, Anna Kochmaryuk, a 36-year-old Mol-
davian schoolteacher, told a visiting reporter recently: "The time
has gone for 'My address is the Soviet Union' [an old platitude of
Leninist Internationalism]. We're sick of slogans about friendship
and peace. Now, everyone needs his own piece of land."[19]

In September 1990, as a crowd of some 100,000 independence-
minded Ukrainians marched through the city of Kiev, one poignant
banner lifted above the throng read: *Mother Moscow: We want to be
orphans.* Indeed, each day now, two flags are raised in front of the
Ukrainian Parliament building—one the official Soviet republican
flag, and the other the historic yellow and blue banner of the new
"sovereign" Ukraine.[20]

The Ukraine is not alone in either its sentiments or its actions.
In recent months the nation's fifteen union republics have declared
themselves sovereign over their own affairs and resources. They
have been joined in this process by many of the Soviet Union's
smaller ethnic homelands and, as sassy as it sounds, even regional
districts and individual cities. "For the most part," says Armenia's
new nationalist president, Lavon Ter Petrosian, "the centre is

politically bankrupt—reduced to the level of a theatrical prop."[21]

In addition to the declarations and resolutions, nationalist rioting or other forms of civil disobedience are now chronic in most of the U.S.S.R.'s ethnic enclaves. Two *National Geographic* reporters on a recent assignment in the Baltic republics were told repeatedly: "Tell the Russians to go home. They were not invited here. They have brought fear and mistrust and a haggardness of spirit. They have changed us, eaten at our soul. We have had enough of them."[22]

Many conflicts have turned bloody. In recent separate incidents in Georgia and Latvia, "Black Beret" troops shot and clubbed peaceful demonstrators to death using gunstocks and sharpened spades. On the flip side, police trying to keep regional ethnic conflicts from spiraling out of control in Nagorno-Karabakh, Abkhazia, Moldavia and the Fergana Valley have themselves been assaulted and killed. Throughout the Caucasus and Central Asia, Party, police and KGB headquarters have been subject to numerous rock and firebomb attacks, while in the Baltics, Latvian and Lithuanian peasants have struggled with state security forces over control of media facilities and border posts.

Weapons stolen from military warehouses are everywhere. Even machine guns and rocket launchers are available on the black market. In Kiev, the prospect for civil war is not far from anyone's mind. "I figure there can only be war," said 28-year-old Alexey Nikolaychuk. "When life is getting so hard, what are the desperate people to do? They can only turn against each other."[23]

An equally pessimistic viewpoint was offered by Soviet economist Yakov Urinson on BBC television during the first week of March 1991. "I see an abyss ahead—economic, political, and social; a return to the horrible times that we lived through . . . in the past." When pressed for more specifics, Urinson said: "I mean the famine of the 1930s, and the repressions of 1937."[24]

Soviet Muslims: Swelling Ranks of Discontent

If civil war does break out anytime soon, it is an almost foregone conclusion that the Soviet Union's ballooning Muslim population

will be a crucial, if not decisive, factor. Aside from the fact that they, like most other Soviet minorities, despise Moscow's economic mismanagement, cultural chauvinism and political heavy-handedness, they also happen to be sitting on top of some thirty percent of the country's total land space (which includes the Caspian oilfields and numerous other strategic resources).

With a base population exceeding 57 million, the U.S.S.R.'s Muslim community already represents one out of every five Soviet citizens,[25] and accounts for nearly a third of all conscripts in the Red Army.[26] Growing at five times the rate of the remaining population, Soviet Muslim minorities are projected to experience a seventy percent increase in their numbers by the end of this decade. By the end of the *next* decade, they will account for more than forty percent of all new entries in the Soviet labor market, and nearly fifty percent of the conscripts serving in the Soviet army.[27] Thirty years from now, according to some estimates, they will outnumber ethnic Russians.[28]

Proud of the fact they are now responsible for every second baby born in the U.S.S.R.,[29] Muslims in Central Asia and Azerbaijan frequently cite their high birth rates as "our secret weapon" against European domination. As an example of this weapon in action, British journalist Martin Walker draws attention to a recent bulletin of the Supreme Soviet listing its new "Hero Mother" awards (bestowed upon women who have ten children or more). Although "there was one such award among the 10 million Belorussians," Walker noted there were "530 among the 19 million inhabitants of Uzbekistan, 242 for the 16 million inhabitants of Kazakhstan, and 45 for the 7 million people of Azerbaijan."[30]

Though they are technically full members in the Soviet power structure, most Soviet Muslims feel they are treated almost as if they were a colony. Anger abounds over Moscow's bleeding off of local resources such as Uzbek cotton and Azerbaijani oil, as well as a host of other religious, environmental and economic issues.

Gross environmental mismanagement over the past decades has led to conditions that can only be termed catastrophic. In Soviet Bashkiria, an autonomous Muslim republic near the Ural Mountains, pollution is now so bad that, in the words of KGB General

Vladimir Podelyakin, "if urgent measures are not taken in the very near future, life in Bashkiria will be doomed."[31] In Central Asia the human-induced evaporation of the Aral Sea has caused severe damage to local agriculture and water resources through massive salt and dust storms. Combined with exposure to fertilizers and pesticides applied at fifty times the standard toxicity levels, this tragedy has resulted in a virtual epidemic of cancer and intestinal illness in eastern Uzbekistan.[32] At the Ulbinsky metallurgical works in neighboring Kazakhstan, 120,000 people were contaminated by toxic beryllium-oxide gas following a September 1990 explosion at the plant.

With per capita social expenditure in Central Asia thirty percent lower than the Soviet average and declining,[33] poverty and attendant sickness in some areas of the region have reached third-world proportions. Infant mortality rates are estimated to be ten times higher than those of most European countries and, in Soviet Turkmenistan, children in their first year of life receive an average of 300 injections (as compared to three or four for American children).[34] Says Yuri Kirichenko, a pediatrician working out of a health institute in the Turkmenian capital of Ashkabad: "This is not Africa—children are not starving to death in the same blatant way—but there is no way to hide it anymore: We are poor and we are suffering."[35]

Widespread unemployment—an estimated two million are jobless in Uzbekistan alone—merely adds to the growing discontent over food rationing and inadequate medical care. At the same time, many seem to feel that, if left to their own devices, the bulk of these problems could eventually be alleviated—and they may be right. From the days when the Silk Road wound its way through Central Asian oases en route to China, local Muslims have made stable lives for themselves as traders and farmers. Then, as now, their society was shaped around the Qur'an and the rigors of life at the edge of a fiercely hot desert. Then, as now, lack of meat for guests at a son's wedding feast served as cause for lasting shame.[36]

For many Soviet Muslims today more than shame is at stake. It is also a question of survival—national, spiritual and even physical. With conditions deteriorating daily, patience is seen as less and less of a virtue. Summing up regional sentiments, one youth in the ancient city of Samarkand growled: "We don't want Communists or their damned system."[37]

If Moscow does not take the hint and Central Asia explodes, one Uzbek nationalist says "it will make the unrest in the Baltic republics look like a tea party."[38] Although some scholars are quick to dismiss such statements as hyperbole, the horrific intensity of several recent conflicts in the area has caused others to take them at face value.

In December 1986, for example, upward of 300,000 anti-Russian Muslim demonstrators spilled onto the streets of the Kazakh capital of Alma-Ata. The rush was so ferocious that radio announcements warned Russians in the city to stay off the streets on the second day. A Russian woman living in Alma-Ata was reported as saying: "The Kazakhs were coming in from the countryside, commandeering buses." When one bus driver tried to keep rioters out of his bus, they "bludgeoned [him] to death with scaffolding poles."[39]

During February 1990, similar resentments exploded in the Tadzhik provincial capital of Dushanbe. Thirty-seven people were killed and eighty wounded when crowds stormed the Central Committee building and skirmished with authorities in more than two hundred locations around town. Many rioters went deliberately after Russians. In a report from the area shortly afterward, *Time* magazine senior correspondent David Aikman wrote that "next to the violence, the most striking aspect of the uprising was its Islamic character. The insurgents demanded that Islam be declared the republic's official religion and that Arabic script be reinstated. Some of their supporters terrorized Tadzhik women who did not wear head scarves in public."[40]

Throughout 1990, incidents of serious violence were also documented in the Muslim-dominated republics of Turkmenistan, Kirghizia, Uzbekistan and Azerbaijan. Besides causing millions of dollars' worth of property damage, activists have been accused of murdering scores of Party and police officials. While the extent of these latter charges is still a matter of investigation, there is no question that ethnic Slavs living in these republics have been harassed to the extent that they are now migrating to the Russian heartland in droves. *(Siberia, very few Muslims)*

Fuel for the Fire: International Islamic Support

Pulled along by the twin engines of religion and nationalism, Soviet Central Asia and the Caucasus have become, in the words of Soviet Muslim affairs commentator Igor Belyaev, "a very receptive milieu" for foreign interference.[41] In fact, in a recent article in the influential Soviet weekly *Literaturnaya Gazeta*, Belyaev recounts a meeting in Lebanon with a senior Iranian mullah who talked openly of a "third Moslem revolution" in the Soviet Union— after Iran and Afghanistan.[42]

One of the first steps taken by the new revolutionary regime in Teheran was to set up a special committee for "Reviving the Message of Islam in the U.S.S.R." According to author Amir Taheri, Iran then began a major radio war against "Soviet atheism" using three powerful transmitters in northern Iran to broadcast a total of 200 hours of multiple-language programming into the U.S.S.R.[43] In a "Mutt and Jeff" programming approach, broadcasts emanating from Radio Gorgan and Radio Tabriz have been generally low-key and clever,[44] while Radio Teheran has dished up more strident fare—including messages encouraging listeners to separate themselves from Soviet society and join the Muslim *umma*, or world community. Since 1986, this sound-only propaganda has been supplemented by well-watched Turkmen-language telecasts.[45]

Iran is hardly alone in its revivalist efforts. Special Islamic theology courses are presently beamed into the Soviet Caucasus and Central Asia by no fewer than 38 radio stations situated in Turkey, Egypt, China, Jordan, Saudi Arabia, Abu Dhabi, Qatar and elsewhere. Taheri reports that "Riyadh Radio began a series of broadcasts especially designed for the Soviet 'servants of the faith' in 1980."[46]

Furthermore, proving that Islam's appeal in the U.S.S.R. is magnetic in more ways than one, audiocassettes with Islamic readings, sermons and music have been turning up in settings ranging from discreet home gatherings to officers' clubs. Tape recorders purchased on the black market are used for copying Iranian, Saudi and Chinese[47] radio broadcasts, and for listening to pre-packaged cassettes of Qur'anic lessons or speeches by Islamic leaders such as the Ayatollah Khomeini.[48] From 1986 to '87 alone, Iran invested a total of nearly $10 million to produce special audio and videotapes for use by Soviet Muslims in Azerbaijan. Other Qur'anic cassettes produced in Turkey were smuggled into the republic recently by a group financed, ironically, by U.S. Republican Party supporters.[49]

International helping hands are also providing Soviet Muslims with Islamic literature—both legally and illegally. On the official side, $150,000 needed to purchase the paper necessary to print 50,000 copies of the Qur'an for Muslims in the Volga region of the U.S.S.R. was pledged recently by Muslims in Tokyo and Finland,[50] while a well-publicized gift shipment of one million Qur'ans from Saudi Arabia arrived in 1990 aboard Soviet Aeroflot jets.

At the same time, fundamentalist Afghan *mujahedin* loyal to radical Hezb-i-Islami chieftain Gulbuddin Hekmatyar have been engaged in a smuggling operation across the Amu Darya River since the mid-1980s. In addition to thousands of Qur'ans, the rebels also claim to have taken in more incendiary literature dealing with the concept of *jihad*, or holy war. Wrapping their illicit cargo in plastic, the Afghans swim over to the Soviet side of the river and transfer their goods to prearranged contacts—some of whom, the *mujahedin* claim, are members of the Soviet security forces.[51]

One candid guerilla commander declared: "Every revolution spills over its borders. I want to take the revolution of God from this country and see its influence spread in the Soviet Union."[52] Obviously on the same page, Ayatollah Ardebili, a former Iranian chief justice, announced during the January 1990 riots in Baku that Soviet Azerbaijan is now a "great market for the introduction of Islam."[53]

The Mosque and the Popular Front

In the June 15, 1989, issue of the Paris daily *Le Monde*, Mikhail Gorbachev expressed apprehension about a "revival of Islamic fundamentalism" in the U.S.S.R. He had good reason to be concerned. Not only were an increasing number of Muslim parents at the time naming their newborn children "Ayatollah" (after the religious leaders in nearby Iran), but the head of the Tadzhik KGB, General Vladimir Petkel, had warned the republic's Communist Party Central Committee that unofficial Muslim clerics were "calling for a *jihad* against the existing system."[54] As a result of these and other ominous developments, conservative-minded Soviet journalists were warning readers that Islam was spreading through the land "like a cancer."[55]

A mere seven months after Gorbachev's comments in Paris, the Soviet president looked like an uncomfortable prophet when throngs of Soviet Azeris gathered along the Soviet-Iranian border and hollered with vein-popping intensity: "God is great!", "Khomeini is the leader!" and "Azerbaijan is awake and defends the Islamic revolution!"[56] During the subsequent festival of *Ashura*, Muslims on the Iranian side of the Araks River (which forms the U.S.S.R.'s southern boundary with Iran) reported hearing their Soviet brethren honoring Imam Hussein with passion chants accompanied by drums and cymbals.

After rooting out scores of underground Islamic organizations during the 1980s, Soviet policymaking at the beginning of the 1990s took a distinct turn in the direction of accommodation. Moscow was apparently finally reaching the same stoic conclusion verbalized in 1982 by the Kazakh Party chief in Karaganda: "Islam is so deeply entrenched among the popular masses that nothing can be done to extirpate it anyhow."[57]

The first eye-opening signal of the changes to come occurred in 1989 when the mufti over Central Asia, a man widely regarded as a Kremlin stooge, was replaced by Mukhammadsadyk Mamayusupov, a charismatic 36-year-old who received his theological training in Libya. A popular figure, Mamayusupov was greeted in Tashkent by thousands of jubilant supporters waving banners reading: *Islam is the only true way.*[58]

By 1990, there was no longer any mistaking it: Soviet Muslims were in the midst of an energetic spiritual reawakening. Friday prayer gatherings and Qur'anic readings were televised regionally

and, for the first time in more than seventy years, religious ceremonies observing the Islamic month of Ramadan were held in
hundreds of mosques throughout the Soviet Union.[59] As one Central Asian mullah put it: "The number of believers is growing.
Everybody wants to go to Mecca."[60]

Since the Islamic revolution in Iran, mosques have mushroomed
throughout the Soviet Muslim republics. Official mosques in Central Asia alone have more than tripled, while estimates of the
number of informal or underground centers range between 2,000
and 5,000.[61]

Dispensing knowledge and offering leadership to millions of
Soviet Muslims are an estimated 50,000 unofficial "servants of the
faith."[62] Many are self-educated and itinerant, and hold clandestine religious training seminars in *chaikhanas*, or tea houses.[63]
Other concealed mosques function in clubs, on collective farms
and, in at least one case, a funeral parlor.[64] Apparently one
method used to camouflage what, from the Soviet perspective, may
be questionable or even illegal religious instruction is for students
to obtain employment in the same secular workplace as their teachers, or for an individual to become a domestic servant in the home
of his mentor.[65] The influence of these unofficial mullahs is said to
be very high.[66]

Taheri puts the number of active members (*murids*) in the
U.S.S.R.'s underground Sufi network at about half a million. At
the same time, he draws attention to the fact that, beginning in the
1930s and peaking after Iran's Islamic revolution, a number of
other smaller but more militant movements have also emerged on
the Soviet scene. "Many of [these]," he says, are "committed to the
eventual overthrow of the Soviet system, which they describe in
their literature as satanic and in revolt against God."[67]

Referring to underground groups that seek a total break with
Moscow, one Tajik dissident bragged, "We are many, and we are
growing."[68] Another radical who favors establishment of an
Iranian-style Islamic republic said: "We need to raise the people
up." It may take "two, three, or four years," he added, and "it has
to be done very quietly."[69]

While elements of these new revolutionary groups are active in all of the Soviet Muslim republics, the vanguard of the movement appears to be concentrated for the most part in Azerbaijan and Tadzhikistan. In the latter republic, security forces in 1989 arrested and imprisoned more than fifty Muslim militants belonging to five different politically active fundamentalist cells.[70] An autumn 1990 CBS Evening News report revealed that during the first week of October, Tadzhik Muslims, apparently undeterred, had announced formation of a radical new Party for Islamic Renaissance. At the same time, in Uzbekistan, an underground Islamic party calling for a regional Islamic federation independent of Moscow is also reported to be gaining rapid support.[71]

"If we don't act now, we shall never act," said Talat Tajidin, the mufti of European Russia and Siberia, in a moving 1989 speech urging Muslims to stand together and take advantage of the current religious revival.[72] Somebody, obviously, was listening. In many cases today, the Communist Party is not only failing to neutralize Islam, but Islam, at least in the Muslim republics, may be co-opting the Party.

As a consequence, in June 1990 an extraordinary meeting of top Party and government officials from all five Central Asian republics took place in the city of Alma-Ata. Their purpose, which was in great measure achieved, involved the development of a sweeping regional compact between the republics of Kazakhstan, Kirghizia, Tadzhikistan, Uzbekistan and Turkmenistan. Roughly equivalent to an embryonic Muslim Common Market, the compact calls for negotiation of multilateral accords in twelve major political, social and economic areas. An attendant document released at the meeting's conclusion declared that "the memory of [our] great ancestors today calls on us to unite our efforts to strengthen the historic ties of brotherhood."[73]

Waiting in the wings should this effort fail are a growing number of Popular Front organizations. The Azerbaijani Popular Front, for instance, has grown dramatically since it was launched in August 1989, and has earned the quiet support of the local Shi'ite religious establishment.[74] In Uzbekistan, the local popular front, Birlik, has grown even more quickly. Kicked off in November 1988, it now has more than 300,000 members and has conducted several mass demonstrations. Another group, the Erk Democratic Party, is a split-off faction of Birlik, and in the words of its chairman, Muhammad Salih, is "working towards independence for Uzbekistan."[75]

With their empire unraveling at the fringes, and finding precious little room for political maneuvering, tension among Soviet decision-makers is mounting by the hour. At the bottom of the deck, says former U.S. National Security Advisor Zbigniew Brzezinski, is the question of "whether the Soviet Union will be transformed by force or by accommodation."[76] Recent events in Central Asia and the Caucasus have been especially unnerving to the Russians, and there are legitimate fears that a new holy war could unleash the hatred of centuries. Gorbachev has spoken of possible civil war, and former Soviet Foreign Minister Eduard Shevardnadze has cautioned against a possible "social explosion" that could, in his words, "ignite the enormous stockpiles of nuclear and chemical weapons."[77]

The unfolding drama, according to Tajik writer Salim Ayub, is a "struggle between the brown-eyed and the blue-eyed"[78]—and both sides have plenty of nightmares and prejudices to bring to the table. With the fearsome imagery of their brutal 250-year[79] subjugation by the Tatar-Mongol hordes stamped on their collective memory, Russian mothers have since medieval times frightened naughty children with the threat that "the Tatars are coming." In Moscow, some taxi drivers still call any dark-looking passenger a Tatar—a common and derogatory name for all Muslims.[80] At the same time, few admirers of Saint Basil's Cathedral—Ivan the Terrible's architectural masterpiece on Moscow's Red Square—realize that the church's multicolor onion-shaped domes were originally intended to symbolize the severed, turbaned heads of eight Muslim chiefs who fell in battle against Russian troops.[81]

In its most benign form, Muslim response toward Slavs residing in Central Asia or the Caucasus could be described as "cool ostracism." One locally produced pamphlet dealing with the alleged "Slav colonization of Islamic lands" invites the faithful to "separate ways" wherever and whenever they come into contact with "those who have no right to be in a land that is not theirs."[82] In practice, this can mean anything from denying non-Muslims entrance to local restaurants to refusing to learn the Russian language. According to one Central Asian expert, no Slav, even with the best of intentions, can survive in a Uzbek village for more than six months. "If ostracism doesn't force him out, harassment will."[83]

Increasingly, this same hostility is also being felt in the region's major cities—places like Tashkent, Frunze, Dushanbe and Baku. Confronted with rapidly deteriorating social conditions, thousands of Slavs are now throwing in the towel each year and heading north. Whereas in 1970 the Slavic population of Central Asia numbered about 21 percent of the total, today it is about 13 percent and decreasing.[84] In a deliberate effort to fuel this exodus, fanatical Muslim elements are spreading fear through rumors of impending violence. (In August 1990, for example, the word on Uzbek city streets was that every Russian would be gone or dead by October 1—a threat taken all the more seriously after February 1989 attacks on Russian nationals left several victims with their throats slashed.)[85]

Christian churches in the area, whose membership rolls include a preponderance of ethnic Slavs and Germans, have been particularly hard-hit. Threatened on both religious and national grounds, believers are leaving in large numbers. A Baptist superintendent in Central Asia reported that 16 of the 32 churches within his jurisdiction were now without leadership. One fellowship in the Kirghiz capital of Frunze has lost nearly eighty percent of its members since January 1990. When an American missionary preached recently to the remaining congregation on the challenge of reaching Muslims, several parishioners approached him after the service and said, "Please forgive us, but we must leave."[86]

Backlash: *Pamyat* and the Rise of Russian Fascism

In January 1990, during the height of bitter three-way fighting between Russians, Armenians and Azerbaijanis in Baku and Nagorno-Karabakh, the Soviet newspaper *Trud* reported that a Muslim pogrom had ensued against the ethnic Russians in the area. So intense was the situation that Moscow took the unusual step of evacuating 15,000 dependents of the military and KGB divisions stationed in Azerbaijan.[87]

In an attempt to frame the government's current predicament, New York professor Michael Rywkin (who was himself raised in Central Asia) observed during a recent interview: "There are pogroms against Russians. They've left villages and now they're leaving the cities. Soviet leaders face the same dilemma as Charles De Gaulle in Algeria, whether to just get out."[88]

The Russians themselves are divided on this question. While many nationalists embrace their empire as a symbol of greatness, and even a divine right, others like Alexandr Solzhenitsyn see it as their undoing. Arguing that the Soviet empire "sucks all juices" from the Russian heartland, the dissident writer recently called for all non-Slavic republics to secede or be cut off.[89]

Likewise, most Communist Party reformers, although they would tend to couch both the problem and its solution in somewhat different terms, are generally agreed that the empire's minority republics should be free to chart their own course. Led by such figures as Boris Yeltsin, Eduard Shevardnadze and the mayors of both Moscow and Leningrad, this endangered faction has also expressed open concern about the potential revival of the Soviet totalitarian system.[90] Realizing that Russia itself cannot be free as long as it oppresses others, more and more of them are willing to let go of empire for the sake of a free and democratic Russia.

Growling on the other side of the aisle are the formidable conservatives. Appalled by the forces let loose by *glasnost* and *perestroika* (especially the territory-ceding policies of both liberal nationalists and democratic Party reformers), these self-styled patriots are fiercely committed to preserving what is left of their empire. If this leads to an arm's-length relationship with the West, so much the better. At a street rally in early 1990, one uniformed army officer denounced what he called efforts to turn the military "into a prostitute, used for experiments that win applause in the West."[91] During the subsequent Communist Party Congress in Moscow, Pacific Fleet Commander Admiral Gennady Khvatov charged that liberal reformers had squandered every geopolitical gain made by the Soviet Union since before World War II. "We have no allies in the West, and we have no allies in the East," he barked. "As a result, we have returned to the 1939 situation."[92]

Even the KGB has chimed in. In an extraordinary open letter to President Mikhail Gorbachev, members of the agency's headquarters staff vowed to take whatever measures were necessary to preserve order and the union. "Gambling on glasnost and the pluralism of opinions," they wrote, "loud-mouthed advocates of certain social interests denigrate the sacred name of Lenin and the notions of Motherland, patriotism and October [the Bolshevik Revolution] that are so dear to every Soviet person."[93]

By mid-1990, it had become clear that a counter-reform movement launched by the conservatives several years earlier was evolving into a juggernaut. Sensing the shift, a July editorial in the liberal *Moscow News* lamented: "We indeed hoped there was no road back to the past. But the road, we found, was still there and in good repair. Not just an untravelled country road, but a modern expressway."[94]

Closing ranks with conservatives in the armed forces, the KGB and the Communist Party today are a growing number of fascist-oriented Russian nationalist organizations. While many of these groups are officially stationed on the political fringes, their popularity, stridency and highly placed government connections[95] have caused some reformers to find them even more menacing than the Communists in power.[96]

Outside of the powerful *Soyuz* (Union) bloc, which dominates official conservative politics in the U.S.S.R., the majority of these new right-wing organizations are overtly nationalist and maintain strong links with the Russian Orthodox Church. The most well-known of these is *Pamyat,* or Memory. Headquartered in Moscow and Novosibirsk, the society lists members in such places as the Ukraine, Latvia, Kazakhstan and Yuzhno-Sakhalinsk in the Soviet Far East.[97] Founded in 1980 ostensibly to foster patriotism and the preservation of monuments, Pamyat has instead prompted fascist Black Hundreds–style ideas. (The "Black Hundreds" were an extreme right-wing group active in the 1905 pogroms against Jews, liberals and other intellectuals.)[98]

Pamyat, along with sister organizations like *Otechestvo* (Father-land) in Sverdlovsk and *Spaseniye* (Salvation) in Leningrad, per-ceives all manifestations of separatism and inter-ethnic conflict in the U.S.S.R. as being "the result of dirty Zionist-Masonic provocation."[99] In a March 1990 *Time* magazine sidebar entitled "Whispers of Hatred," an account is given of a January encounter between some fifty Pamyat supporters and a gathering of liberal writers. "Waving anti-Semitic banners and shouting racist slo-gans, one hooligan warned the crowd, "We have come this time with a megaphone—but next time with a gun." Another protester, whose actions were captured on video, shouted, "Neither the KGB nor the Party can help you now. We will be masters of the country, and you bastards should take off for Israel."[100]

At the helm of the Russian nationalist movement are two par-ticularly noteworthy figures: Dimitri Vasilyev of Pamyat, and Gen-nadi Shimanov of the far-right Ultras. Both speak of a united Indivisible Russia[101]—a sort of Slavicized Third Reich. In his treatise *The Ideal State*, Shimanov calls it a "Mystical Organ-ism . . . under the leadership of the Russian people."[102]

For their messianic vision to be fulfilled, however, Russia her-self must first be cleansed from the disastrous effects of Soviet "cosmopolitanism"—a term the nationalists define as power-sharing and race-mixing. This process will require all non-Slavic peoples to leave the nation's heartland and return to the equivalent of territorial reservations. Only within the context of this large-scale *apartheid* can Russia regain her spiritual bearings and begin to mold her empire into what Shimanov calls a "Little Mankind."[103]

Surrounded by black-shirted henchmen in the manner of the Aryan nation or Louis Farrakhan's Nation of Islam, Pamyat's Va-silyev cuts a sinister figure. When reminded that not all of the Soviet Union's white population cares to be a part of this mystical Russian nation, Vasilyev declared with twisted sincerity, "It's the Zionists who have persuaded the Ukrainians to believe that they are not Russians. It is they who persuaded the Lithuanians to believe that they are not Slavs."[104]

In the face of impending social chaos, many Russians are jumping on board the nationalist's bandwagon—especially since Shimanov, in the words of Soviet affairs analyst Alexander Yanov, "has managed to construct an ideological justification for the Orthodox masses' intuitive drive to make peace with the [Soviet] regime."[105]

Shimanov's reasoning is clever, invoking elements of guilt, pride and fear. While acknowledging that "the Soviet system can no longer seriously strive toward the spectre of Communism," he hastens to add that neither can it "abandon the grandeur of its tasks." Why? Because "otherwise it would have to answer for fruitless sacrifices which are truly innumerable."[106] To redeem these sacrifices and bring about what Shimanov calls "the Great Transformation of the World" (which fallen Western society can no longer accomplish), the Soviet system must jettison Communist cosmopolitanism and adopt in its place Russian Orthodoxy.[107] Without this nationalist vision, the Soviet system has no goal; but apart from the Soviet system and its institutional dictatorship, Russian (and global) civilization will either disintegrate into lawlessness, or be overrun by contemporary Tatars.

There are alarming signs today that the dictatorial Soviet system and nationalist ideology are indeed merging to form a new facist monster. Nikolai Makushev, a Communist worker at the Kaustik chemical plant, makes no bones about what he would like to see. "People like order," Makushev said. "If they have order and a decent life, they don't give a damn whether the government is Nazi, fascist, communist or socialist. And neither do I. After four or five years of rule by an iron hand, the country will begin to prosper—but in our Russian way."[108]

For its part, the Orthodox Church has not only thrown its weight behind the regime's efforts to keep the union intact, but, even more offensively, has elected to keep Black Hundreds emblems and banners in its cathedrals.[109] As for the army, at least one expert, Professor John Erickson of Edinburgh University, sees it becoming steadily more Russian and less Soviet. Besides the fact that the *Military History Journal* now proudly displays photographs of priests and patriarchs blessing Russian troops, a growing number of military officers—like Leningrad's Lieutenant General Grig-

ori Samoilovich—are turning up on the membership rolls of
societies like Pamyat. [110]

What is more, there are those who think that the Soviet military
may be looking for a fight. Generals are disgusted by Gorbachev's
soft line toward the West and by his rush to cut military budgets.
They are also more than a little displeased with the high incidence
of draft evasion, [111] and with the treatment their units are getting
in outlying republics. (Some Russian soldiers assigned to quell
ethnic unrest in Kirghizia, for instance, were beaten and had
stones hurled at their departing trains.)[112] As a consequence of
these and other factors, troops in some cities are now patrolling the
streets alongside regular militia, while others have been seen staging their own demonstrations.

Return of the *Basmachi*: Walking the Precipice of War

As the Soviet military learned in Afghanistan, fighting "holy
warriors" on their own terms and terrain can be a difficult assignment. That message was sent home thousands of times during the
war in the form of sealed coffins and body bags. As the carnage
accumulated, observers who did their homework discovered that it
was not the first time the Red Army had encountered angry Muslim
guerillas.

In the years immediately following the 1917 Russian Revolution, fresh battle lines were drawn throughout the Muslim homelands of Central Asia and the Caucasus. On one side were the
militant torchbearers of the Bolshevik ideal and, on the other, the
anti-Communist soldiers of Allah. After the first few skirmishes,
the Muslim defenders were dubbed *Basmachis* (phonies or bandits) by Lenin's advancing troops. While the label was clearly
intended as pejorative, it soon became "synonymous with courage
and dedication to Islam."[113]

For two decades, from 1919 to 1939, the Basmachis dueled with
the Bolsheviks. During this time their ranks were bolstered by
warriors from Afghanistan, China, Iran and Turkey. Even Enver
Pasha, one of the wartime Ottoman triumvirate, fought and died in

Central Asia out of devotion to his visionary pan-Turkic ideals.

While Stalin eventually crushed the Muslim partisans through a combination of military action and starvation, the mental uprising against Communist usurpation continued. Today there is fresh evidence that the Basmachi rebellion may be on the verge of staging a comeback.

In most Central Asian republics, for example, poems and short stories related to the anti-Communist Basmachi movement are immensely popular. Not only have Kirghiz Party officials complained about the phenomenon, but a 1989 Radio Liberty Focus Group Analysis recommended that future radio programming take care to portray the Basmachi not as bandits, but as partisans fighting for their villages.[114]

Furthermore, raids by local guerillas imitating Basmachi fighters are being reported with increasing frequency. Some radicals have even been seen wearing red headbands of martyrdom.

An example of how fast things can move given the right catalyst was provided in the Dushanbe riots of 1990. In a May 1990 article in the Soviet daily *Pravda*, TASS observer Viktor Ponomarev asserted that, once the demonstration turned to violence, "it was then that a call rang out in the tea-houses which had been turned into prayer-houses: 'Wake up, Muslims! The people are rising up!' Speeches by Islamic fundamentalist leaders were distributed on audio and videotape: 'It is time to establish an Islamic state!' "

Ponomarev connects these calls with the appearance in Dushanbe of what he calls "envoys" from Baku and implies that these were responsible for the ensuing violence. He links the formation of a "provisional national committee" on the second day of the riots with "groups of militants, galvanized by local mullahs, [who] were already hastening to the capital from outlying areas, shouting demands for the establishment of an Islamic republic."[115] The committee, according to Ponomarev, was headed by none other than Buran Karimov, the Deputy Chairman of the republican Council of Ministers and Chairman of the State Planning Committee.[116]

On February 21, 1990, *Literaturnaya Gazeta* published a document emanating allegedly from the Rabita Da'awa Institute in Peshawar, Pakistan, giving precise instructions to Soviet Muslims on how to start *jihad*.[117] The radical Afghan group *Hezb-e-Islami*, moreover, now claims a membership of 3,000 inside Central Asia[118]—a contention that gained substantial credibility when KGB Major General Vladimir Petkel admitted in a 1987 speech that cross-border infiltration was taking place, and that underground networks have been uncovered.[119] Even more ominous, however, are confirmed reports that the infamous *Hizballah* is now active on Soviet soil.[120]

During the recent anarchy in Azerbaijan, the Soviet daily *Izvestia* reported that Muslim extremists commandeered three trains carrying soldiers and military equipment. In all of 1990, theft of weapons and ammunition from Soviet military bases rose an astonishing fifty percent.[121] This spread of lethality—in some cases, at least—is evidently taking place with official connivance. Referring specifically to the Caucasus, a major general with the Interior Ministry revealed: "The police [said] the weapons were stolen from them, but actually they handed the guns over."[122]

Rumors are also rampant of arms from Afghanistan being collected in the Fergana basin, some 300 miles east of Tashkent. "The Uzbeks want to dominate Central Asia and they are armed up to their eyes," said a non-Uzbek intellectual in Samarkand.[123] Furthermore, on New Year's Eve 1990, as many as 40,000 Soviet Muslims crossed illegally into Iran and returned with weapons.[124]

All this prompted a respected Soviet ethnographer to remark: "Moscow does not have enough troops, and it will not be able to manage if anything really blows." This is doubly true if the revived Basmachi take to the hills, and unrest occurs simultaneously in other parts of the U.S.S.R. While Mr. Gorbachev attempted to counter the growing threat recently by appointing the hard-line Boris Pugo (former Latvian KGB chief) and General Boris Gromov (the former Afghan theater commander) to run the Interior Ministry, there is a growing concern over even the army's reliability.

The biggest problem is the high percentage of military personnel with Muslim backgrounds. The composition of Interior Ministry (MVD) units responsible for internal security, for example, is said to be about fifty percent Central Asian. In the 1980s, at least one air base near Alma-Ata was secured by a guard company consisting of eighty percent Muslim conscripts.[125]

Central Asian troops are increasingly bitter over their treatment in the military. Many report that Slavic NCO's regularly insult them with epithets like "black asses" and "slant eyes." In one air defense brigade, two Kazakh Tatars were harassed by Russian troops who, knowing they did not eat pork, proceeded to put a pig's ear in their soup; others placed a foot cloth on their heads while they slept.[126]

Some are starting to fight back. In addition to a huge fight that reportedly broke out a few years ago between Russians and Azerbaijanis in a training unit at Novosibirsk, serious conflicts have also taken place at the top-secret nuclear installation near Tomsk. One young Uzbek, fed up with the ceaseless harassment, took a machine gun and ambushed the entire guard detail. A similar case was reported in the model Tamansk Division when two frustrated Central Asians walked off with high-caliber weapons and ammunition before being hunted down and killed in an exchange of fire.[127]

Apparently several top Soviet military and political leaders have begun to realize just how vulnerable many of their strategic resources and installations are. When, in January 1990, well-armed Azerbaijani extremists roamed the streets of Baku in stolen Red Army armored personnel carriers, special KGB troops were hurriedly dispatched to guard a nuclear-warhead depot a scant sixteen miles away.[128] Eight months later, Army Chief of Staff General Mikhail Moiseyev signaled a "retreat" of sorts when he announced that all such weapons had been removed from potential trouble spots.

Even with their nuclear weaponry moved out of harm's way, the Kremlin still has a great deal of strategic exposure in the Muslim republics. The Glavnebtemesh factory in Baku, for instance, produces more than seventy percent of the machinery and spare parts used by the Soviet oil and petroleum industries. Without it, energy production would be paralyzed and the Soviet economy would shudder to a halt. Moreover, Azerbaijan itself produces about fourteen million tons of high-grade petroleum annually.[129] The vulnerability of Azerbaijan's petroleum industry was further highlighted when, during a recent military crackdown in the republic, captains of more than fifty merchant ships from Caspian Sea oil refineries blockaded Baku Harbor, threatening to blow up tankers and drilling platforms.[130]

Also located in the Muslim heartland are the Semipalatinsk nuclear test site, the strategic Baikonur Cosmodrome (the equivalent of Cape Canaveral) and nearly all the country's nuclear plants, air-conditioner factories and cotton fields. While Moscow is not likely to hand over these arteries of the Soviet economy to Muslims without a fight, time is running out for the Kremlin leadership to propose serious alternatives.

Notes

1 Originally published in the Latvian People's Front newspaper, *Atmoda;* subsequently cited by Paul Goble in a Radio Liberty Research article entitled "Soviet Citizens Blame System for Ethnic Problems," June 29, 1990.

2 Radio Liberty, Special Daily Report: Soviet Party Congress, July 4, 1990.

3 See Ezekiel 38 and 39.

4 As chapter 9 will show, the biblical land of Magog encompasses only parts of today's U.S.S.R., a departure from the long-standing idea that the two are synonymous. This does not mean that Russia itself (possibly biblical *Rosh*) is suddenly a non-player. It probably will be a prophetic participant although, in my opinion, a secondary one to Muslim influence.

5 While the recent liberation of Eastern Europe is unquestionably a grade-A story, it is unlikely to have much impact on the major events of tomorrow.

6 "Underlying Issue: Possible Collapse of Soviet Union," *The Seattle Times*, May 29, 1990.

7 "Old Style Communists Lick Their Wounds," *The Guardian*, July 13, 1990.

8 Frederick Starr, "The Disintegration of the Soviet State," *The Wall Street Journal*, February 6, 1990.

9 John Barry, "Riding the Tiger," *Newsweek*, December 4, 1989.

10 Figures as of spring 1991.

11 Marc Fisher, "Deserter Walked Out of His Barracks and Headed toward Sun," *The Seattle Times*, November 17, 1990.

12 Soviet economic sources in early 1991 predicted a sixteen percent drop in Soviet GNP, a fifteen percent decline in industrial output and a total collapse of domestic capital investment. (Gosplan report excerpted in *The Seattle Times*, March 12, 1991.)

13 Report by Jim Laurie, ABC News "Nightline," October 16, 1990.

14 "Hundreds of Thousands Swamp Shops in Moscow," *The Seattle Times*, May 27, 1990.

15 *"Vremya"* newscast, July 5, 1990.

16 "Nightline," October 16, 1990.

17 Scott Shane, "Freedom Opens Door for Crime in the Soviet Union," *The Seattle Times*, October 21, 1990.
18 David Broder, *International Herald Tribune*, July 9, 1990.
19 Scott Shane, "Will Ethnic Strife Sap Remaining Unity in Soviet Union?", *The Seattle Times*, November 1, 1990.
20 Igor Zaseda (deputy chief of the Ukrainian branch of the Novosti Press Agency in Kiev), special to *The Seattle Times*, October 12, 1990.
21 "American Rebels to Join Police," *The Independent*, August 11, 1990.
22 Priit Vesilind, "The Baltic Nations," *National Geographic*, November 1990.
23 Mariusz Ziomecki, Knight-Ridder newspapers, October 4, 1990.
24 R. C. Longworth, " 'A Return to the Horrible Times,' " *The Seattle Times*, March 12, 1991.
   Note: Millions of Soviet citizens perished during this period, either of starvation or after being swallowed up in Stalin's infamous gulag system. (See Alexandr Solzhenitsyn's *Gulag Archipelago* for additional insight into this period.)
25 *Soviet Muslims Brief*, Vol. 5, Nos. 5–6, 1990.
26 Alexander Alexiev and S. Enders Wimbush, *Ethnic Minorities in the Red Army, Asset or Liability?*, A Rand Corporation Research Study (Boulder, Col.: Westview Press, 1988), p. 122; *Wall Street Journal*, "Gorbachev and His Generals," January 24, 1990.
27 Amir Taheri, *Crescent in a Red Sky: The Future of Islam in the Soviet Union* (London: Hutchinson & Co., 1989), p. xix.
28 Taheri, *The Times* (of London), July 20, 1989; see also *Washington Times*, "Kremlin Policy, Islam Collide in Soviet Central Asia," July 22, 1987.
   Note: While citing what he calls "explosive growth" among the U.S.S.R.'s Muslim population, Ward Kingkade of the Census Bureau's Center for International Research does not see them reaching majority status for at least sixty years. See Robert Pear article, "Islamic Population Gain a Challenge to Soviets," *New York Times*, January 24, 1990.
29 In an article in *Time*, "Karl Marx Makes Room for Muhammed," March 12, 1990, David Aikman cites the fact that Muslims accounted for half the total population increase of the past decade; Kingkade projects Soviet Muslims account for roughly half of all growth through 2010, and nearly two-thirds of growth through 2050.
30 Martin Walker, "Fundamental Problems in Soviet Islam, Where M Is a Hero They Call Mother," *The Guardian*, April 13, 1988.
31 TASS news report picked up by Reuters and reprinted in *The Seattle Times*, March 13, 1991.
32 Anthony Hyman, "The Greening of the Soviet Muslims," *The Middle East*, November 1989.
33 Alex Alexiev, "Muslim Unrest Grows Inside the Soviet Union," *Los Angeles Times*, January 4, 1987.
34 David Remnick, "As Soviet Central Asia Children Die, There's No Hope, to Be Honest," *The Economist*, September 22, 1990; David Remnick, "As Soviet Central Asia Children Die, There's No Hope, to Be Honest," *International Herald Tribune*, May 23, 1990.
   Note: While in the United States infant mortality figures have fallen to under ten per

1,000 live births, the rate in Soviet Central Asia is as high as one hundred per 1,000 births.

35 *Ibid.* (*Tribune*).
36 See Associated Press, "Talk Grows in Central Asia of 'Decolonization' by Soviets," June 10, 1990.
37 *Ibid.*
38 "A New Scourge in the Land of Tamburlaine," *The Independent*, June 6, 1990.
39 *Central Asia Survey*, Vol. 7, No. 4 (1988).
40 Aikman, "Karl Marx Makes Room for Muhammad."
41 *Literaturnaya Gazeta*, May 1987.
42 Xan Smiley, "Russia Warned About Islamic Subversion Threat," *London Daily Telegraph*, May 22, 1987.
43 Taheri, p. 186.
44 This assessment comes from a July 1990 interview with Marie Broxup, daughter of the late Soviet Muslim expert Alexandre Bennigsen and head of the Society for Central Asian Studies in London.
45 "The Mullahs vs. Moscow," *Washington Post*, September 25, 1988.
46 Taheri, p. 195; see also Alexandre Bennigsen in *Orbis*, Vol. 32, No. 3 (summer 1988).
47 Radio Urumchi.
48 "The Magnetic Appeal of Islam, U.S.S.R.," *Arabia*, March 1985.
49 Taheri, p. 195. Some sources believe the figure could be as high as fifty percent.
50 Radio Liberty Research, "Muslims of Middle Volga to Celebrate Two Anniversaries," July 20, 1989.
51 "A Silent War of Infiltration Against the Soviet Union," *Time*, January 29, 1990.
52 *Ibid.*
53 Bruce Nelan, "Occupational Disease," *Time*, February 5, 1990.
54 Report on "parallel Islam" delivered by General V. V. Petkel at the Eighth Plenum of the Tajik Communist Party Central Committee in December 1987. Cited by Bennigsen, "Islam in Retrospect," *Central Asian Survey*, Vol. 8, No. 1, 1989.
55 V. Rabiev, *Kommunist Tadzhikistana*, February 12, 1987.
56 Associated Press, Nicosia, February 12, 1990.
57 Q. Zmanbaiev, *Qazagstan Kommunisti*, No. 8, August 1982.
58 *London Financial Times*, March 15, 1989.
59 United Press International, "Tashkent Radio Says Religious Ceremonies Held in Uzbek Mosques," March 29, 1990.
60 Aikman, "Karl Marx Makes Room for Muhammad."
61 In a March 16, 1990, article, "Soviet Islam's Freedom Road," the *Toronto Globe & Mail* reported that there are now more than 3,000 mosques (official and informal) in the Azeri capital of Baku alone, compared with just three fifteen years ago. Both *Time* ("Islam Regains Its Voice," April 10, 1989) and *The Daily Telegraph* ("Russia Warned About Islamic Subversion Threat," May 22, 1987) list the number of unofficial mosques at around 1,800 (a figure almost certain to have gone up by now). The figure for official mosques is taken from *Time*, March 12, 1990, and does not include 56 new Muslim communities that, according to the Soviet news agency TASS on August 16, 1989, were newly registered in the European part of the

U.S.S.R. and Siberia. The August 1989 *Central Asia and Caucasus Chronicle* (Vol. 8, No. 4) added that, by the beginning of 1990, an estimated 200 restored mosques were slated to reopen in the autonomous region of Daghestan.

62 Taheri, p. 194.
Note: At the heart of unofficial, or "parallel," Islam in the Soviet Union are the Sufi brotherhoods. Predating the Soviet system in the area by centuries, the Sufis possess, in the words of the late French scholar Alexandre Bennigsen, "an exceptionally effective organizational framework around which political dissent with Muslim coloring could coalesce and be directed." This framework includes "strong and strict hierarchies, a developed style of discipline, and a strong spirit of dedication and sacrifice." Bennigsen goes on to add that there is evidence of clandestine Sufi courts and even local defense groups used against the enemies of Islam, and suggests that the KGB has found the brotherhoods exceedingly difficult to penetrate. See Ursula King, review article on Bennigsen's book *Mystics and Commissars: Sufism in the Soviet Union* in *The Journal of Communist Studies*, Vol. 4, No. 3, September 1988.

63 Radio Liberty report on the U.S.S.R., March 10, 1989; *Pravda*, December 1, 1986.
Note: In the early years of Soviet power in Tajikistan "red *chaikhanas*" were used as agitation centers.

64 Muriel Atkin, "The Survival of Islam in Soviet Tajikistan," *Middle East Journal*, Vol. 43, No. 4, autumn 1989.

65 *Ibid.*
Note: This also provides a way for the students to pay their teachers.

66 Daniel Sneider, *Christian Science Monitor*, June 12, 1990.

67 Taheri, pp. 196–197.

68 Mort Rosenblum, "Samarkand: Ancient Magic, Current Unrest," *The Seattle Times*, October 21, 1990.

69 Associated Press, "Soviet Central Asia Buffeted by Islamic Resurgence," May 5, 1989.

70 Taheri, p. 197.

71 Ahmed Rashid, "Uzbek Unrest," *Far Eastern Economic Review*, July 12, 1990.

72 Dusko Doder, "Central Asia: The Rise of Moslems," *U.S. News & World Report*, April 3, 1989.

73 Paul Goble, Radio Liberty Research, July 5, 1990.

74 Said Zafar, "Soviet Islam's Freedom Road," *Toronto Globe & Mail*, March 16, 1990.

75 Adrian Karatnycky, "Summer of Discontent for Soviet Turks," *Asian Wall Street Journal*, July 31, 1989; *Central Asia and Caucasus Chronicle*, Vol. 9, No. 2, May 1990.
Note: Erk, which proclaimed itself operational on April 11, 1989, is named after a political party founded in western Turkestan in 1919. The aim of the original Erk Party was the emancipation of Turkestan from Russian colonialism; and, as the *Chronicle* points out, it seems that the new Party has set itself a similar goal.

76 Zbigniew Brzezinski, special to the *Washington Post:* "Should the Soviet Union Be Saved?"; reprinted in *The Seattle Times*, March 10, 1991.

77 Martha Brill Olcott, "Soviet Central Asia: Next to Erupt?" *Christian Science Monitor*, January 29, 1990.

78 Said Zafar, "Soviet Islam's Freedom Road," *Toronto Globe & Mail*, March 16, 1990.

79 This period lasted roughly from the Tatars' first deep-penetration cavalry raids in 1237 to the Russian decision in 1480 to cease paying tribute to the Golden Horde.

80 "Islam Rises, Moscow Trembles," *The Independent*, June 13, 1990.

81 Taheri, p. ix.
    Note: More recently, the Tatar capital of Kazan has been divided into "reserved territories" by up to 150 Muslim and Slavic gangs. A Soviet newspaper reported that no fewer than fifteen teenagers were killed in gang warfare between 1985 and 1987, and then added: "Nearly all of the city is now under the control of the gangs in one way or another" (p. 201).

82 *Ibid.*, p. 200.

83 Conversation with Marie Broxup.

84 Alexiev, *Los Angeles Times.*

85 Broxup. See also Wybo Nicolai, "Muslim Radicals Gain Strength in Soviet Central Asia," *News Network International*, July 10, 1989.

86 Conversation with Steve Weber in Seattle, September 12, 1990.
    Note: In the Tien Shan mountains separating the U.S.S.R. and China, a Soviet believer has worked among Muslim Kirghiz villagers for the past three years. Twelve have accepted Christ. In Tashkent, a Russian woman in her forties, who has managed a local factory for a number of years, has a burning passion to reach the local Uzbek people. Already she has witnessed to several professional colleagues and coordinated evangelistic meetings out of the main Baptist church in the city. In spite of these positive developments, however, fewer and fewer workers are available to attend to the spiritual needs of the area.

87 "Occupational Disease," *Time*, February 5, 1990.

88 Associated Press, "Talk Grows in Central Asia of 'Decolonization' by Soviets," June 10, 1990.

89 From an article in *Komsomolskaya Pravda*, September 1990; cited in *Time*, October 1, 1990.

90 This was accomplished via two dramatic strokes in 1990: the resignation speech of Foreign Minister Eduard Shevardnadze, and an open letter to Gorbachev signed by 47 prominent politicians, scientists, journalists and army officers (including Yuri Ryzkov, head of the Moscow Aviation Institute, sociologist Tatyana Zaslavskaya and top Americanologist Dr. Georgi Arbatov).

91 Aikman, "Karl Marx Makes Room for Muhammad."

92 Radio Liberty, Special Daily Report: The Party Congress, July 7, 1990.

93 Michael Parks, "KGB Warns It Will Act to Protect Socialist System," *The Seattle Times*, March 9, 1990.
    Note: In an attempt to silence the one man conservatives considered the biggest loudmouth of all, Boris Yeltsin, the KGB dipped deep into its infamous bag of tricks. In addition to launching anonymous death threats, the state's "brave" and "patriotic" agents also organized a crude smear campaign accusing Yeltsin of being an alcoholic. When these efforts failed to diminish either the drive or popularity of the maverick leader, KGB security guards were seen placing anti-Yeltsin leaflets in the Russian Parliament building on the eve of the May 1990 republican elections.

Confirmation of these charges was provided by retired KGB General Oleg Kalugin. See Scott Shane article in *Baltimore Sun*, July 6, 1990.

94 Leonid Treyer, "The Summer of Our Discontent," *Moscow News*, July 15, 1990.

95 A July 31, 1987, article in *Russkaya Mysl* suggests that at least one ultra-nationalist organization, Pamyat, has key supporters in military circles, the Ministry of Internal Affairs, the KGB and in certain parts of the Party apparatus. Two specific names mentioned were Yuri Prokofyev, a secretary of the Moscow City Party Committee, and K. G. Levykin, the director of the State Historical Museum. A Pamyat board member in Novosibirsk, Alexander Kazantsev, is a physicist at the nearby Institute for Semiconductors. He was expelled from the Communist Party only after accusing top Party officials of conspiring with Zionists and Freemasons against the Russian people.

96 See David Shipler, *Russia: Broken Promises, Solemn Idols* (New York: Penguin Books, 1983), p. 327.

97 Julia Wishnevsky, "The Origins of Pamyat," *Survey*, Vol. 30, No. 3, October 1988, p. 84.

98 Peter Duncan, "The Fate of Russian Nationalism: The *Samizdat* Journal *Veche* Revisited," *Religion in Communist Lands*, Vol. 16, No. 1, spring 1988, p. 52.

99 Article #50, Manifesto of the National Patriotic Front "Pamyat."

100 In her *Survey* article, Julia Wishnevsky shares a sobering report by *Moscow News* reporter Valeri Voskoboinikov that placed "dozens" of police, as well as district and provincial Communist Party officials, at a recent Pamyat meeting in Leningrad. Reportedly, none made any attempt to intervene when speakers called for marriages to be banned between Russians and non-Russians, and for the immediate deportation of Jews and other minorities to "their places of historic origin" (p. 83).

101 Initially defined in *The Nation Speaks*, a "Russian patriots' manifesto." See Alexander Yanov, *The Russian Challenge and the Year 2000* (Oxford: Basil Blackwell, 1987), p. 158.

102 Gennadi Shimanov, *Ideal'noye gosudarstvo* (The Ideal State), p. 16; cited by Yanov, pp. 240–241.

103 While Lenin also had a messianic vision to mold a "Little Mankind," his actions were propelled by history rather than God. Furthermore, he saw the Party—as opposed to the Russian people—assuming the leading role.

104 Dimitri Vasilyev, interview with the French magazine *Actuel*, May 1989.

105 Yanov, p. 237.

106 Gennadi Shimanov, *Kak ponimat' nashy istoriu* (How to Understand Our History), p. 6.
   Note: To summarize Shimanov's thinking on this point, Yanov writes: "The regime, by nature mobile, whose dynamism is based on movement toward a clear and exalted goal, has lost its goal and consequently become immobilized. Movement was first reduced to marching on the spot, then 'putrefaction.' The nation is disoriented and degraded, and hence dying in a spiritual sense. This is shown by the catastrophic drop in social and labour discipline, which undermines the vital forces of the nation. The colossal sacrifices made by the people on the road to the supposed goal have lost their meaning. The Revolution, the Civil War, the Gulag, the deaths of millions, famine and collectivisation, World War II, self-sacrifice—

everything which could be justified by the movement toward Communism—has proved to be meaningless" (p. 233).

107 *Ibid.*

108 Paul Quinn-Judge, "Industrial Town Awaits Capitalism with Trepidation," *The Seattle Times*, October 19, 1990.

109 From Walter Laquer's *Russia and Germany*, p. 85; cited by Yanov, pp. 62–63.

110 *The Jerusalem Post*, "The Soviet Threat of Nuclear Civil War" (by arrangement with the *Sunday Telegraph*), no date; Sobesednik, No. 32, 1987, pp. 4–5; cited by Wishnevsky, p. 86.

111 In Lithuania and Georgia, only about one-third of the eighteen-year-olds called up in 1990 actually reported; in Armenia, a mere 7.5 percent showed up.

112 "An Angry Army," ABC "World News Tonight with Peter Jennings," March 26, 1991; *Newsweek*, "A Bitter Homecoming," July 30, 1990.
Note: There are other problems as well. Some 200,000 younger officers are plagued with inadequate housing—a factor that reportedly played a part in a recent threat by soldiers to desert a missile base if conditions there did not improve.

113 Taheri, p. 100.

114 Radio Liberty Focus Group Analysis, "Islam and Soviet Central Asia," July 1989.

115 Ponomarev also alludes to an informal group called *Rastokhez*, whose program and statutes, for all their fine words, "amount to the overthrow of Soviet power in Tadzikistan," and whose "popularity is growing by virtue of the demogoguery of its leaders." See *Central Asia and Caucasus Chronicle*, Vol. 9, No. 3 (June 1990).

116 The Buro of the Central Committee of the Tadzikistan Communist Party discussed Ponomarev's article on May 22, 1990, and found that "the conclusions reached by the author in many respects correspond to the situation in the city of Dushanbe during February 1990."

117 *Central Asia and Caucasus Chronicle*, Vol. 9, No. 2 (March 1990).

118 U.S.S.R. News Brief No. 10 (1984); quoted in *Central Asian Survey*, Vol. 6, No. 1, 1987.

119 See footnote 55.

120 Conversation with Marie Broxup, and Soviet press reports.

121 David Wood, "Underlying Issue: Possible Collapse of Soviet Union," *The Seattle Times*, May 29, 1990.

122 *Time*, "Eyewitness to Hatred," February 5, 1990.

123 Marie Broxup, *Far Eastern Economic Review*, July 12, 1990.

124 *The Seattle Times*, January 20, 1990; "Occupational Disease," *Time*, February 5, 1990.

125 Alexiev and Wimbush, pp. 148–150.

126 *Ibid.*, p. 182.

127 *Ibid.*, pp. 185–186.

128 David Wood, "Underlying Issue: Possible Collapse of Soviet Union," *The Seattle Times*, May 29, 1990.

129 *Soviet Muslims Brief*, Vol. 5, Nos. 5–6, 1990.

130 *Time*, "Occupational Disease."

9

Days of Rage and Wonder

We, Soviet Moslems, affirm that we were and still are a part of the Moslem Umma [nation]. . . . The Moslem world is not a geographical conception but a huge international power.

> Talat Tajidin, Mufti of Russia,
> in a recent address to the
> Islamic Conference Organization[1]

The Qur'anic prophecy of the inevitable victory of Islam will be realized following the advent of the Mahdi who will . . . establish a world order based on the Islamic teachings of justice and virtue. Thereafter there will be only one religion and one government in the world.

> Shaykh Yusufali Nafsi[2]

And I saw another beast coming up out of the earth. . . . And he exercises all the authority of the first beast in his presence. And he makes the earth and those who dwell in it to worship the first beast. . . . And he performs great signs. . . .

> Revelation 13:11–13 (NASB)

The Decade of Evangelism is now in full swing. For the first time in centuries—and perhaps ever—the enemy's camp has been forced to expend as much energy guarding its spiritual prisoners as it does in taking new captives. With its iron portals shaken ajar by persistent intercession, shafts of Gospel light have reached the darkest huddles of satanic dominion.

Sensing their time is short, Satan and his entourage are struggling feverishly to close these new evangelistic openings—such as in the U.S.S.R. and the Middle East—so that they can get on with preparations for their own final offensive. While, for now, God has His foot planted firmly in the door, once it is removed, mankind will almost certainly enter the most intense period of spiritual conflict the world has ever known.

Defining the parameters of this period is a difficult task. For most Christians, in fact, trying to interpret prophecy, especially the apocalyptic variety, is a little like building a house with blueprints consisting of blurry hieroglyphics. Even so, recent epoch-changing events such as the Iranian revolution, the breakup of Eastern Europe and the Gulf War have convinced many of these same believers that we have reached a stage of history in which the "end times" have become "our times."

If this conclusion is accurate—and the preponderance of evidence suggests that it is—then the great prophetic passages of Daniel, Ezekiel and Revelation must be viewed not merely as the curious highlights of eschatological tour books, but as strategic road maps for tomorrow.

While projecting specific timetables or chronologies is not our goal here, there is a growing consensus in the Church today that, in light of recent world events, perhaps the time has come to rethink some of our assumptions about the days to come. We do this not out of idle curiosity, but because we have been called to leadership. If we are to minister responsibly in the future—our future—then we must know something about what tomorrow holds in store.

Like most things written about the future, however, this chapter should be taken with a grain of salt. The future has a way of fooling people—especially dogmatists. Beyond a commitment to rigorous research, I can claim no special gifts or powers. There are other views on the subject that also merit study, and I hope readers will take the time to review this larger body of evidence before committing themselves to any position. To this author, the important issue is not whether dispensationalism or any other dogma is correct or incorrect, but what the Church is doing to better understand her responsibilities in light of the spiritual forces at work in today's world.

Apostasy and Desecration: Provoking the Ultimate *Jihad*

Nearly all Bible scholars agree that one of the most important end-time events is an all-out invasion of Israel by a powerful, northern-led confederacy. The prophet Ezekiel writes about this in some detail (see chapters 38 and 39). Although the popular Christian view has attributed this invasion to a lust for oil, this rationale seems too weak to fit the circumstance. Not only are many of the coalition members oil-rich states but, in light of the recent performance of the U.S. military against Iraq, it is highly improbable that economic interests alone would override their instinct for self-preservation.

Another standard assumption that warrants reevaluation is that this invasion will somehow be Communist-led (or -inspired). While Russia may well participate in the conflict, it is extremely doubtful that she would do so while still touting the ideology of Marx and Lenin. In addition, there are strong indicators—some of which we have already discussed—that Russia may also be heading toward a divorce from her present empire (the Soviet Union).

Where, then, does that leave us? From the clues afforded us in Scripture, the most likely scenario is that the confederacy mentioned by Ezekiel will be an essentially Islamic force, an alliance forged and motivated into battle for powerful *religious* reasons. Russia, finding common cause with these Muslim forces, will also wade in on religious grounds, although these will not be of an Islamic nature (more will be said on this later).

While Israel is clearly the primary target of this ultimate *jihad*, it may not be the first. There are actually several holy sites throughout the Near East today of concern to Muslims. Some of these are under the *de facto* control of infidels, while others are in the hands of Muslim tyrants or apostates. To Islamic fundamentalists, it makes little difference. Each of these sites must eventually be liberated.

Outside of Israel and Saudi Arabia, the biggest sore spots are found in the Soviet Union and Iraq—nations that in various ways and at various times have desecrated holy places like Bukhara, Samarkand, Baku, Kufa, Najaf and Karbala. Since the Scriptures suggest that these latter nations will be full participants in the ultimate *jihad*, there is also good reason to believe that their holy sites will be emancipated prior to the events of Ezekiel 38–39.

Which brings us back to Israel and Saudi Arabia. Of Islam's shrines, none is more revered by Muslims than Mecca (the site of the Grand Mosque), Medina (the location of Muhammad's tomb) and Jerusalem (the location of The Most Noble Sanctuary). While Mecca and Medina are administered currently by the outwardly straitlaced Saudis, many fundamentalists view the Arabian regime as compromised and corrupt.[3] In fact, so strongly do these elements disapprove of Saudi guardianship that any major *jihad* against the infidel Israelis will almost surely endeavor to topple the "apostate" House of Saud en route.

In early 1988, more than four hundred Muslim radicals—many of them on the watch lists of various Western and Arab intelligence agencies—gathered at the Royal National Hotel in London for a three-day conference to discuss, among other things, Saudi Arabia's stewardship of the holy shrines. Describing the Saudis as "the arm of U.S. imperialism extending into the heart of the Islamic world," the conference called for the formation of an international Muslim committee to replace the Saudi government as the primary custodian of Mecca and Medina.[4]

The recent U.S. military buildup in Saudi Arabia has done nothing to dispel radical concerns. While the Saudis justified their recent decision to invite non-Muslim forces into the country by soliciting—and receiving—the blessing of religious leaders at an emergency meeting of the Muslim World League in September 1990, the Iranians ridiculed the conference. Calling it an orchestrated bid to "alter the facts of Islam," Iranian spiritual leader

Ayatollah Ali Khamenei called for a *jihad* to drive the infidels away from the holy cities.[5]

While fundamentalists cannot bear the thought of Western, and particularly American, troops casting their shadow across Islam's most sacred shrines, officials in the Gulf are conceding privately that there will be some U.S. military presence—including at least limited ground forces—in the area for many years. If this proves true, then it is only a matter of time before hard-liners, chafing at this sacrilege, resurrect Saddam's call to "save Mecca and the Tomb of the Prophet from occupation."[6]

An even surer way to trigger *jihad*, of course, would be for some misguided zealot to desecrate Jerusalem's Temple Mount—known to Muslims as *Haram al-Sharif*, or The Most Noble Sanctuary. As the site of two of Islam's holiest places, the landmark Dome of the Rock and the smaller Al Aqsa mosque, this strategically placed 35-acre tract atop Mount Moriah is viewed as a serious obstacle by those Jewish and Christian fundamentalist groups who want to see a third Temple built on the site.

While official Israeli policy on the Temple Mount issue has generally been one of tolerance and sensitivity, since 1967 there have been at least six major attempts to destroy the Muslim complex by religious radicals. The majority of these incidents has involved Jews. (An Australian was also arrested by authorities.) One plan that quite literally never got off the ground involved an aerial bombing by the radical Jewish Underground organization. According to authorities, the plan was scrapped only when the terrorists themselves concluded that the blast might cause collateral damage to the Wailing Wall.[7] In August 1990, Israeli police discovered a formidable arms cache, including shoulder-held missiles, in the ultra-Orthodox neighborhood of Mea Shearim. The weapons reportedly belonged to a radical Jewish group intent on destroying the Dome of the Rock, and were originally stolen from the Israeli Defense Forces by Shimon Barda, the leader of a mystical, cave-dwelling sect.[8]

These and a good many other Israelis—nearly twenty percent, according to a 1983 poll[9]—feel it is time to rebuild the Temple. Since the Romans destroyed the second Temple in A.D. 70, one of the eighteen benedictions recited daily by religious Jews humbly requests, "May it be thy will that the *beit hamikdash* [Temple of Holiness] be rebuilt speedily in our day." Tired of waiting, Gershon Soloman, leader of the activist Faithful of the Temple Mount organization, says that the Muslim mosques should "be taken back to where they belong—in Mecca."[10] Others like Zev Golan, the director of the equally proactive Temple Institute, believe the Jews will have to wait a little longer, but adds: "Every day's delay is a stain on the nation."[11]

Meanwhile, Golan says, "Our task is to advance the cause of the Temple and to prepare for its establishment, not just talk about it." During nearly eight years of scriptural research, the Institute has reconstructed dozens of ritual implements—including incense vessels, musical instruments and priestly vestments—that will be necessary if and when Temple sacrifices are restored.[12] The Institute and other groups are also involved in breeding red heifers and in gathering building materials for the Temple walls. (An attempt by Soloman's group to hold a cornerstone-laying ceremony at the Western Wall was blocked by police in 1989.)[13]

As of 1990, religious Jews represented about fifty percent of Israel's total population. This group can be broken down into religious Zionists (about thirty percent), messianic Zionists (five percent) and ultra-Orthodox, non-Zionist Jews who are waiting for the Messiah (about fifteen percent).[14] Each of these categories can, in turn, be subdivided into multiple levels and emphases.

Some of the more significant sects in Israel today include *Ataret Cohanim, Shavau Banim*, the Young Israel Movement, and *Chabad*, an Orthodox messianic group actually headquartered in Brooklyn, New York. The latter, who acknowledge Rabbi Mendel Schneerson as their spiritual leader, believe strongly in the imminent return of the Messiah, and have gone so far as to build a home for him in Israel.[15] The Young Israel Movement is based in the Muslim Quarter of Jerusalem and teaches what one publication calls "a mixture of Greater Israel theology and Temple lore."[16] The group was founded by Rabbi Nahman Kahane (the brother of the late radical nationalist Meir Kahane) and maintains close links with the virulently anti-Arab *Kach* party. The *Ataret Cohanim*, also

based in Jerusalem, serves as an elite *Gush Emunim yeshiva*.[17]
Housed near the Temple Mount, the members of *Ataret Cohanim*
are actively preparing themselves to assume priestly duties when
the third Temple is built. They have received considerable material support both from the Israeli government and from Christian
groups in the United States.[18]

Where is all this activity leading? According to Gershon Soloman, Israel's faithful "will not pause until the Temple Mount
belongs totally to the Jews."[19] At the same time, however, a cleric
at the Al Aqsa mosque recently made it known that Muslims "will
defend the Islamic holy places to the last drop of their blood."[20]
With so many peoples, nations and religions claiming a stake in
the issue, no one is likely to argue with the words of a former
British intelligence officer who said during the summer of 1990: "It
is therefore on the platform of Palestine and at the gates of Jerusalem that the present epoch will face its ultimate drama."[21]

Black Hundreds and Green Flags: Forging the Ezekiel Alliance

The prophet Ezekiel defines the anti-Israel coalition in chapter
38 as including the land of Magog, Persia, Ethiopia, Libya, Gomer
and all his bands, and the house of Togarmah and all his bands.
With the exceptions of Persia, Ethiopia (Cush) and Libya (Put/
Phut), which are all easily identifiable modern nations, the other
allies alluded to here by the prophet have sent biblical scholars
and prophecy buffs scurrying for maps of the ancient world to
search out identifying clues.

While, in many cases, the results of these studies have turned
up more questions than answers, a thorough historical review does
present us with two important facts about this confederacy: 1) its
inherently Islamic character, and 2) its lack of correspondence to
modern political boundaries.

Regarding this latter point, it is highly probable that several of
the participants mentioned by Ezekiel are major ethno-linguistic
people groups rather than individual political nations. While this

observation may at first seem to complicate matters, it actually
provides a critical link between current events and biblical
prophecy—especially where the projected breakup of the Soviet
Union is concerned.

Take the land of Magog, for example. While it is almost universally considered synonymous with Russia or the Soviet Union,
it is also associated ethnically with Gomer and Togarmah in Genesis 10:2–3. Magog, Gomer, Meshech, Tubal and Togarmah—as
the descendants of Japheth, all mentioned in Ezekiel 38—are said
in Genesis 10:5 to be the progenitors of the Gentile nations. Looking to the north of Israel, we can conclude that their descendants
include not only the modern Russian people, but also the millions of non-Semitic Turkic peoples who dwell presently in
"Turkestan"—a wide band extending from Turkey (Asia Minor)
across the southern U.S.S.R. and into China.

Gomer and all his bands (or related people groups) are widely
regarded to be the ancient Cimmerians who originally inhabited
the Volga River basin north of the Caucasus and the Sea of Azov.[22]
Driven out of southern Russia by the Scythians toward the end of
the eighth century B.C., many Cimmerians ended up in what is now
eastern Turkey. The house of Togarmah, descended from Gomer,
would be ethnic kin. Known to the Assyrians as Til-garimmu,
these people along with those descended from Tubal and Meshech
(Tabalu and Mushki to the Assyrians) were likely among the early
inhabitants of Turkey, the Caucasus and southern Russia.[23]

While it is difficult to envision the present Communist leadership of the Soviet Union sanctioning major military action against
Israel, the impending threat of national dissolution conjures an
entirely different set of possibilities. If the house of Togarmah "of
the north quarters"—tens of millions of Soviet Turkic Muslims—
were suddenly freed from Moscow's yoke, their participation in the
ultimate *jihad* becomes plausible.

While Turkestan itself remains a political dream, the nearly 150
million Turkish-speaking peoples occupying twelve million square
kilometers of land between the Balkans and China are living facts.
Their presence and potential political clout—if they were ever to
be united—cannot be denied.

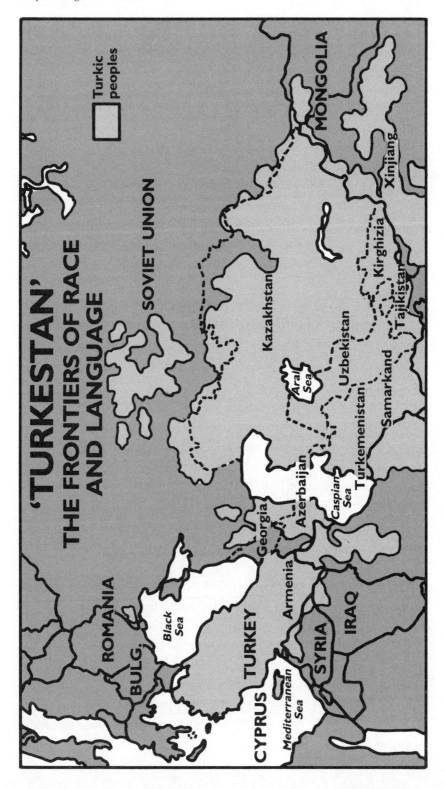

'TURKESTAN'
THE FRONTIERS OF RACE
AND LANGUAGE

Turkic peoples

SOVIET UNION

MONGOLIA

Xinjiang

Kirghizia

Tajikistan

Kazakhstan

Uzbekistan

Samarkand

Aral Sea

Turkemenistan

Caspian Sea

Azerbaijan

Georgia

Armenia

ROMANIA

BULG.

Black Sea

TURKEY

CYPRUS

Mediterranean Sea

SYRIA

IRAQ

In fact, there are increasing signals today that Turkic-Muslim unity may not be all that far-fetched—or far off. In November 1989, for instance, representatives of the U.S.S.R.'s burgeoning Turkic community (including Uzbeks, Meskhetian Turks, Azerbaijanis and various Tatar groups), gathered in the city of Baku to call for the creation of a Turkish federation within the Soviet Union.[24] When Red Army troops moved into the city two months later to quell ethnic violence, thousands of demonstrators poured onto the streets of Istanbul demanding aid for their "Turkish brothers in Asia."[25] While government officials could offer no more than moral support, Turkish State Minister Ercument Konukman managed to stir up a major political duststorm by predicting that "soon several states with Turkish flags will be established in the U.S.S.R. and China."[26]

In mid-1990, the underground Kazakh newspaper *Alas* took matters a step further by demanding that Turkestan be established as an Islamic republic.[27] The paper, distributed after Friday prayers at the central mosque in Alma-Ata, did not express an isolated opinion. After Kazakh, Kirghiz and Uigur minorities rioted in China's Xinjiang[28] province in April 1990, Chinese officials charged that the unrest was fomented by an underground Islamic party that is also active in Soviet Uzbekistan and Tadzhikistan. Moreover, in a recent article in the *Far Eastern Economic Review*, correspondent Ahmed Rashid reported unconfirmed rumors that this same party is building up links with Turkic Muslims in Afghanistan as well.[29] What does this cross-border cooperation mean? It means, as one Turk observed, "that we are the fingers of one hand."

While Turkey's pro-Western rulers have long endeavored to steer clear of such pan-Turkic ideas, a recent rejection of the country's application for early membership in the European Community may change things. The rebuff has already encouraged the spread of Islamic fundamentalism, and if Muslim revivalists manage to work their way into power, many experts envisage Turkey as a potential catalyst for a religiously dominated Turkestan.

Even if Turkey does fulfill this role, however, the question remains as to who will provide individual leadership. Although no obvious star has yet arisen, New York professor Edward Allworth believes that circumstances are so ripe for change that "if any charismatic figure emerges waving a green [Islamic] flag, people will rally behind him." When asked whether Allworth was right, Anvar Khadyrov, an Uzbek professor of philosophy at Tashkent University, said, "Yes, I am afraid they would follow."[30] Offering a clue as to *where* they might follow such a leader, Tadzhik Imam Khatib Mukaramov charged: "The Israelis have trampled [the] holy commandment under foot. It is the duty of every Muslim to help our tormented Palestinian brothers and sisters secure peace and national independence."[31]

If the great Turkic masses from the north do descend on Israel, the Scriptures make it clear that they will be joined by equally zealous Arab and Persian Muslims. While some of these allies— notably Iran and Iraq—are designated as part of the northern attack force, several others, including Libya, Ethiopia and probably Sudan and Somalia,[32] come up from the south.

When Jewish arsonists damaged the Al Aqsa mosque two years after the 1967 Israeli conquest of East Jerusalem, an incensed Ayatollah Khomeini recited a sura (verse) from the Qur'an to a group of Shi'ite disciples in Najaf, Iraq: "Prepare against them whatever force you can muster and horses tethered."[33] Putting his own spin on this passage, Khomeini declared, "If the Muslims had acted in accordance with this command and . . . made the necessary extensive preparations to be in a state of full readiness for war, a handful of Jews would never have dared to occupy our lands, and to burn and destroy the Masjid al-Aqsa. . . ."[34] As part of their effort to keep the retrieval of Jerusalem in the forefront of Iranian minds, the Khomeini regime during the war with Iraq code-named one of their major offensives *Tariq al-Qods*, or Path to Jerusalem.[35]

It is of no small significance that the first foreign leader to visit Khomeini after his accession to power in 1979 was P.L.O. leader Yasir Arafat. As Richard Pipes points out, not only did this embrace add a crucial Islamic tone to the Palestinian conflict with Israel, but "Arafat's battle cry, 'Today Teheran, tomorrow Tel-Aviv,' made an explicit connection between the two movements."[36]

Recognizing that Israel will not be overcome by religious fervor alone, however, Muslim leaders from Pakistan to Libya have since echoed Khomeini's call for the appropriate arming of *jihad* forces. In an April 1990 dispatch monitored in Rome, Libyan strongman Muammar Gaddhafi called on Arab nations to work together as "one single country" to develop a nuclear arsenal "within the next 20 years."[37]

There is also evidence—both prophetic and political—that this grand Islamic coalition may be joined in common cause by Russia. This is certainly the popular notion among prophecy buffs who frequently connect the latter with Rosh, a people mentioned in some translations (NASB, KJV) as a member of the anti-Israel alliance of Ezekiel 38. Whether or not this particular association is accurate, there is enough evidence in the passage as a whole to make a decent case for Russian—as opposed to Soviet— participation. (The Soviet Union at the time of this invasion is likely to be a historic relic.)

Adding persuasive fuel to this fire is the deeply rooted anti-Semitism found among many Russian people and institutions. Dating back to Czarist times, these sentiments have manifested themselves, often violently, with the acquiescence (if not outright connivance) of the Russian Orthodox Church. During the vicious pogroms that darkened the years between 1905 and 1911, Russian extremists calling themselves the Black Hundreds[38] robbed, beat and murdered thousands of Jews across Russia and the Ukraine. Composed largely of landlords, police officials, bureaucrats and Orthodox clergy, the Black Hundreds' support of an Orthodox autocracy was, in many ways, little more than a Christianized version of Khomeini's Islamic fundamentalism.

As the twentieth century has progressed—at least in a chronological sense—many Russian nationalists have sought to portray the Jew (and, to a lesser extent, Freemasons) as the centerpiece of various diabolical plots. Often linked allegorically with the serpent, Jews are seen as satanically energized in a drive for world domination.[39] In feeding these notions to the Nazis in the 1930s, Grigorii Bostunich dug up a vintage map of Europe being encoiled by a snake. According to Walter Lacqueur, Bostunich then proceeded to demonstrate how the Jews had "broken" various states that obstructed their malevolent goals.[40] In the end, Bostunich was rewarded for his "breakthrough" research by being made an honorary professor in the German SS.[41]

Today there are frightening and abundant signs of the Black Hundreds' return to fashion. Not only are young fascists in swastika-emblazoned armbands seen celebrating Adolf Hitler's birthday and marching to chants of "Heil Hitler!" and "Sieg Heil!", but many have lately been turning to the tactics of arson and beatings that characterized their forebears.[42] Furthermore, as Yanov points out, "It is becoming exceedingly fashionable to praise the firmness of the leaders of the Third Reich," and books about the Nazi reign are gaining an avid readership "especially among young functionaries."[43]

Driving this unwholesome movement is an unremitting hatred of the Jews coupled with a sincere belief that a Jewish-Freemason conspiracy is threatening to overwhelm Russia by the year A.D. 2000. Fearing extermination and/or enslavement at the hands of this diabolical alliance, Russia's nationalists have increasingly thrown their weight behind a strong Soviet military dictatorship as "the only powerful barrier standing in the way of Zionism's march to its year 2000."[44] In his mystical, nationalist treatise entitled *Moscow: The Third Rome*, Gennadi Shimanov bestows religious anointing on the dictatorship—a viewpoint that L. Borodin notes is "extremely popular among the nationalistically inclined Russian intelligentsia."[45]

Illustrating the dynamics of religiously sanctioned anti-Semitism, Yanov cites a passage from a nationalist magazine entitled *Russian Self-Awareness*, which reads: "The Semites have spoiled our motherland, and only anti-Semitism will save her. Revulsion toward kikes is implanted in us by the Lord God himself. Anti-Semitism is a sacred emotion. He who stifles it in himself is not only sinning, but also ruining both himself and his country."[46]

Those who dismiss this nationalist rhetoric as too extreme to be taken seriously would do well to consider the observation of English historian Norman Cohn. "There exists a subterranean world,"

Cohn wrote in his 1966 book *Warrant for Genocide*, "where pathological fantasies disguised as ideas are churned out by crooks and half-educated fanatics for the benefit of the ignorant and superstitious. There are times when that underworld emerges from the depths and suddenly fascinates, captures, and dominates multitudes of usually sane and responsible people. . . . And it occasionally happens that this subterranean world becomes a political power and changes the course of history."[47]

Gog and the Spirit of Totalitarianism

If the identities of the partners in Ezekiel's prophesied invasion of Israel are slowly emerging, not so that of their leader. While the prophet does disclose the name of this end-time ringleader—the infamous *Gog*—and even further identifies him as the "chief prince" of Magog, Rosh, Meshech and Tubal, affixing these clues to a specific personality is still only extravagant speculation.

Based on the context of Ezekiel 38 and the fact that Gog appears again after the millennial reign (Revelation 20:7–9), the editors of the *Living Bible* suggest in textual notes associated with the passage that "Gog seems to be a symbol rather than a historical figure like Nebuchadnezzar."[48] Indeed, the considerable time span between the Ezekiel 38 invasion (which most scholars contend predates Armageddon) and the end of the Millennium would appear to rule out the possibility that Gog is any kind of normal human being.

The fact that Gog is identified as the chief prince of a specific region and also appears as a warlike mobilizer in different eras leads us to another intriguing theory: Neither man nor symbol, Gog is rather a *territorial strongman* that rules over the lands and peoples of Magog, Meshech and Tubal—a geographical belt that presently encompasses portions of Turkey, Iraq, Iran and the Soviet Union. If this theory is correct, then the spirit of Gog— totalitarianism—has incarnated various human vessels in the region over the course of many centuries.

Certainly few other places on earth can match the number of

powerful and bloody dictators who have arisen in the lands between and south of the Black and Caspian Seas. Besides producing
such ancient despots as Nebuchadnezzar, Sargon the Great and
Sennacherib, more recent history has offered up the likes of Joseph
Stalin (who hailed not from Russia, but from the Caucasian republic of Georgia) and Saddam Hussein. While it is, of course,
impossible to measure the collective carnage left behind by these
and other regional tyrants, it can safely be said that nowhere else
has the lamp of human life and happiness been extinguished
so consistently or cruelly. (Though the fiery furnaces, show
trials, gulags and megalomania of many of these leaders are
well known, not so the devastating raids of the Assyrian mon-
archs—Sennacherib claimed in his annals that he had "poured out
terror over the broad lands of Elam"[49]—or the genocidal Turkish
massacre of the Armenians.)

Although two of the cruelest tyrants of all time, Ghengis Khan
and Adolf Hitler, commanded empires situated outside the land of
Magog, both had salient connections to the region. While the
Mongol advance sowed violence among the region's Muslim population and cut Russia off from the Renaissance, the Russians
later carried their gospel of fascist anti-Semitism to the Germans.
(N. E. Markov, one of the early leaders of the Black Hundreds
movement, reportedly ended his days as a consultant to the Ge-
stapo for Russian affairs.)[50]

Viewed objectively and over time, striking similarities in the
tenor and tactics of the region's totalitarian regimes become apparent. While it is true that dictators tend to embrace their own
kind (hence the current popularity of Hitler's writings in the
U.S.S.R. and Iraq), it is also possible, if the lands of Magog,
Meshech and Tubal are viewed with spiritual eyes, to detect
the shadowed visage of a puppetmaster named Gog. Seeing him
skulking behind the scenes as Ezekiel's end-time axis aligns, one
cannot help but wonder which of his puppets he will animate
next.

The Expected One: *Al-Mahdi* and His Miracles

Sliding down the pages of Ezekiel's prophecy, we learn that God will intervene supernaturally to frustrate the ultimate *jihad*—at least once it has reached the mountains of Israel. Not only are the allied invaders themselves to be decimated, but their own land of Magog is also subject to the fiery wrath of God. Because of the nature and scope of this destruction, the nations—including, presumably, those within the Muslim fraternity—will be brought face to face with the reality and sovereignty of God.

While it is safe to predict that many inhabitants of the earth will turn to Christ at this time, equally certain is the fact that many more, whether out of skepticism or pride, will not. The Muslim community itself is likely to be split into two camps: genuine truth-seekers who will embrace Jesus as Savior, and demoralized fundamentalists who will attribute the miracles to *al-Dajjal* (the Antichrist of Islamic eschatology).

If we assume that the apocalyptic seven-headed beast rising out of the sea in Revelation 13 is representative of human political kingdoms and systems—the primary vehicle through which Satan works on this earth[51]—then we might also consider the Islamic military defeat of Ezekiel 38–39 to be the mortal wound spoken of by John in Revelation 13:3 (see appendix). In any case, the resounding defeat of the Islamic armies in Israel will represent an emotional low point for many Muslims paralleling the experience of Jesus' disciples in the immediate aftermath of His crucifixion.

It is into just such a situation that Islamic eschatology inserts a messianic, miracle-working figure known as *al-Mahdi*, or "The One Who Is Guided by Allah."[52] In the words of Sheik Yusufali Nafsi, "He will reappear on the appointed day, and then he will fight against the forces of evil, lead a world revolution and set up a new world order. . . ."[53]

Although many sincere Muslims would no doubt resent the comparison, Islamic traditions of the Mahdi's emergence and actions are eerily akin to those associated with the false prophet in John's Revelation. As the false prophet, for example, "performs great signs, so that he even makes fire come down from heaven on the earth in the sight of men,"[54] one mirror-like Shi'ite *hadith* (tradition) says that at the Mahdi's appearance in Mecca, "God will command the light to raise itself in the form of pillars, rising from earth upwards to the heavens, so that the inhabitants of the earth will see it."[55]

Could it be that the Mahdi will be that miracle-working leader who will manage to heal the wounded head (the global Islamic empire) of the beast by resuscitating the faith of Muslims in the hour of their darkest defeat? That Islam is the ultimate systemic incarnation of the beast is suggested by: 1) the fact that the false prophet exercises the authority of the beast—thereby implying the system is essentially religious in nature; 2) the fact that no other global religion exists with traditions matching the descriptions of Revelation 13 and 17; and 3) the fact that the nations following the beast hate and make war on the scarlet woman (the spirit of materialism and wantonness)[56]—a graphic description of the sentiments and desires of today's Islamic fundamentalists vis-à-vis the "Great Satan."[57]

Unlike many Sunni Muslims, most Shi'ites believe that they know the identity of the Mahdi—at least in name. He is Muhammad bin al-Hasan al-Askari, the Twelfth Imam, or Expected One.[58] Although he has not formally interacted with his followers since A.D. 940, he is said to be alive somewhere in Saudi Arabia and to be a regular participant in the annual *hajj*.[59] That the Imam is capable of spanning more than ten centuries without dying is explained by his decidedly supernatural origins. Born in Samarrah, Iraq, to a slave girl named Narjis—ostensibly a virgin who showed no signs of pregnancy up to the very moment of giving birth to the Mahdi—the Imam's first act in life was to prostrate himself in prayer and bear witness to Allah and Muhammad.[60] Whether or not these details can be taken uncritically, there are numerous *hadiths* designating al-Mahdi as the descendant of Muhammad's daughter, Fatima, and more particularly, her son Hussein (the famous martyr of Karbala).[61]

Interestingly, a well-known prophetic *hadith* states: "A people will appear in the East who will pave the way for the *Mahdi*'s rise to power."[62] Many Muslims, particularly Shi'ites, like to view this as a direct reference to Iran (which is indeed located to the east of the former Imamate base in Iraq). In launching his fundamentalist revolution, the Ayatollah Khomeini was certainly conscious of such a role, and his efforts and influence may yet prove pivotal in relation to the rise of the Mahdi, or biblical false prophet.[63]

According to New York professor Abdulaziz Sachedina, "Before the Mahdi rises on the day of Ashura, his name will be called out on the twenty-third night of the [fasting] month of Ramadan." This night, in Shi'ite theology, is considered to be "The Night of Power" during which the Qur'an was revealed, and in which "the angels descend with the decrees from God about the events that will take place during that year."[64] The Mahdi's initial public appearance will be, not surprisingly, at the site of the *Ka'aba* inside the Grand Mosque of Mecca. As he stretches forth his arm, light will emanate from his hand as he declares: "This is the hand of God; it is from his direction and through his command." Moments later, as the sun begins to rise in the sky, a voice in the direction of the sun's rays calls out in eloquent Arabic: "O inhabitants of the universe! This is the Mahdi from among the descendants of Muhammad." This supernatural announcement will be heard in all the earth.[65]

Before launching out to destroy unbelievers in Saudi Arabia, Iraq and elsewhere, the Mahdi will lean on the *Ka'aba* and recite various scriptures as a further sign of his authenticity.[66] Shi'ite traditions also portray Jesus descending from the heavens to Jerusalem where He will espouse the cause of the Mahdi[67]—at which point Christians and Jews will reportedly recognize the Mahdi's true status and abandon their faith in the Godhead.[68]

At this stage, Islamic (at least Shi'ite) eschatology matches closely the prophetic passage contained in Revelation 13:11–18 in which the false prophet "causes the earth and those who dwell in it to worship the first beast, whose deadly wound was healed." Each citizen will be required to bear a mark of the system, without which they will be unable to buy or sell. Those who refuse outright to worship the system will be killed. According to Shi'ite belief, "The first thing that will occur under the rule of the *Mahdi* will be the *Islamicizing of the whole world.*"[69] This he will accomplish by force under another of his prophetic titles, *sahib al-sayf,* or Master of the Sword.[70] In the works of Shi'ite scholar Nu'mani we read that the Mahdi "will not accept repentance from anyone, nor will the rebuke of his adversaries deter him from carrying out the command of God."[71]

As for the infamous mark of the beast, there exists already in many Muslim nations—Pakistan, Malaysia and Iran, for example—an Islamic identification system that allows for discrimination against non-Muslims. This is also true in some North African states, which often refuse passports and other privileges to such people. In light of the miraculous exploits of the Mahdi, it is not difficult to envision how rejuvenated believers could see fit to expand and zealously enforce such systems.

Two Reapers, Three Frogs and Seven Angels: On the Eve of Armageddon

Between the ultimate *jihad* of Ezekiel 38–39 and the great and terrible battle of Armageddon—which nearly all Bible scholars believe will bring a close to human kingdoms—the Scriptures relate that there will be a major ingathering of souls into the Church. An especially powerful passage on this theme is Revelation 14:14–16.

> Then I looked, and behold, a white cloud, and on the cloud sat One like the Son of Man, having on His head a golden crown, and in His hand a sharp sickle. And another angel came out of the temple, crying with a loud voice to Him who sat on the cloud, "Thrust in Your sickle and reap . . . for the harvest of the earth is ripe." So He who sat on the cloud thrust in His sickle on the earth, and the earth was reaped.

Here we are presented with a thrilling final harvest scenario immediately prior to a time of great violence and trouble on the earth. While the dimensions of this harvest are apparently enormous, the window of opportunity will be open only for a limited time. For when the first reaper has completed his work, a second angelic reaper is told to thrust his sickle into the earth to gather the famous grapes of wrath (Revelation 14:17–20).

As God unleashes the seven angels of judgment in Revelation 15, the earth and its rebellious inhabitants are subject to a devastating assault by the Almighty. Within a short span, the waves of unprecedented disease, death and destruction exact such a toll that Satan and his hosts—including the false prophet—decide to launch a climactic counterstrike. As part of the enemy's all-out mobilization effort, John records that three unclean spirits in the form of frogs crawl out of the mouths of the dragon, beast and false prophet to summon support.

> For they are spirits of demons, performing signs, which go out to the kings of the earth and of the whole world, to gather them to the battle of that great day of God Almighty.[72]

Apparently in an effort to hasten the day of victory, God Himself orders the sixth angel of wrath to pour out his bowl on the Euphrates River—thereby drying up the tributary "so that the way of the kings from the east might be prepared."[73] In this final act on the eve of Armageddon, God reverses the original role of the serpent in Eden by infiltrating the heart of Satan's territorial stronghold and perpetrating an act that will lead his rebellious followers to their ultimate judgment.

While the name *Armageddon* has a chilling ring to it—and indeed, to those men and women who are determined to walk in their own counsel it should—to Christians it is also the blessed gateway through which God's Kingdom rule is finally returned to this earth. That this gateway should be stained with the blood of men and women was never the Master's intention.

Notes

1 Reuters, "Mosques Rise As Soviet Moslems Emerge Under Perestroika," February 16, 1990.

2 Quoted in *The Awaited Saviour*, Ayatollahs Baqir al-Sadr and Murtaza Mutahery (London: Islamic Seminary Publications, 1979), p. 13.

3 To the Iranians, and indeed to most Shi'ites, Saudi Arabia's guardianship of the holy shrines of Mecca and Medina is only a continuation of the usurpation of the rightful leadership of the Prophet's descendants through Ali.

4 Adel Darwish, "Islamic Extremists Talk in London," *The Independent*, January 15, 1988.
   Note: Although most conference delegates were Sunni Muslims, they voted to accept the Ayatollah Khomeini as the "authentic voice" of Islam.

5 "Purse Strings and Prayer," *The Economist*, September 22, 1990.

6 *The Independent*, "Saddam's Call to All Muslims," August 11, 1990.

7 Jacob Young, "Retaking the Temple Mount," *Newsweek*, October 29, 1984.

8 *Haaretz* report, "Jewish Sect Believed Ready to Attack Shrine," excerpted in *The Seattle Times*, August 30, 1990.

9 Reported by Richard N. Ostling in *Time*, "Time for a New Temple?", October 16, 1989.

10 Geoffrey Hanks, "Temple Blocked But Plans Rise," *Christian News World*, February 1990; Charles Richards, "Builders of Third Temple Thwarted," *The Independent*, October 17, 1989.

11 Ostling, "Time for a New Temple?"

12 *Ibid.*

13 Hanks, "Temple Blocked But Plans Rise"; Richards, "Builders of Third Temple Thwarted."

14 "Israel Gropes for Line Between State, Religion," *The Seattle Times*, May 4, 1990.
   Note: The messianic Zionists who form the backbone of the settlement movement believe that by redeeming the land, God will redeem the people.

15 These sentiments flared in late 1990 when *Chabad* followers compared events in the Middle East to recent reinterpretations of ancient tracts that prophesied major confrontations between Muslim nations.

16 Mike Dumper, *MEI*, "Settler Groups in the Old City of Jerusalem," April 27, 1990.

17 The *Gush Emunim* are widely regarded as being the vanguard of the Orthodox settler groups. A Jewish *yeshiva* is roughly analogous to a Christian seminary.

18 Dumper, "Settler Groups in the Old City of Jerusalem."

19 Young, "Retaking the Temple Mount."

20 Quoted by Richard Ostling in *Time*, October 16, 1989.

21 *Special Office Brief*, July 10, 1990.

22 See, for example, *Unger's Bible Dictionary* (Chicago: Moody Press, 1957/1971), p. 419; also, *Encyclopædia Britannica, Micropædia*, Vol. 2, p. 938.

23 H.W.F. Saggs, *The Greatness that Was Babylon* (London: Sidgwick & Jackson, 1962/1988), pp. 130–131; also, *Unger's Bible Dictionary*, p. 1120.

24 Radio Liberty B-Wire, "Pan Turkism Makes the Soviet Union and Turkey Nervous," March 12, 1990.

25 "Turks Awake, Russians Quake," *Asiaweek*, April 13, 1990.

26 *Ibid.*

27 *Far Eastern Economic Review*, "USSR—The Islamic Challenge," July 12, 1990.

28 While the Chinese may call their northwestern province Xinjiang, Yusuf Donmez, the Istanbul-based author of *The Turkic World*, says, "We call it Dogu (East) Turkestan."

29 *Far Eastern Economic Review*, "USSR—The New Silk Road," July 12, 1990.

30 Associated Press, "Talk Grows in Central Asia of 'Decolonization' by Soviets," June 10, 1990.

31 TASS report, December 13, 1989.

32 In several translations *Put* or *Phut* are substituted for *Libya*. Unger and others place these ancient civilizations in northeast Africa near Egypt and Ethiopia—territory occupied presently by the fiercely Muslim nations of Sudan and Somalia.

33 *Qur'an*, 8:60.

34 Hamid Algar, *Islam and Revolution* (Berkeley: Mizan Press, 1981), p. 46.

35 Robin Wright, *In the Name of God* (New York: Simon & Schuster, 1989), p. 102.

36 Daniel Pipes, *In the Path of God* (New York: Basic Books, 1983), p. 327.

    Note: In subsequent years the secularist Palestine Liberation Organization (P.L.O.) has been replaced in the hearts of Palestinian fundamentalists by the Islamic *jihad* and *Hamas*, a semi-clandestine organization founded by Sheikh Ahmed Ismail Yassin. The name of the movement, which means "zeal" or "courage," is also an acronym for Islamic Resistance Movement. Strict zealots, *Hamas* leaders present the equivocal P.L.O. leadership as "eaters of pork and drinkers of wine." See Michael Sheridan, "An Eye for an Eye in Hotbed of Islam," *The Independent*, May 7, 1990.

37 "Arab Nuclear Arsenal Backed by Gadhafi," *The Seattle Times*, April 22, 1990.

38 Also called the League of the Russian People.

    Note: While the pogroms of the Black Hundreds were more extensive and better known, the first anti-Jewish pogroms in Russia were launched in 1881 after the death of Czar Alexander II.

39 As Yanov points out, even Solzhenitsyn has not been immune to such tendencies. In his novel *August 1914*, Solzhenitsyn likens the Jew, Mordechai Bogrov, to a coiled snake who strikes down Peter Stolypin.

40 These states purportedly included Athens in 429 B.C., Rome under Augustus, Spain under Carl V, France under Louis XIV and Russia in 1917.

41 Walter Lacqueur, cited in Alexander Yanov, *The Russian Challenge and the Year 2000* (Oxford: Basil Blackwell, 1987), p. 213.

42 From *samizdat* article appearing in *Strana i Mir*, Nos. 1–2, 1984, p. 51; cited by Yanov, p. 252.

43 Yanov, p. 254.

44 Excerpt from *Novyi Zhurnal*, No. 118, 1975, p. 227; see Yanov, chapter 12.

45 *Moskovskii Sbornik*, No. 1 (London: Keston College Archives), p. 68, cited by Yanov.

46 Published by Nikolai Tetenov; quoted in *Zerkalo* (The Mirror), No. 3, 1985, p. 2.

47 Norman Cohn, *Warrant for Genocide* (New York: Harper & Row, 1966), pp. 17–18.

48 *The New Layman's Parallel Bible* (Grand Rapids: Zondervan, 1981).

49 Saggs, p. 113.

    Note: According to Saggs, the Assyrian king's description of the campaign against the Elamites included "Assyrian chargers wading through blood; the plain littered with mutilated bodies of the slain, hacked to bits for the sake of their rings and bracelets or for mere blood lust; terrified horses plunging madly across the battlefield dragging chariots of the dead. . . ."

50 Yanov, p. 44.

51 See chapter 4 for additional information on this subject.

52 Some Islamic traditions place the appearance of *al-Dajjal* after that of *al-Mahdi*. In his *Muquaddima*, for instance, Ibn Khaldun writes: ". . . At the end of time a man

from the family [of the Prophet] will without fail make his appearance, one who will strengthen Islam and make justice triumph. Muslims will follow him, and he will gain domination over the Muslim realm. He will be called the Mahdi. Following him, the Antichrist will appear, together with all the subsequent signs of the times."

53 Sheik Yusufali Nafsi in *The Awaited Saviour*, p. 20.

54 Revelation 13:13.

55 Shia *hadith* (tradition) of conversation between al-Mufaddal and Imam al-Sadiq concerning the appearance of the Mahdi; from Muhammad Baqir Majlisi, *Mahdi-yi maw'ud*, cited by Abdulaziz Abdulhussein Sachedina, *Islamic Messianism* (Albany, N.Y.: State University of New York Press, 1981), p. 161.

56 A careful reading of Revelation 18 offers few alternative identities for the scarlet woman or Babylon the Great.

57 See the appendix for further interpretive comparisons.

58 See chapter 6, "Establishing God's Government."

59 Sachedina, p. 75.

60 *Ibid.*, pp. 70–74; see especially the account by Ibn Babuya.

61 Jassim M. Hussain, *The Occultation of the Twelfth Imam* (London: The Muhammadi Trust, 1982), p. 17.

62 Ibn Maja, *al-Sunan*, II, 1368, cited by Hussain.

63 Khomeini was seen by many as a *mujaddid*—a restorer or renewer of the faith who appears every century to regenerate the Islamic spirit and to defend the traditions against innovation, worldly skepticism and impiety. Viewed in relation to the Mahdi, Khomeini would thus be a sort of John the Baptist.

64 Sachedina, p. 158.

65 *Ibid.*, pp. 162–163.

66 According to Sachedina, the Mahdi will preface his readings with the following declaration: "Truly anyone who wishes to see Adam and Seth, should know that I am that Adam and Seth. Anyone who wishes to see Noah and his son Shem, should know that I am that Noah and Shem. Anyone who wishes to see Abraham and Ishmael, should know that I am that Abraham and Ishmael. Anyone who wishes to see Moses and Joshua, should know that I am that Moses and Joshua. Anyone who wishes to see Jesus and Simon, should know that I am that Jesus and Simon. Anyone who wishes to see Muhammad and 'Ali, the Amir of the Believers, should know that I am that Muhammad and 'Ali. Anyone who wishes to see al-Hasan and al-Husayn, should know that I am that al-Hasan and al-Husayn. Anyone who wishes to see the Imams from the descendants of al-Husayn, should know that I am those pure Imams. Accept my call and assemble near me so that I will inform you whatever you wish to know. Anyone who has read the heavenly scriptures and divine scrolls, will now hear them from me." (Compare with Luke 4:17–21.)

67 After the death of the Antichrist, Shi'ites believe that Jesus will establish a rule of justice for forty years, after which He will die and be buried in Medina next to Muhammad. Some Sunni Muslims doubt the future role of a Mahdi in destroying the Antichrist, however, arguing that "while there was no mention of Mahdi in the Qur'an, the return of Jesus was well established in the signs of the Hour, and he, not the Mahdi, will kill the Dajjal." See Sachedina, p. 172.

68 Nafsi in *The Awaited Saviour*, p. 18.

69 Sachedina, p. 174.

70 This title is in keeping with the Shi'ite tradition of the Imamate (the succession of twelve Imams from the family of Muhammad). Each Imam inherited three symbols of authenticity from his predecessor: 1) the Prophetic light, or knowledge (*al-'ilm*); 2) the Books (*al-kutub*); and 3) the Prophetic weapons (*al-silah*). The "light" ostensibly allowed each Imam to attract people through various transcendental distinctions, while the "Books" included the Prophetic scroll of Fatima, legal instructions from Ali, and the biblical Psalms, Torah and Gospels. The "weapons," which included the Prophet's sword, armor and spear, paralleled the significance of the Ark of the Covenant to the Israelites. The sword was especially noteworthy, not only because it was believed to have been brought out of the heavens by the angel Gabriel, but because it would be used by the Master of the Sword against apostates and unbelievers in the end times. (See Sachedina, pp. 21–22.)

71 Muhammad bin Ibrahim bin Ja'far al-Nu'mani, *Kitab al-ghayba*, Tabriz: Maktabat al-Sabiri, 1383/1963, cited in Sachedina.

72 Revelation 16:14.

73 Revelation 16:12.

Note: While the identity of these "kings of the east" is not specified, it is fair to speculate that the populous Islamic nations of Iran, Pakistan, India, Bangladesh, Afghanistan, Soviet-Chinese "Turkestan" and perhaps even Indonesia and Malaysia are involved.

10

Responding to the Times: A Strategic Checklist

> In this hour when men skilled in their natural gifts and
> abilities are fainting, God is awakening many to see
> how imperative it is to expect the supernatural.
>
> DeVern Fromke[1]

> The vision of faith has ideas about the future which are
> God's ideas. God himself is the one who "summons
> things that are not yet in existence as if they already
> were" (Romans 4:17). Vision is not a matter of seeing
> what is and asking why. It is far more a matter of seeing
> what has never yet been and asking why not.
>
> Os Guinness[2]

> I have a hope that the world will see Christ through his
> church before they see him with his church.
>
> Steve Fry[3]

The future, it has been said, is a foreign country; they
do things differently there.[4] For many of today's corporations and
public institutions, acquiring advance insight into the preferences
of this new world is vitally important business. Indeed, the political and economic well-being of these institutions, and in some

cases their very existence, is dependent largely on how successful they are in knowing what to expect next.

Curiously, with few exceptions, the Christian community has not shown nearly the same degree of interest in anticipatory information as its secular counterparts. The future, to the extent that it is contemplated at all, is viewed by many believers as simply a reprise of the present. For them, the subject is best summarized by the writer of Ecclesiastes who declared: "Is there anything of which one might say, 'See this, it is new'? Already it has existed for ages which were before us. . . . So, there is nothing new under the sun."[5]

For others, the future conjures up fearful images of divine judgment. I knew of a Christian woman who was absolutely terrified of the book of Revelation. She would never read it because, as she said, it gave her nightmares. And she is not such a rarity as one might think. In her mind, and those of thousands like her, the "end times" do not represent global evangelistic opportunities, but shadows of apocalypse and Armageddon. Daily headlines do not elicit optimism but despair. The "signs of the times" are not happy omens of promise and reunion, but a countdown to cataclysm. To them we are all on a runaway freight train without any ability to control impending events.

Whether we realize it or not, our vision of the future will have a great deal to do with the way we behave in the months and years that lie before us. "If," as futurist Alvin Toffler pointed out, "tomorrow's society is simply an enlarged, Cinerama version of the present, there is little we *need* do to prepare for it. If, on the other hand, society is inevitably destined to self-destruct within our lifetime, there is nothing we *can* do about it." The irony is that "both these ways of looking at the future generate privatism and passivity . . . both freeze us into inaction . . . both lead to the paralysis of imagination and will."[6]

If our spiritual ambitions and institutions are to survive the raging storms of the future, we must first toss overboard all notions of inevitability. If we are going to sink, then there is no reason even to start our engines, let alone try to replace our navigational instruments. Inevitability removes incentive, which, in turn, erodes motivation. If people are convinced their actions will not make a real difference, they simply will not bother—even for God.

Fortunately, the Scriptures do not present us with the prospect of an impotent and meaningless future. (In fact, mere "forms of godliness" are described with contempt.) Rather, God challenges His people to invest vigorously in tomorrow. Christians are to be active agents of a loving, "divine imperialism" throughout the planet. The boredom and futility of ritualism are replaced with the consuming responsibility of leadership. As H. G. Wells once declared in *The Open Conspiracy*, "It is opportunity and not destiny we face."

At the same time, those Christians who assume they can apply 1970s-vintage ministry strategies to 1990s realities are in for a rude awakening. Strategic plans and policy manuals written for yesterday's placid conditions are rapidly becoming museum pieces. Despite Marcus Aurelius' contention that "he who hath seen present things hath seen all,"[7] all of us must admit that the world of today bears little resemblance to the world we lived in three years ago; and the same is likely to be true three years hence.

Accordingly, those ministries most prone to failure in tomorrow's world are those that insist on conducting "business as usual" today. No matter how big or venerable they are, denominations, mission agencies and local churches that fail to adjust to the sweeping changes ushered in by the 1980s will, quite simply, fail to thrive in the 1990s.

Recognizing this fact, the Evangelical Lutheran Church in America, for one, made a major course adjustment in their missions strategy in 1988 by deciding to significantly upgrade their witness to Muslims. One of the chief drafters of the new policy, Dr. Mark Thomsen, declared: "If you can't adapt, you might as well stay home. A static church without capacity to adapt is incapable of significant participation in the mission of God."[8] Some years earlier, in his book *The Church at the End of the 20th Century*, the ever-prescient Francis Schaeffer concurred: "Not being able, as times change, to change under the Holy Spirit is ugly." Moreover, Schaeffer noted, "Refusal to consider change under the direction of the Holy Spirit is a spiritual problem, not an intellectual problem."[9]

Happily, many individuals and institutions today have remained on the cutting edge of ministry by acknowledging the indispensable role of the Holy Spirit in their research and planning operations. As I have observed and conversed with many of these modern-day success stories, it has become clear that their strategic adjustments to the times have centered on four primary issues: 1) the need to identify and target key harvest fields; 2) the need to organize and participate in ministry partnerships; 3) the need to adequately finance the campaign; and 4) the need to acknowledge the importance of prayer and spiritual gifts in the success of frontline ministry. In the pages that follow, we will take a closer look at each of these important issues.

Pulling in the Right Direction: Identifying and Targeting Key Harvest Fields

In the course of his January 1989 address to delegates attending the Global Consultation on World Evangelization held in Singapore, Floyd McClung, Youth With A Mission's International Director, remarked: "I heard a story about a guy who had a rifle and went out to practice shooting. First he shot at the side of a building, and then he went and drew a target around the hole where the bullet had gone in. Then he stood back and said, 'That was a good shot.' I think that's the way it is sometimes in our Christian work," McClung added pointedly. "We target that which we've already hit, but we may not necessarily be hitting that which God wants us to target."[10]

In an effort to get around this problem, many church and agency mission programs endeavor to hit as many targets as possible in the hope that included among them will be at least some of God's strategic intentions. Some dubious wags have dubbed this widespread practice the "buckshot approach" to missions. Aside from the fact that it is quick and easy—requiring no spiritual marksmanship skills—the biggest selling point to this approach is that it gives practitioners a *sense* of great power and coverage. Its primary drawback, of course, is the fact that it is almost completely lacking in strategic focus. By sending low-financed, often ill-equipped mission "pellets" scattering indiscriminately in all directions, buckshot practitioners not only wound and anger many of the Church's primary targets, but cause significant collateral damage as well.[11]

In marked contrast to this expedient and often ineffectual style of ministry, the psalmist's words in Psalm 144—"[God] trains my hands for war, and my fingers for battle"—convey the concept of *precision*—and a timely reminder that spiritual planning and warfare should not be sloppy.

So while Christian personnel and financial resources can be dispatched almost anywhere today, the real question concerns where they should be sent. In light of what we have already examined about God's ways, the times we are living in and the contemporary spiritual battlefield, the answer to this inquiry would seem to be threefold: to *neglected areas, kairos opportunities* and *extraordinary harvests*. While these rationales overlap in various ways, they also stand, as we shall see, as distinct categories.

Neglected Areas

According to missions researcher Dr. David Barrett, the hardcore unevangelized world presently encompasses nearly a quarter of the earth's population (or some 1.25 billion persons).[12] A large proportion of these people can be found in thirty evangelistically underserviced countries within the greater 10/40 Window.[13]

Despite the fact that the 10/40 Window contains close to 95 percent of the world's unevangelized (or unreached) people, Barrett goes on to reveal that, astonishingly, only *one percent* of the Church's global foreign mission force (about 3,000 persons) was dedicated to the area as of 1990![14] Muslims, who constitute the largest block of unreached people in today's world, merited only about *two percent* of all Christian workers (both in and outside of the 10/40 Window).[15]

So where are Christian personnel targeted today? Almost 91

percent are engaged in work with what Barrett describes as "heavily Christianized populations in predominantly Christian lands."[16]
Thus, while many nations of North Africa and Central Asia go
begging for evangelistic resources, church workers from the United
States are bumping into one another in airport baggage claim areas
in Brazil, Mexico and the Philippines. (In fact, the "mission"
experience of many U.S. Christians today involves little more than
being picked up at the airport by friends and transported to mission compounds or churches where they proceed to offer teaching
to nationals who are already Christians.)

Regent University missions professor Dr. Howard Foltz likens
this situation to a fishing trip he took a few years back in Colorado.
Starting his holiday at the popular and accessible South Platte
River, he soon found his line snarled with those of other fishermen
in the crowded waters. Later, having ascended high into the Rocky
Mountains, he suddenly found himself surrounded by an embar-
rassment of riches. Within his line of sight were no fewer than six
lakes—most with no trails to them, but all full of fish. He had
these pristine "fishing holes" all to himself simply because they
were tougher to get to.

While it is obvious to all but a few hyper-Calvinists that current
ministry resource-to-need ratios are not a reflection of divine math-
ematics, mere recognition of the problem is not enough. The
Church needs to act—and act decisively.[17] If Christians—
especially in the West—are truly serious about fulfilling the Great
Commission and bringing back the King, then a major redeploy-
ment of personnel and finances is in order.

While it is understandable that churches and agencies with
extensive relational equity in places like Latin America and the
Philippines should be reluctant to sever or reduce assistance to
their friends, there are other alternatives. One of these is to link
the continued financial and technical aid to the willingness of
various missionaries and national workers to explore ministry options within the 10/40 Window. Latin Americans, for example,
have a great opportunity to minister in Muslim North Africa—
especially among the Spanish-speaking peoples of Morocco's Rif
Mountains and in the Western Sahara (both former Spanish colo-

nial territories). At least two ministries in southern Spain are already receiving and training Latin Americans for service in the area. While an increasing number of Latins are testifying to having a new burden for Muslims, few have the financial wherewithal to travel abroad for training and ministry. If Americans, Canadians and Europeans were to pick up the tab, however, not only would they be encouraging and supporting strategic end-time evangelism, but they would also be keeping important relational links intact.

Kairos Opportunities

As has been mentioned previously, strategic ministry targeting is not related just to location, but increasingly to strategic timeliness as well. Thus, those leaders who are charged with the responsibility of deploying Christian resources in the 1990s must be equally familiar with *windows of need* and *windows of opportunity*.

When it comes to recognizing and responding to historic ministry openings, unfortunately, the Church's track record has been a dismal one. When the great Mongol leader Kublai Khan, for instance, had reached the height of his power, he asked Marco Polo to request missionaries of the Pope to present the claims of Christianity within his realm. At the time, the nephew of the infamous Ghengis Khan ruled over the most far-reaching empire the world has ever known. After a considerable delay, the Church finally dispatched two semi-literate priests who wound up returning home almost as soon as they had arrived. Opportunity lost.

Several centuries later, during the post-World War II Mac-Arthur era in Japan, the call again went out for Christian missionaries to come with their Gospel message. According to Christian historian Kenneth Scott Latourette, the Japanese "were spiritually adrift and wondered whether the reason for the debacle of the[ir] empire had not been a false ideology." Even more significantly, they began to ask "whether the secret of the American victory was to be found in what they deemed the religion of the United States."[18] By and large the Church's response to this opening was meek; and, as a consequence, Japan's post-War openness has been replaced with crass materialism and resurgent national religions like Soka-gakkai.[19] Once again, opportunity lost.

A third, and more recent, example of the Church's failure to seize a golden ministry opportunity involved the millions of Muslim Afghan refugees sent fleeing for their lives by the Soviet Red Army during the 1980s. With the exception of a few stalwart organizations like SERVE, the international Church virtually ignored the chance to minister the love of Christ to the massive numbers of needy and dislocated Afghans in Pakistan and other countries. This, despite the fact that numerous mission strategists and Church leaders held Afghanistan up as an example of one of the most evangelistically difficult-to-access nations in the world.

If the Church of the 1990s is going to fare any better than its predecessors, she will have to start by adopting a proactive mentality. Why? Because history's one great lesson is that reactionaries are losers.

National Hockey League star Wayne Gretzky once told reporters, "The secret to my success is that I have an ability to anticipate where the puck will be and get there before it does." No preacher could have come up with a better description of what the Church will need to do if she is to take advantage of *kairos* opportunities in the coming years. What is lacking are Gretzky's anticipatory skills.

On the positive side of the ledger, many are trying to aid the Church in this regard. My own ministry, The Sentinel Group, is working to develop new mechanisms for detecting, evaluating and responding to emerging windows of ministry opportunity. In keeping with Isaiah's watchman who is instructed to declare to the people what he sees,[20] we feel this is a very sentinel-like assignment. The trick, as always, is coming up with advance information.

While aspects of this new "early warning" tool are fairly complex, one of the primary sources that feeds it couldn't be simpler. As we recalled the numerous home, office and church prayer meetings in which the Lord spoke to His people in detailed and confirming ways, it occurred to us that a marvelous and largely untapped source of strategic information about today's harvest field was represented in the growing ranks of praying Christians around the globe. If the spiritual feedback received by these believers— undoubtedly millions strong—could be systematically harvested and cataloged, surely significant patterns and emphases would emerge that would be helpful to Church strategists. For instance, if significant numbers of mature believers in Norway, Brazil, Egypt and Korea were all to report suddenly that God had impressed them to pray for "open doors" on the Horn of Africa, you would have at least a partial indicator of divine intention.[21]

As these emerging windows of opportunity are detected, they must then be evaluated for such things as their likely duration and the type of ministry response required. Once this is done, reports defining "hot spots" can be sent out with projected "action time-tables" to Christian networks that—in the fashion of a spiritual 911 system—will then be able to respond to these "emergencies" with appropriate resources.

Extraordinary Harvests

Unlike *kairos* opportunities in which divinely engineered (or redeemed) circumstances offer extraordinary evangelistic potential[22]—which the Church may or may not respond to—there are certain areas in the world today where souls are already being saved in large numbers. In these settings local Christian workers may need reinforcements to help pull the nets into the boat (see John 21:6).

While such situations are still relatively rare—at the start of the 1990s genuine examples could be found in Argentina, Indonesia, Algeria, Bangladesh and Zaire—there is ample scriptural evidence to suggest that they will become more common in the future.[23] Before trundling off to rich harvest fields, however, Western Christians should check first with recognized national Church leaders to make sure they are needed.

Pulling Together: The Case for Partnerships

In a 1989 article entitled "Cooperation in World Evangelization," EFMA Executive Director Paul McKaughan writes: "It has

been suggested that the major reason why so many [plans to evangelize the world] have failed has not been due to the lack of
dynamic commitment, lack of resources, or opposition from the
enemy." Instead, McKaughan continues, "the great 'Achilles heel'
of world evangelization has been the unwillingness of the great
[spiritual] entrepreneurs . . . to lay aside their individualistic
dreams and organizational manifestations and cooperate with others equally gifted and equally committed."[24]

A graphic illustration of this attitude at work is provided by
David Barrett and James Reapsome in their "A.D. 2000 Series"
report *Seven Hundred Plans to Evangelize the World.* Of the 788
active plans profiled by the authors, nearly two-thirds were either
non-cooperating or partially cooperating with other groups, and
only 10.5 percent considered cooperation with like-minded traditions and bodies indispensable.[25]

At the root of this failure to cooperate are two familiar themes:
fear and pride. Insecure Christians pull back from collaboration in
order to avert a loss of identity, whereas self-sufficient individuals
simply see no reason to work with others. Such people rarely see
their positions as injurious to Kingdom growth but, in John 17:21,
Jesus cements the relationship between unity and evangelism when
He prays that His followers would be one so that the world would
know that He had truly been sent of the Father.

The truth of the matter is that God's universe has operated on the
principle of *interdependence* from the very beginning. Atomic
structure, the human body and the family unit all testify to this
truth. From one end of creation to the other, nothing is strong
enough or sufficient enough to operate with total autonomy. The
strategy is delightfully coherent: Let material creation reflect the
intrinsic interdependence of the Trinity, and then encourage moral
creation to take note and emulate the divine pattern. The Trinity
is, in fact, the first and best network.[26] Its members are at once
equal in value and standing, but diverse in their roles or expres-
sions. When the apostle Paul spoke of the Church as being "one
body with many members," it was with this same concept in mind.

In an essay in *Fern Seeds and Elephants,* C. S. Lewis suggests
that the basis for our unity within Christ's Body begins not with our

similarity but with our *diversity*. Pointing out that the very word *membership* is of Christian origin, he decries the fact that it has since been taken over by the world and emptied of its meaning. Rejecting the idea that biblical membership has anything to do with inclusion in a homogeneous collective, Lewis declares: "By *members* he [Paul] meant that we should call *organs*, things essentially different from, and complimentary to, one another. . . . A dim perception of the richness inherent in this kind of unity is one reason why we enjoy a book like *The Wind in the Willows;* a trio such as Rat, Mole, and Badger symbolizes the extreme differentiation of persons in harmonious union."[27]

Biblically based networking involves cultivating an awareness of, and an appreciation for, the various members of Christ's Body, and then allowing ourselves to be "joined and knit together" with adjacent members.[28] For the Body to function properly, we need to understand both our role and our limitations. While we are never forced to lose our identity, we *are* asked to dispense with the ludicrous notion that we can do everything alone.

In fact, wrote Herman Melville, if we submit ourselves to Body life, "We cannot live for ourselves alone. Our lives are connected by a thousand invisible threads, and along these sympathetic fibers, our actions run as causes and return as results."[29] Those who insist on clinging to their own lives and identities become either parasites or cancer within the Body.[30] Whereas true members, or "loyalists," always ask, "What's best for the whole Body?" the foremost concern of independent operators tends to be, "What's best for me and/or my organization?"

Writing about what he sees as legitimate "cultural" distinctions between denominations today, well-known Bible teacher Jack Hayford points out that "even in the Apostle Paul's sharpest rebuke against those who did separate themselves by names, saying 'I am of Paul,' 'I am of Apollos' or 'I am of Cephas,' it does not seem to be the *denominating* that disturbs him, but the *dividing*.[31] He affirms in I Corinthians 3:4–6, the distinct ministry of men to whom people may refer as distinct influences upon them, to some as instructors, to others as fathers—4:15. Thus, it seems the 'naming' of groups *within* the Body is not disallowed [*per se*]. What *is* confronted vehemently is the dividing of groups *from* one another by reason of attitudinal differences."[32]

While the impact of these attitudinal divisions on the Body of Christ itself is generally self-evident, the spillover effect on world evangelization is perhaps best summarized in the words of an East African proverb: "If the fingers of one hand quarrel, they cannot pick up the food."[33]

Body unity and ministry also suffer from the more common sins of *neglect*—especially at an international level. Despite the absence of any scriptural justification for a segmented Body, for instance, most Western believers continue to view the subjugation and isolation of certain of their brethren by various manmade barriers and human edicts as simply an unfortunate fact of life. Although fellowship with Christian counterparts in China, Vietnam or the Muslim world is seen as desirable, it is also construed as impossible. The fact that these segregative devices contain nothing more than the *potential* to divide is completely overlooked; and, as a consequence, they are empowered through the Church's passive acquiescence to their intent.

By referring to the Body of Christ alternately as the "persecuted Church" and the "free Church," Christians perpetuate both a distortion of reality (that members of the persecuted Church are essentially victims, and that the so-called free Church is necessarily free) and a harmful and unbiblical "us-them" mentality. In order to break free of this syndrome, an important first step must be to adopt new nomenclature, perhaps the "forward-positioned Church" and the "partner-provider Church," which better reflects the reality of current Body roles and relationships. (These roles, of course, are neither static nor exclusive.)

Those who have investigated their merits find that international ministry partnerships have much to commend them. Looking at the respective assets and liabilities of the forward-positioned and partner-provider units of Christ's Church, it is clear that the strengths of one are the precise remedy for the weaknesses of the other. The partner-provider's problems with language, culture, access and general proximity to the evangelistic front lines, for instance, are overcome through relational linkage with its forward-positioned brother. In similar fashion, the forward-positioned church's lack of manpower, training materials, finances and political freedoms are needs that can be addressed by its partner-provider. Partnership, in other words, is the only means by which the *whole* Church can take the Gospel to the whole world.

Happily, from the mid-1980s onward, international ministry partnerships have grown noticeably in both number and effectiveness. While most of these have forged links between Western churches and agencies and various national enterprises—especially in front-line Hindu, Muslim and Communist countries—others have drawn together previously competitive international agencies.

One particularly bright note in this latter category is a relatively new coalition of radio broadcast ministries called "The World by 2000." Originating out of a historic meeting in September 1985 in which the leaders of the three major international broadcasters—HCJB, Trans World Radio and FEBC—signed a covenant to trust and cooperate with one another, the results have thus far been impressive. With joint projects in Africa, Saipan and elsewhere, the group is making great strides toward its goal of ensuring that every people on the planet will be able to hear the Gospel in a language they can understand by the year 2000. In the words of HCJB President Ron Cline, "We found it's an amazing thing what you can get done when you're working together."[34]

Another shining example of international cooperation is contained in a regionally diverse set of action networks called Strategic Evangelism Partnerships. Established largely through the tireless efforts of Phill Butler and Interdev, these partnerships have provided coherence for a number of otherwise unfocused ministry agencies and initiatives in several difficult areas of the world. Relational healings have been common.

The challenges facing the Church today are enormous, not only in terms of the sheer numbers of unreached people and the immense geographical range that must be covered, but also in relation to the wide diversity of languages and cultures. Add in the resources and intensity of those who are opposing the Gospel message and the furious pace at which things are moving, and the

combined weight is enough to buckle the knees of any one ministry. Only partnerships can distribute, and thereby bear, the pres-
sure.[35]

One of the great byproducts of partnering is *synergy*, a wonderful
term that simply means that whenever people, drugs, animals or
muscles cooperate, the result of their efforts will be greater than
the sum of what they can do separately. As many a surprised
farmer has discovered, one horse can pull six tons of weight, but
two horses harnessed together can haul not twelve but 32 tons! For
most Christians this idea is captured best in the familiar Old
Testament equation that if one can chase a thousand, two can put
ten thousand to flight.[36]

Synergistic unity is to the Church what an unshaven head was to
Samson; it is the secret of our strength. Having recognized this
fact, we must guard against beguiling Delilahs who would seek to
rob us of our power.

Pulling Out the Stops:
Adequately Financing the Campaign

One of the greatest tests of our commitment to a cause is how
much we are willing to pay for it. This is true not only for individuals, but also for companies, ministries and even nations.

When George Bush met with his top military advisors to forge
the American response to Saddam Hussein's August 1990 invasion
of Kuwait, the question of cost surfaced almost immediately. Concerned that the U.S. might once again pursue the halfway measures adopted during the Vietnam campaign, the chairman of the
Joint Chiefs of Staff, General Colin Powell, supported military
action only with the proviso that an insertion of American forces
would be massive and swift. "If you are going to commit the armed
forces of the U.S. to a military operation that could involve conflict
and loss of life," Powell said, "then do it right."[37]

To Powell, it all boiled down to a simple proposition: If leadership is going to ask young men and women to leave their homes
and families and put their lives on the line, then the least that

leadership can do is supply those men and women with the resources necessary to do the job. "Doing it right," we discovered in the Desert Storm operation, involved not only tanks and ammunition, but boots and sunscreen.

The United States military is not the only institution aware of this principle. Communist organizations from the Vietcong to the KGB have applied it for years. In fact, the level of commitment and support given to Soviet overseas operatives in training is almost astonishing. Screened and recruited while still in universities, the finest students are encouraged to finish their studies and then given an additional five years of special education at government expense. In its latter stages, the regimen becomes so intense that success allows for only three to five hours of sleep per night. To remind them that commitment pays, however, the young agents-to-be are taken to watch Olympic champions in training. They are also given rigorous memory training, and a ten percent pay raise for every Western language they learn (twenty percent for every Oriental language).[38]

In Asia, Pakistani Muslims enable their Chinese brethren to make the annual *hajj* (pilgrimage) to Mecca by providing foreign exchange through the Utility Stores Cooperation. The arrangement permits 2,000 Chinese pilgrims to sell up to 25,000 rupees' worth of silk, crockery and other goods during their transit stay in Pakistan. All the goods come through the Silk Route and are handed over to the Cooperation at Gilgit.[39]

Commitment is also a favorite buzzword in most Christian circles. It is sung about, preached about and written about with great gusto. Talk, however, is cheap; and as history demonstrates, Christians have been content to preach and sing themselves to victory for many years. The only way to discover believers' *real* intentions is to follow their wallets.

According to Barrett, as of 1988 the combined annual personal income of church members around the world—both Catholic and Protestant—amounted to a staggering 8.2 trillion dollars.[40] Of this, less than two percent, or $145 billion, was given "to operate organized global Christianity."[41] While $145 billion is unquestionably a lot of money, the fact that it represents such a pitifully small percentage of the Church's overall resources offers an important clue as to Christian priorities.

Despite all of the recent exciting progress reported in global evangelization, for example, foreign missions remain a poor sideshow when it comes to Christian spending habits. Whereas the average Christian family income in 1990 was $19,280, the weekly foreign missions giving per church member was a paltry ten cents.[42] Moreover, most of what is given in the name of "missions" today, at least in America, is used to propagate the Gospel among people who have the opportunity to hear the Good News *up to one hundred times each day*.[43] Only 0.1 percent of all Christian income is spent on direct ministry outside of the Christianized world—and a microscopic 0.01 percent on the hard-core unevangelized world.[44]

So where are most Christian donations being spent today? In addition to a plethora of conferences, seminars and self-help programs, there are such things as new hymnals, Sunday school materials, books, cassettes and bumper stickers. Christian radio and television programs for the faithful consume billions each year, as do ever-popular brick-and-mortar building projects. As of 1979, the total accumulated assets of religious property in America alone amounted to over $130 billion.[45] Observing these close-to-home spending patterns, black evangelist Tom Skinner perhaps summed matters up best when he said: "Let's be honest, we tithe to ourselves."

A growing segment of Christendom has convinced itself that a convenient—and even indulgent—lifestyle is fully consistent with the will of God. The proponents of this position, which include elements of both the faith and prosperity and the church growth camps, are not only growing more numerous, but more willing to practice what they preach. Jim and Tammy Faye Bakker, who stood at the forefront of this doctrine for many years, eventually made *People* magazine's list of twenty definers for the Decade of the '80s. In a 1989 profile on the Bakkers, writer Dave Barry reflected: "I think the Bakkers were successful because they personalized a very appealing, very convenient moral philosophy that flourished in the '80s; a philosophy that can be summarized as follows: You can't do good unto others unless you feel good about yourself, and you can't feel good about yourself unless you have a lot of neat stuff. . . . Their message seemed to be, Hey, if you're doing the Lord's work, the Lord wants you to be comfortable. He wants you to have nice clothes and antique cars and luxury residences with gold-plated bathroom fixtures and air-conditioned dog-houses.[46]

During the course of researching her recent book on direct-selling organizations, sociologist Nicole Woolsey Biggart interviewed a Christian who made it clear where his inspiration came from. "I'm reading *Think and Grow Rich* for the third time," he said. "My mind is sharper today because I read strictly motivational books. . . . I even chose a church that doesn't have a bad attitude, a church that basically has a positive kind of attitude in its religious approach." Biggart also shares an interesting vignette on Mary Crowley, the late founder and CEO of Home Interiors and Gifts. Opening a management training course for 25 women, Crowley turned to the book of Proverbs and said: "Let's read what King Solomon told his sons about how to become leaders. [Because] if any group needs wisdom and understanding, it's management. And what is wisdom but seeing the world from God's point of view? Once you can do that, you just have to succeed at your mission— *our* mission. Which is ensuring that no home in America is ever dull or unattractive."[47]

While attractive homes, successful businesses and big churches are not inherently evil, if we "seek our own" and "not the things which are Jesus Christ's,"[48] then not only do we run the risk of misdefining our true mission, but we also leave a door open for the enemy to animate our idols. "We do not care much whether we see our gods with our eyes or with our minds," Joseph Haroutunian wrote back in 1940. "But we do care that they are bearers of our ideals, champions of our happiness, and ultimate vindicators of our ways."[49]

While demonic agents have recently made effective use of Islamic and Hindu resources to counterattack Christian gains in Africa and India, it may well be that Satan's most brilliant stroke to date has been his ability to use materialism to keep the Church's

potent financial resources out of the hands of Christian warriors.
With 98 percent of all Christian income removed from the battle
right off the top, and then 99.9 percent of the remaining "loose
change" being consumed within the Christian world, there is almost nothing left for frontier action.

It is increasingly obvious that if the Church is to sustain the
thrilling evangelistic momentum of the past thirty years *and* mount
a credible assault on the enemy's final strongholds, Christians are
going to have to open their pocketbooks and "do it right." As one
Atlanta-area pastor said while announcing the morning offering to
his congregation, "It's Kingdom investment opportunity time!"
While a few bright lights have appeared on the recent horizon—
the Calvary Charismatic Center in Singapore, for instance, gives
more than $250,000 per month to missions[50]—a constellation of
such stars is needed.

Further progress on this issue will most likely be determined by
three things: 1) a revolution in contemporary notions of stewardship; 2) a reasonable redistribution of existing mission resources;
and 3) harnessing Christian entrepreneurs to the cause of world
evangelization. In each case, believers on duty in the 1990s will
need to ask whether the things they are giving themselves to are
appreciating or depreciating in value.

This first issue, stewardship, is perhaps the simplest and the
most difficult to process. To fully understand the concept, as Gregory Lewis points out in his book *Is God for Sale?*, we must first
recognize that "there is something spiritually deceitful [in placing]
our trust in what belongs to us instead of in the One to whom we
belong."[51] Until we begin living our lives as if one hundred percent of everything we have belongs to God, we have not mastered
the concept.

A better grasp of stewardship in the Church will also impact
upon the second issue—that of redistributing existing mission resources. Again, what we are looking for here is appreciation in
value, investments that are paying dividends, talents that are mul-
tiplying (see Matthew 25:14–30). If and when we find that this is
not what is occurring, good stewardship requires that we take
action. In many cases this action will involve pruning back un-

productive programs, personnel and/or infrastructure, and reallocating liberated resources into more profitable and strategic ministry investments. It is often difficult to admit that a cherished program has reached the end of its usefulness. Yet, in the manner of ballplayers entertained beyond their prime, if no changes are made they will begin to cost us our winning edge.[52]

Part of the Church's difficulty in this regard has to do with her primary orientation. Whereas the corporate and scientific worlds place a premium on the effective management of resources, the Church is known as a community whose specialty is holding meetings. As a consequence, while the Church might be well-stocked with vision, she does not do a good job of accounting for her resources. Handicapped by a lack of measurable goals (the ability to picture what success would look like if it were achieved), the Church continues wastefully to subsidize a prodigious number of stale programs and "shotgun" mission policies.

It is not that the Church lacks access to competent resource managers; she simply does not *recognize* them. Waiting patiently within her ranks are thousands of highly gifted managers, analysts and entrepreneurs who are looking for a way to express latent spiritual ambitions and callings.[53] Because she has largely failed to challenge these people, the Church has experienced a classic brain drain, hemorrhaging much of her finest talent to temporal pursuits. Unable or unwilling to make use of this creative mindpower, the Church has instead seen it harnessed almost exclusively by leading corporate, academic and political institutions.[54]

As the Church maneuvers toward the terminus of history, the final campaigns to liberate spiritual hostages from the bowels of enemy strongholds promise to be both complex and expensive (even with supernatural assistance). If we are to entertain high hopes for success, the skills of motivated laity—especially entrepreneurs—must be added to the Church's arsenal.

Entrepreneurs are possibility thinkers. They rearrange their existing resources to create opportunities that do not presently exist. They are innovators who, observing that pursuit of the status quo will result in future inadequacy, will form a "locomotive of change" to pull their fellow men and women in new directions.

To ask such persons to concentrate on giving financially to Kingdom causes is to misapply their skills in much the same way an agent would if he contracted Luciano Pavarotti to sing children to sleep in nursery schools. He could surely fulfill the assignment, but it would be a limited use of his gift. While entrepreneurs are likewise capable of *giving* wealth, their real talent lies in *creating* it.

When the Proverbs speak of "witty inventions,"[55] it is a reminder that on her final approach to the year 2000, the Church of Jesus Christ cannot afford a failure of imagination. As A. W. Tozer once admonished, we must tune our ears to the fact "that the creative voice of God is constantly sounding throughout the creation."[56] At the same time, we must dream big, because as Malcolm Muggeridge wrote in the early 1970s, "Experience shows that those who ask little tend to be accorded nothing."[57]

Pulling Strings: The Role of Prayer and Spiritual Power

While the world has always been a supernatural battlefield, for many Western Christians this fact has remained little more than theological theory—until recently. Over the past decade, thousands of previously nonchalant parishioners have been aroused to the reality of unseen spiritual forces by such things as the vivid novels of Frank Peretti[58] and a rising number of credible reports detailing spiritual power encounters on the foreign field. More and more, doctrinal disagreements over issues like the reality of demons and the validity of miracles in this modern age are being resolved without argument.

As Gary Kinnaman writes in his book *Overcoming the Dominion of Darkness:*

> Orthodoxy is necessary, but it is not enough. If it is true that our battle is not against flesh and blood, then we need spiritual insight and power of our own to make a fight of it. Correct doctrine—as necessary as it is for the long-term stability of the Church—is not adequate to bring down the legions of spiritual darkness arrayed

against her. While carefully defined truth is necessary to confront and overcome error, we must realize that error does not exist merely in the intellect.

The Bible gives every indication that the closer we come to the return of Christ, the more the battle is going to heat up. In fact, the unprecedented advance of the Church in the last part of the twentieth century, the resurgence of apostolic-like signs and wonders, and the rising consciousness of spiritual warfare are as much a sign of the nearness of the Lord's return as many of the geopolitical events in the Middle East.[59]

The Role of Spiritual Gifts and Power

Now that Christians are beginning to accept the fact that the material world represents little more than the thin outer skin of Reality—John Dawson reminds us that "Jesus walked through walls in His resurrection body because He was the solid object and the walls were misty and ethereal"[60]—the next step is to find strategies and weapons that will work effectively in the more substantial spiritual dimension. Prayer, which we shall discuss shortly, is both a strategy *and* a weapon. So, for that matter, are fasting, unity and deliverance (the latter being necessary whenever people or places are inhabited and/or disturbed by demonic agents). In addition to the powerful sword of truth, useful weapons today include the biblical gifts of knowledge, wisdom, healing and miracles.

Addressing those who question the validity of such supernatural tools, Howard Snyder writes:

> Spiritual gifts cannot be depreciated without a corresponding devaluation of the biblical understanding of the church and the Spirit-filled life. The *charismata* are not something artificially tacked on; neither are they temporally or culturally bound. They are cross-culturally valid, and it is their presence in the church which makes the church cross-culturally relevant.[61]

It is this cross-cultural relevance that has, in recent years, attracted the attention of an impressive contingent of veteran missionaries, among them cultural anthropologist Chuck Kraft. Dr. Kraft recalls his days on the field in Nigeria:

As missionaries we had brought an essentially powerless message to a very power conscious people. The Nigerians "knew" that
whatever power Christianity brought, it wasn't adequate to deal with
such things as tragedy, infertility, relational breakdowns, and trou-
blesome weather. It didn't meet many of their deepest spiritual
needs. Even though this was puzzling to them—given the fact that
Christian leaders talked such a good game—they simply accommodated by developing a kind of dual allegiance: a loyalty to Christianity to handle certain needs paralleled by a continuing loyalty to
traditional religious practitioners to handle their power needs. As
missionaries we decried this practice, but we had no effective an-
tidote.[62]

Echoing Kraft's observation, another long-term missionary to
Pakistan and the Arab world, Vivienne Stacey, remarked: "After
spending 32 years in the Muslim world I have come to the conclusion that Christians have underestimated the hold of folk religion." Citing the widespread practice of occult rituals in many
areas of Muslim South Asia, Stacey argues that "there is a need for
more than intellectual persuasion and head knowledge" to coun-
teract this situation. "Theology has its place, but teaching should
be clinical, practical, and event-oriented so that its relevance is
apparent."[63] Dr. Paul Hiebert, chairman of the School of World
Mission and Evangelism at Trinity Evangelical Divinity School,
agrees. "Our invitations to Muslims to follow Christ," writes Dr.
Hiebert, "should include demonstrations of God's power."[64]

The most significant support for this philosophy in recent years
has come from the spiritual marketplaces of the third world. In
many lands, including Uganda, Zaire, Algeria, Indonesia, Guatemala, Pakistan, Nigeria, Brazil, Thailand, Argentina, Nicaragua
and the Philippines (to name only a few), power-oriented
Pentecostal/charismatic churches have experienced phenomenal
growth. Other non-third world countries such as South Korea,
Romania and the United States have been similarly affected.

During some of the worst years of the brutal Mengistu regime in
Ethiopia, miracles not only brought many into the Kingdom of
God, but kept some people out of the grave as well. On one
occasion in the early 1980s, an Ethiopian evangelist was arrested

in the act of preaching by revolutionary guards and taken at gunpoint to a house for interrogation. After the questioning had begun, one of the political cadres asked mockingly: "So you believe in God. Do you think He will save you from us?" The guards then lifted their prisoner up on top of a table, and unscrewed a bulb from the ceiling light socket. The evangelist was then given the choice of putting his finger into the live socket or being summarily shot. Knowing the cadres were serious, he placed his finger into the socket and cried out, "In the name of Jesus!" Instantly all the lights went out in the entire district. At this, the Communist guards cowered under the table while the evangelist stood praising God. The cadres asked him meekly to curtail his preaching but, not surprisingly, they found him at it again the very next day. This time he was taken and beaten with thorns and, like the apostle Stephen during his stoning, he saw a vision of the Lord and did not feel the pain. After this beating he became a fire for the Kingdom in Ethiopia.

The ultimate target of the "weapons of our warfare" are, of course, the demonic hosts of darkness. It is this foul throng that we are called to "bind," "put to flight" and "cast out." Because these spiritual creatures cannot be seen or heard with human faculties (except when they choose to manifest themselves through mortal vessels whom they have been permitted to possess), their conquest can, at times, prove challenging.

When we speak of territorial strongmen or princes, the odds against us are even greater. "At this level," declares Tom White, a noted (and balanced) authority on spiritual warfare, "we are in a sense describing the 'Board Room of Hell'—acknowledging that there are high ranking C.E.O.'s (Chief Executive Officers) responsible for the major movements of deception and destruction of human life in our world."[65] In combat with forces of this caliber and stature, our task is less that of *expulsion* than it is of *binding* and *contending*—in other words, tying up their resources with distracting action (such as angelic "ambushes" set up through intercessory prayer) so that our ministry "raids" can be conducted successfully behind enemy lines.

While "setting lives free from evil spirits is normative for Gospel ministry," White told an audience of Christian leaders at the 1989 Lausanne II Congress on World Evangelization in Manila, "tackling the fortresses of Satan is not (except where there is a sovereign selection of a saint to do it under the extraordinary leading of God)." At the same time, White believes that the contemporary move of the Spirit within the Church worldwide may indicate that God is raising up soldiers "to roll back the forces of hell for a season of unprecedented harvest."[66]

In his foreword to *Christianity with Power*, Canadian theologian Dr. Clark Pinnock writes:

> Brothers and sisters, our risen Lord has triumphed over the powers of evil. He now reigns at God's right hand, having all authority on heaven and earth. King Jesus now wills to save and heal human beings in every dimension of their fallen condition: in body, mind, and spirit. . . . Shall we not then exercise faith in the victorious power of Jesus to fight everything that enslaves and oppresses humankind? Shall we not take authority over all the power of the enemy? Shall we not determine to live our lives as those who expect miracles to come from the hand of God our Father—forsaking the paths of functional unbelief?
>
> Fellow Christians, Jesus Christ is now challenging us to help set aright the disorder and pain of a fallen creation by going forth in his authority and power. He sends us forth in his name to proclaim the good news of the kingdom, to heal the sick, and to cast out demons.

While Pinnock does not explicitly say so, this going forth under the influence of the Holy Spirit is precisely "that which was spoken" of by the prophet Joel (2:28) and alluded to by Peter on the day of Pentecost (Acts 2:14–18).

The Role of Prayer

With effects as boundless as the God whom it stimulates, prayer is easily the single-most important weapon in the believer's arsenal today. It is, writes Walter Wink, "spiritual defiance of what is, in the name of what God has promised. Intercession visualizes an alternative future to the one apparently fated by the momentum of current contradictory forces. It breathes the air of a time yet to be into the suffocating atmosphere of present reality."[67]

John Robb points out that intercessory prayer, mentioned more than thirty times in the book of Acts alone, preceded virtually all "major breakthroughs in the outward expansion of the early Christian movement."[68] Evidencing its timeless value, prayer also played a pivotal role in the exemplary revivals of Jonathan Goforth (China and Korea) and Charles Finney (U.S.A. and Britain), and is widely considered responsible for the dramatic opening of Eastern Europe. It is also possible to link it directly with recent Gospel penetrations deep into the Muslim world.

Helping pave the way for the current exciting move of God in Afghanistan (upward of 2,000 to 3,000 new national believers), for instance, was a single intercessor by the name of Flora Davidson. In an article on the topic of prayer for Muslims, Dr. Christy Wilson describes how Miss Davidson, originally from Scotland, lived during the 1940s in a two-story earthen house in the city of Kohat on the northwest frontier of British India—now northwest Pakistan, not far from the famed Khyber Pass. "In front of a window that looked out on the mountains of Afghanistan in the distance," Dr. Wilson recalls, Miss Davidson "would spend hours on her knees praying that God would open that country to the gospel."

As early as 1945 her efforts began to pay off as Dennis Clark and others, including the Wilsons, were permitted to enter the country as tentmaker missionaries. Since that time—including during the dark years of the Soviet occupation—a steady stream of Christian workers has managed to enter Afghanistan and fan the spiritual embers lit by Flora Davidson.[69]

On a recent trip to Rochester, New York, I spoke with a middle-aged missionary[70] who in the 1960s led a team of young Americans in prayer on the very site of Raymond Lull's fourteenth-century martyrdom in Algeria. Praying that God would redeem the seed of Raymond Lull's poured-out life and send a move of His Spirit, the team helped to lay the groundwork for a sovereign outpouring of divine grace fewer than twenty years down the road.

In many ways the ancient cultures of Asia and Africa lend themselves to such intercession. Citing the experiences of Abraham and Moses, Walter Wink sees biblical prayer—which he describes as "impertinent, persistent, shameless, and indecorous"—as "more like haggling in an outdoor bazaar than the polite monologues of the churches."

Happily, more Christians are praying today than ever before. (This is undoubtedly one of the primary reasons for the stunning success of global evangelization over the past several decades.) As of 1990, an estimated 170 million persons across the planet were praying daily for world mission. Twenty million of these were involved in full-time prayer ministry, many as members of 22 active global intercessory prayer networks or one of ten million weekly prayer groups.[71]

On the down side, the practices of a stout percentage of these contemporary intercessors tend to bear a striking resemblance to Iraqi anti-aircraft gunners during the recent Gulf War. While adept at lighting up the night sky, they may not be hitting much in the process. Among the primary reasons for this: poor training and even worse target intelligence.

What can be done? John Robb believes that "the most strategic thing we can do for frontier missions is to stimulate the formation of ongoing prayer and spiritual warfare networks focused on particular unreached peoples, cities and countries." He cites as a case in point the experience of OMS International under the leadership of Wesley Duewel. After 25 years of ineffectual ministry in India, the organization decided to "recruit 1,000 people in their homelands to pray 15 minutes a day for the work." The results were startling. In just a few years the work grew from 25 churches with 2,000 believers to 550 churches with more than 73,000 believers.[72]

In this same spirit, and in order to encourage breakthroughs in the world's twenty most severely underserviced frontiers, The Sentinel Group has launched what we call our 20-20 Program. We plan to recruit thousands of no-nonsense individuals over the next several years who will contribute to the softening of enemy defenses in these spiritually resistant bastions in two ways: 1) by praying at least twenty minutes a week for the territories listed on the Target Group Twenty roster (see pp. 253–254), and 2) by giving at least twenty dollars a month to support outreach to these territories. Our commitment in return: to provide quality prayer intelligence in the form of monthly *Target Updates*, and to use our extensive network of contacts within the restricted-access world to channel financial resources into strategic front-line ministry projects.

Does this sort of thing work? It surely has in the case of Russian Christian Radio (RCR), an Estes Park, Colorado, ministry headed by Earl and Pirkko Poysti that sends out meaty information faithfully to stimulate informed intercession. Consider the following from an early 1991 bulletin:

> In our November [1990] letter, we mentioned the influence of the occult and psychic healing in the Soviet Union. Please continue to pray against these powers of darkness. We praise God that He has already begun to answer. The top psychic healer, Kashpirovsky, who has had daily programs on Soviet television and has had a tremendous influence on the people, has finally fallen out of favor. His programs have been cancelled. Thank you for your prayers!

Soliciting continued prayer on this matter, RCR offered the following excerpt from a letter written by a Soviet listener:[73]

> "The memory of feeling is much greater than the memory of the mind," says the Soviet parapsychologist and psychic healer Kashpirovsky, [whose] seances are transmitted over television all over the country. The results are very impressive, a leg that was shorter is stretched to be the same length as the other, a completely blind person begins to distinguish between day and night, the hair of a balding western actress begins to grow back, many diabetics are healed, etc. A sister from Novorossisk was reported to have become demon-possessed after one of these television seances. People coming under his spell fall asleep, others laugh, some cry. Some don't feel anything, others have hallucinations.
>
> The Soviet central television has begun to show a program every other Sunday about moral issues. . . . Except for a timid reference to the Bible or to some ancient books, it is difficult to detect in their "sermons" anything divine or relating to God. These programs seem so uninteresting when compared to Kashpirovsky that they hardly present any alternative to him.

Despite the counterfeit power of the enemy, God has promised that, if His people will but ask, He will give the nations to them as an inheritance (Psalm 2:8).

Pulling It Off: Cultivating an Activist Mentality

Activism—a term not to be confused with busyness—is the inevitable result of a soul that moves into close proximity to the heart and purposes of God. It is the natural response to the realization that the will of God is the highest and most profound cause that may be served.

Jeremiah cried under the weight of prophetic anointing: ". . . His word was in my heart like a burning fire shut up in my bones; I was weary of holding it back, and I could not."[74] Peter and John argued before the Sanhedrin: "For we cannot but speak the things which we have seen and heard."[75] The apostle Paul reasoned with the Corinthians: "For if I preach the gospel, I have nothing to boast of, for necessity is laid upon me; yes, woe is me if I do not preach the gospel!"[76] And Jesus declared to His disciples: "I must work the works of Him who sent Me while it is day; the night is coming when no one can work."[77]

The Nigerian novelist Chinua Achebe tells the true story of a medical doctor living in Angola toward the end of that country's colonial period. Throughout the guerilla war against the Portuguese, the doctor (who was also a poet) remained apolitical. One particular day, however, this doctor witnessed an extraordinarily brutal act perpetrated by the colonial regime. Realizing he could no longer remain uninvolved, he shut down his medical practice and took to the bush. In the months that followed, two lines of his poetry made their way to the front lines and became the rallying cry for the liberation forces: *"I wait no more. I am the awaited."*[78]

For Christians today, the circumstances are the same. The last of the giants have bared their teeth and the hour for "business as usual" has passed. In light of the challenge, God is now imploring His Church to renounce what Calgary pastor Kenn Gill notes as a tendency toward inordinate softness.[79]

Once we acknowledge the will and purpose of God, activism is no longer contingent upon guidance, but becomes instead a matter of obedience. To the Christian who has indulged in the blessing of the Father's house without considering the corresponding responsibilities of discipleship, the notice is out: "Let him that stole steal no more: but rather let him labor. . . ."[80]

One of the most poignant cries to activism ever recorded comes, ironically, not out of the mouth of a great prophet or patriot but from dying lepers. The account, found in the book of 2 Kings, offers an interesting sidelight to surrounding stories chronicling the rise and fall of kings. The main characters, four rag-tag lepers, are seated at the entrance to the gate of Samaria, which was besieged by the armies of the Syrian king, Ben-Hadad. They had been there long enough to take stock of their situation and found it wanting. Outside the city, the Syrian army perched like vultures awaiting their prey. Inside the city, starvation had taken its toll and panic was beginning to set in. In the midst of it all, their own diseased flesh was decaying unto death. Realizing the scene was not going to mend of its own accord, and that passivity would only guarantee the status quo, the previously ludicrous notion of activism flooded their minds suddenly like an elixir of youth. Turning to one another, they asked: "Why are we sitting here until we die?"[81]

Like these lepers, many Christians today are immobilized and ineffectual simply because they have been asking the wrong question. Passivity results from asking *how*, and withholding commitment until there is an answer. The activist mentality, on the other hand, is stirred by a lack of results and asks, *"Why* am I not going anywhere?"

Others, while more than willing to attempt divine tasks, are less inclined to finish them. Their reasons for dropping out range from tedium to a fear of persecution. Without dismissing altogether the rewards of a job well done, they are generally satisfied to have at least "given it a go."

An activist, by contrast, does not even entertain the notion of partial victory. To abandon a commitment when God's work and reputation are at stake cannot be justified under any formula.

Required is a straightforward proposition of counting the cost in advance so that the Kingdom is not discredited later by the spectacle of a half-built monument.

After a tour of U.S churches and media ministries in the late 1980s, a Polish pastor was asked to summarize his impressions. His reply was piercing. "The American Church," he said, "is captive to freedom." Later, when asked to explain his comments, he responded: "To American Christians the most important thing about freedom is that they have it. To those of us in Eastern Europe, however, the most important thing about freedom is what one does with it." It has often been said, in this regard, that God will not judge a man on the basis of what he has done, but on the basis of what he could have done and did not.

As the Church proceeds toward the year 2000, no other reminder is more appropriate to the occasion. Multitudes still wait in the valley of decision; the question is simply who will reach them first. Never before has the competition for souls been so fierce. Never before has the Church had to contend with such a diverse assortment of rivals committed so utterly to the principles of activism. Fortunately, it is into just such an hour that God has promised through the prophet Joel to pour out His Spirit upon all flesh.[82]

This is indeed good news. It also means, as Francis Schaeffer noted, that "the more the Holy Spirit works, the more Christians will be used in battle."[83] Given the abundant signs that God's latter-day rain has now begun to fall on the earth, we may soon find ourselves, like the character in the Robert Frost poem, with "promises to keep." For, as Peter Wagner reminds us, while "God brings the harvest to ripeness, *he* does not harvest it."[84] That privilege He has left to His Church.

> Whatever your hand finds to do, do it with your might; for there is no work or device or knowledge or wisdom in the grave where you are going.
>
> Ecclesiastes 9:10

Notes

1 Quoted in *And Signs Shall Follow*, Gary Kinnaman (Tarrytown, N.Y.: Chosen Books, 1987), p. 18.

2 Os Guiness, *In Two Minds* (Downers Grove, Ill.: InterVarsity, 1976), p. 286.

3 From a message delivered at the *World Mandate* Conference in Dallas, Texas.

4 Quoted in *Profiles of the Future*, p. ix.

5 Ecclesiastes 1:9–10 (NASB).

6 Alvin Toffler, *The Third Wave* (New York: Bantam, 1981), pp. 11–12.

7 Marcus Aurelius Antonius, *Meditations*, IX, 28.

8 "Ministries to Muslims Highlighted," *The Lutheran*, November 23, 1988.

9 Francis Schaeffer, *The Church at the End of the Twentieth Century* (Downers Grove, Ill.: InterVarsity, 1970), pp. 67, 77.
Note: Schaeffer explained this declaration by pointing out that "there is a bad concept of old-fashionedness and there is a good concept. The good concept is that some things never change because they are eternal truths. These we must hold to tenaciously. . . . But there is [also] a bad sense. I often ask young pastors and professors who are wrestling with these things a simple question: Can you really believe that the Holy Spirit is ever old-fashioned in the bad sense? The obvious answer is No. So if we as evangelicals become old-fashioned—not in the good sense, but the bad—we must understand the problem is not basically intellectual, but spiritual. It shows we have lost our way. We have lost contact with the leading of the Holy Spirit. . . ."

10 Floyd McClung, "Targeting for the Countdown," *Countdown to A.D. 2000*, ed. Thomas Wang (A.D. 2000 Movement, Inc., 1989), p. 23.

11 This "collateral damage" generally results from the lack of training and/or resourcing afforded many of today's field personnel (both long- and short-term) that can lead in turn to an anesthetizing of various people groups to the Gospel message. Another problem is that "buckshot ministry" is not particularly results-oriented and often draws vital resources away from truly strategic targets.

12 Barrett and Johnson, *Our Globe and How to Reach It* (Birmingham, Ala.: New Hope, 1990), Global Diagram 12, p. 25.
Note: This number is based on what Barrett calls "demographic evangelization" where families, groups or ethno-linguistic peoples represent the primary components of evangelistic scorekeeping. The total number of unevangelized rises by nearly 500 million persons if tallying is done on the basis of persons who have received the opportunity *individually* to respond to the Gospel by joining a local church of their own culture.

13 The author's own ministry, a Seattle-based agency known as The Sentinel Group, is dedicated to the evangelization of the world's most severely under-serviced mission frontiers. These spiritually needy frontiers, dubbed Target Group Twenty by ministry staffers, are listed below:

- Afghanistan
- Albania
- Bhutan
- Cambodia
- Djibouti

- The Gulf States *(Saudia Arabia, Kuwait, Qatar, United Arab Emirates, Bahrain and Oman)*
- India (northern)
- Iraq

- Libya
- The Magreb
  (Algeria, Morocco, Tunisia
  and the western Sahara)
- Maldive Islands
- Mauritania
- Mongolia

- North Korea
- Pakistan (western)
- Somalia
- Soviet Central Asia
- Tibet
- Turkey (eastern)
- Yemen

While all but one of these areas (western Sahara) contain at least a handful of Christian believers, organized and mature churches may be found in only two-thirds of them. In those areas where churches do exist, the challenges to evangelism are formidable—but by no means impossible!

14 Barrett and Johnson, Global Diagram 14, p. 27.
Note: There are 133 million newly evangelized each year in the unevangelized world, which number is offset, unfortunately, by 142 million new births a year. Thus, despite the new converts, we are still losing ground every year in this category. See Global Diagram 20, p. 33.

15 Robert Douglas, "The Challenge of the Muslim World," *World Evangelization*, November–December 1988.
Note: Happily, this number is growing today as more and more Christians awaken to the challenge of Islam. Still, more than 930 different ethno-linguistic groups need churches planted among them—a task calling mainly for cross-cultural missions.

16 Barrett and Johnson, p. 98.

17 According to Barrett, the Christianized world as of 1990 was the beneficiary of 99 percent of all Christian literature, 99.9 percent of all Christian radio and TV broadcasting, 94 percent of all Christian finances and 87.2 percent of all foreign missions money. See *Ibid.*, p. 99, Table 9.

18 Kenneth Scott Latourette, *A History of Christianity*, Vol. II (New York: Harper & Row, 1953/1975), p. 1450.

19 *Soka-gakkai* (literally, Value Creation Society) is a militant Buddhist offshoot religion related to the Nichiren-sho-shu sect. Its membership is now almost certainly in the range of 20–25 million and growing.

20 Isaiah 21:6.

21 This vital new initiative, which is known by the acronym STEP (Strategic Target Evaluation Program), uses a computer as a sort of glorified notebook to record all that God seems to be saying to His people, and then to help sort this information into meaningful "big picture" patterns and categories. Once this is accomplished, the information is added to other trend-tracking data to help pinpoint and analyze emerging ministry opportunities.

22 See John 4:35.

23 See chapter 9, section entitled "Two Reapers, Three Frogs and Seven Angels."

24 *World Evangelization*, March–April 1989.

25 Barrett and Reapsome, *Seven Hundred Plans to Evangelize the World* (Birmingham, Ala.: New Hope, 1988), pp. 49–50, 69.

26 On several occasions I have been approached by individuals asking whether I was aware that the term *networking* was actually a New Age word. My response each time has been that I am operating under the assumption that it is, in fact, an English word. In my view, people who give up using words in their own language simply because some heathen cult or movement has endeavored to co-opt them for their own use are only ceding ground to the enemy—something I refuse to do.

27 C. S. Lewis, *Fern Seeds and Elephants* (New York: Fontana, 1975), p. 15.

28 See Ephesians 4:16.

Note: By *adjacent members* we do not mean solely those of our own kind or neighborhood, but also those to whom we must be connected in order to function in the Body. Knees, for example, are connected not only to the femur, tibia and fibula bones, but also to various muscles, ligaments and blood vessels. So in the spiritual Body, a missions strategist may be connected to pastors, teachers and psalmists for personal nurture, and to researchers, computer specialists and evangelists for operational reasons. No matter how exemplary a knee may fancy itself to be, it must never lose sight of the fact that, apart from the body, it is a nigh-unto-useless instrument.

29 Quoted in *Fearfully and Wonderfully Made*, Paul Brand, M.D., and Philip Yancey (Grand Rapids: Zondervan, 1987), p. 43.

30 *Ibid.*, p. 20.

31 1 Corinthians 1:12–13.

32 Jack Hayford, "Dependently and Independently Interdependent"

33 Collected by Dr. Jan Knappert; quoted in *The World & I*, Vol. I, No. 6 (June 1986), p. 159.

Note: Compare with Matthew 12:25.

34 Ron Cline, "World by 2000: A Journey of Cooperation," *Countdown to A.D. 2000*, p. 95.

35 Many ministries in recent days, having overestimated their capabilities, have found themselves overcome and rendered ineffectual by the pace and complexities of the 1990s. See Revelation 3:17.

36 Deuteronomy 32:30.

37 "Ready for Action," *Time*, November 12, 1990.

38 See Victor Suvorov, *Inside the Aquarium: The Making of a Top Soviet Spy* (New York: Berkley, 1986).

39 From Gairdner Ministries (now People International) newsletter, *Islam in Britain*.

40 Barrett and Reapsome, *Seven Hundred Plans to Evangelize the World*, Appendix H, p. 116.

41 *Ibid.*, p. 25. In 1990 Barrett and Johnson placed combined church and agency income at $157 billion per year. See *Our Globe and How to Reach It*, Global Diagram 14, p. 27.

42 Barrett and Johnson, *Our Globe and How to Reach It*, Global Diagram 14, p. 27.

43 Information gleaned from a leader of an international mission organization.

44 Barrett and Johnson, Global Diagram 12, p. 25.

45 Gregory Lewis, *Is God for Sale?* (Wheaton, Ill.: Tyndale, 1979), p. 96.

46 *People* magazine supplement (fall 1989).

47 Nicole Woolsey Biggart, *Charismatic Capitalism* (Chicago: University of Chicago Press, 1989), p. 137.

48 Philippians 2:21.

49 Joseph Haroutunian, *Wisdom and Folly in Religion* (New York: Charles Scribner's Sons, 1940), p. 51.

50 *Mission Frontiers*, January–February 1988.

51 Lewis, p. 107.

52 This relates back to comments on page 228 about the way churches often respond to long-supported nationals and missionaries working in non-strategic fields or activities.

53 Some Christian entrepreneurs have decided that the best route to achieve this is by establishing a "company for Christ." The idea is championed by the Atlanta-based Fellowship of Companies for Christ and has taken off across the United States. Among the numerous contemporary examples of this concept are the Albuquerque-based Tetra Corporation, a high-tech research and development firm specializing in pulsed power and plasma physics, electrical engineering and computational physics; and the Santa Cruz, California, computer software company called Metaware. Both companies have found numerous ways to serve the cause of Christ through their business activities.

54 Careers today absorb more than just hours and weeks. New research suggests that in addition to consuming nearly fifty percent of our time, our jobs also soak up a whopping 95 percent of our emotional energy. This is why job satisfaction has become such an important issue in recent years. So important, in fact, that *Personnel Journal* reported in 1988 that U.S. workers now rate job satisfaction as more important than job security.

The prophet Isaiah asked, "Why do you spend money for that which is not bread, and your labor for that which does not satisfy?" In the Gospel of John, the Lord Jesus declared that His joy should remain in us and that our joy should be full (or complete). If we as Christians lack this joy in our careers, it is time for us to examine (or reexamine) why this is so. To say that secular work is dignified may be true but it isn't enough.

Note: For more information on the subject of finding God's maximum in the workplace, write to The Sentinel Group and request a copy of the article by George Otis, Jr., entitled "Full Extent Ministry."

55 Proverbs 8:12. Most modern translations read *discretion*, which, in context, still connotes a shrewd sorting out of values and priorities.

56 A. W. Tozer, *God Tells the Man Who Cares* (Harrisburg: Christian Publications, 1970), p. 14.

57 Malcolm Muggeridge, *Jesus Rediscovered* (New York: Doubleday, 1974), p. 116.

58 *This Present Darkness* and *Piercing the Darkness*, both published by Crossway Books.

59 Gary Kinnaman, *Overcoming the Dominion of Darkness* (Tarrytown, N.Y.: Chosen Books, 1990), pp. 24, 30.

60 John Dawson, *Taking Our Cities for God* (Lake Mary, Fla.: Creation House, 1989), p. 139.

61 Howard Snyder, *The Problem of Wineskins* (Downers Grove, Ill.: InterVarsity, 1976), p. 131.

62 Charles Kraft, *Christianity with Power* (Ann Arbor, Mich.: Servant, 1989), p. 4.

63 Vivienne Stacey, "The Practice of Exorcism and Healing," *Muslims and Christians on the Emmaus Road* (Monrovia, Cal.: MARC, 1989), pp. 292–293.

64 *Ibid.*, Dr. Paul Hiebert, "Power Encounter and Folk Islam," p. 56.

65 Tom White (Mantle of Praise Ministries), "A Model for Discerning, Penetrating, and Overcoming Ruling Principalities and Powers"—a paper presented at the Lausanne II Congress on World Evangelization in Manila, July 1989.

66 *Ibid.*
Note: Pointing out that neither Wesley nor Finney majored on dealing directly with the devil but concentrated on obedience to truth, labor in prayer and dependence on the Spirit, White warns that "power encounter, like any other aspect of ministry, is not to become a preoccupation. There is danger here of a holy crusade to rid the world of evil strongholds. If the vision of the heart of God aching for the lost is blurred by a commando operation to storm the gates of hell, we miss the point of the Great Commission."

67 Walter Wink, "Prayer: History Belongs to the Intercessors," *Sojourners*, October 1990.

68 John Robb, "Prayer as a Strategic Weapon in Frontier Missions"—a paper delivered to the International Society for Frontier Missiology, September 13–15, 1990.

69 J. Christy Wilson, "The Experience of Praying for Muslims," *Muslims and Christians on the Emmaus Road*, pp. 326–327.

70 Dick Dreyer, now with Elim Fellowship.

71 Barrett and Johnson, *Our Globe and How to Reach It*, Global Diagram 14, p. 27.

72 Robb, "Prayer as a Strategic Weapon in Frontier Missions."

73 As a result of his radio preaching, Earl Poysti is perhaps the most widely known and beloved Christian personality in the U.S.S.R. today.

74 Jeremiah 20:9.

75 Acts 4:20.

76 1 Corinthians 9:16.

77 John 9:4.
Note: While these statements have in recent days become the credos of a growing company of Christian activists, an equal number of modern churchmen find such displays of spiritual passion both intrusive and intimidating. Generally uncomfortable with anything that disturbs their pedestrian pace, these individuals construe activist references to the urgency of the hour as alarmist and unnecessary drama. Though they will not say so, their philosophy of service is summed up in the notion that "if God wants me, He knows my address." Such people view themselves not as partners in but as observers of God's work.
   At their more deliberate pace, many passive-minded Christians find plenty of time to criticize their more active brethren. They don't much care for the new church outreach program; they don't consider it wise or ethical to smuggle Bibles into restricted countries; they don't understand why anti-abortion activists need to be out picketing every weekend. The fiery Dwight L. Moody, finding himself thus criticized, once replied, "I prefer my way of doing things over your way of not doing them."
   There are, of course, more "spiritual" reasons given for sedentary living. The most popular of these, "I am waiting on the Lord," has a particularly legitimate ring to it.

What must be remembered, however, is the fact that waiting without expectation will always go unrewarded. When a soldier waits on his commander, he does so with the certainty that orders will soon be forthcoming. By making himself eligible for battle, he has opened himself to specific guidance. His civilian buddies, on the other hand, may frequent the military post all they wish, but they will not be addressed by the commander.

True waiting upon the Lord, in other words, always leads to activism. The rest of faith has nothing to do with a cessation of activity and should never be used as an excuse for lifelessness. Paul exhorts the Romans to be "not lagging in diligence, fervent in spirit, serving the Lord" (12:11). Proverbs 24:10 declares, "If you faint in the day of adversity, your strength is small." An even stronger admonition is found in Jesus' Parable of the Talents in which indolent servants are called "lazy" and "unprofitable" and given their dread release (Matthew 25:26–30).

78 Quoted in an interview with Bill Moyers, *A World of Ideas* (New York: Doubleday, 1989), p. 336.
79 In this plea Gill declares, "God is not urging us to be radical, but to be normal."
80 Ephesians 4:28a (KJV).
81 2 Kings 6:24–7:20.
82 Joel 2:28–29.
83 Francis Schaeffer, *No Little People* (Downers Grove, Ill.: InterVarsity, 1974), p. 72.
84 C. Peter Wagner, *On the Crest of the Wave* (Glendale, Cal.: Regal, 1983), p. 121.

Epilogue

Risky Safety

The risk-free life is a victory-free life. It means lifelong surrender to the mediocre. And that is the worst of all defeats.

Jamie Buckingham[1]

Daring ideas are like chessmen moved forward; they may be beaten, but they start a winning game.

Goethe[2]

It is not enough to count the hidden costs of saying yes to new enterprises. We must also learn to count the hidden costs of saying no.

Freeman Dyson[3]

The popular idea that it is possible to achieve progress without entertaining risk has no basis in fact. This idea is false not only in the spiritual arena but in all other categories of life. As Christians we are reminded that we live in a fallen world and that at least some measure of damage is unavoidable. As University of California public policy professor Aaron Wildavsky points out in his recent book, *Searching for Safety,* "The trick is to discover not how to avoid risk, for this is impossible, but how to use risk to get more of the good and less of the bad. . . . Playing it safe, doing nothing, means reducing possible opportunities to benefit from chances taken, and can hurt people."[4]

History is not prescriptive; and as one astute writer has pointed out, "Neither heroism nor invention emerged from doing things as one did them in the past." For progress to be achieved in the spiritual or any other arena of life, prevailing assumptions about what is necessary and possible must be periodically challenged—not out of a juvenile desire to be deliberately provocative, but rather from the understanding that times change and that many assumptions held widely in the past have proven faulty and inaccurate.

In the scientific realm, for instance, people held fast to the belief that the world was flat, and that, in fact, the sun revolved around it. The year before the Wright brothers' successful flight at Kitty Hawk, astronomer Simon Newcomb proclaimed, "Flight by machines heavier than air is unpractical and insignificant, if not utterly impossible." In 1923, Nobel Prizewinning physicist Dr. Robert Millikan demonstrated a similar pessimism when he declared, "There is no likelihood man can ever tap the power of the atom."

On the spiritual plane, evangelistic progress continues to be hampered by many such negative and false assumptions. Perhaps the biggest of these—that evangelism cannot be conducted in so-called "closed" societies—is no more sound than the prevailing notion in earlier ages that the world was flat.

In truth, many of us need a fresh revelation from God as to what is possible and what is not. A good starting point might be admitting that we have confused government opposition to Christianity with rejection of the Gospel by the resident people groups; and that we have judged these mission fields not "white unto harvest" without having first attempted seriously to evangelize there. (In other cases, we have failed to recognize that it may not be the Gospel being resisted but rather our methods of presenting it!) By acknowledging that our notions are untested and that we have based our determinations on assumption rather than experience, we clear the way for God's purposes to be revealed.

Risk avoidance is nothing more than an effort to avoid regret. The reasoning is that if you cannot predict the future with certainty, then it is best to live out theoretician John Rawls' advice and "choose as if you would end up in the worst possible position." A biblical parallel to this is found in Jesus' Parable of the Talents. The prime figure in the story, a particularly conservative servant, elects to carry out his fiduciary responsibility by burying, rather than investing, the capital entrusted to him during his master's absence. For him, the *potential for loss* was of far greater concern than the *failure to gain*. As a consequence, the possibility of not doing better was sacrificed on the altar of not doing worse. The story ends, of course, with the servant's worst fears being realized. The very steps taken to alleviate loss in fact promoted it.

Much the same thing is occurring today, tragically, relative to evangelism and church growth inside many of the world's more restrictive mission fields. In an unfortunate number of cases, our passion to protect the Church from its external enemies is resulting instead in the unwitting eradication of her influence from within. By wrapping our talents in the napkin of discretion, we, too, may be stumbling toward our greatest fear—the effective silencing of Jesus Christ's primary voice on earth.

All this raises significant questions when it comes to sharing our faith with others—particularly when doing so will likely stir up fierce opposition. If, for example, we know there will be persecution, should we attempt to gauge its probable severity before we extend a witness? If the reaction will be severe, even life-threatening, can we biblically justify a decision to avoid the confrontation?

Should the Church in politically or socially trying circumstances remain covert to avoid potential eradication by forces hostile to Christianity? Or would more open confrontation with prevailing spiritual ignorance and deprivation—even if it produced Christian martyrs—be more likely to lead to evangelistic breakthroughs?

Islamic fundamentalists claim that their spiritual revolution is fueled by the blood of martyrs. Is it conceivable that Christianity's failure to thrive in the Muslim world is due to the notable absence of Christian martyrs? And can the Muslim community take seriously the claims of a Church in hiding?

Surely there is biblical precedent for strategic seclusion. David hid from the relentless anger of Saul. Rahab hid the Jewish spies in Jericho. Joseph and Mary took the infant Jesus into Egypt to escape Herod's massacre of the innocents. The question is not whether it is wise at times to keep worship and witness discreet, but rather how long this may continue before we are guilty of "hiding our light under a bushel."

Open Doors and the Gates of Hell

The first book of the prophet Samuel records a dramatic encounter between God's people and the spirit of fear and intimidation. The account involves the armies of Israel and Philistia who had set themselves for battle in the Valley of Elah. As they faced each other atop parallel ridges, a monstrous Philistine warrior broke ranks with his fellows to defy Saul's troops. For forty days this giant presented himself morning and evening before the armies of God. As he bellowed his hostility across the valley, we are told that "all the men of Israel, when they saw the man, fled from him and were dreadfully afraid."[5]

Fear can be a deadly enemy. It possesses the capacity to disarm, disorient and paralyze the most stable of souls. Its two faces include *terror*, which arises in the face of imminent peril, and *dread*, a distortion of reality brought on by imagining the unknown. In the latter case many are immobilized not by what is happening, but by what might happen. As finite creatures, we all face the spread of the unknown; and if we cannot find reassuring knowledge of the future, or at least a safe harbor in which to wait for it, we will be overcome by the debilitating effects of dread.

In these modern times our fears over what *might* happen have resulted in an increasing incidence of missionary detours and evangelistic paralysis. The primary question being asked by would-be missionaries and mobilizers today is not, "Is the field ripe?" but, with increasing frequency, "Is it safe?" If relative freedom and safety cannot be affirmed satisfactorily, the only prudent option is to step back and wait for God to "open doors."

But what is meant by the term *open doors?* By popular definition, the concept clearly involves more than mere assurance of personal safety. Opportunity and feasibility are cast as equally important components, demanding in the first case some kind of legitimatizing invitation or welcome to minister, and in the second a realistic resources-to-challenge ratio. With either of these factors absent, the assumption is made that the doors to effective ministry are, for the time being, at least, "closed."

Despite the prevalence of such notions, a careful reexamination of the New Testament places them in clear conflict with the view and practices of the early Church. The idea, for instance, that God's servants must be welcomed in their ambassadorial roles is nowhere encountered. The record shows that from Jerusalem and Damascus to Ephesus and Rome, the apostles were beaten, stoned, conspired against and imprisoned for their witness. Invitations were rare, and never the basis for their missions.

No Fair Fights

It is a salient fact of spiritual engagement that God almost never calls His people to a fair fight. The recurring theme of Scripture is one of giants and multitudes. Time and again Christian warriors were asked to face foes whose natural resources exceeded their own.

The script is the same for us today. As we face the emerging powers of darkness manifest in the challenges of urbanization, massive refugee populations, militant Islam and growing numbers of totalitarian governments opposed to the spread of the Gospel, there are no fair fights. And, no, the field is *not* safe—but neither is walking in unbelief.

The greatest battles most of us face when it comes to taking godly initiatives, however, come not from without but from deep within our own minds and spirits. What we harbor in these secret realms is, in turn, often the product of our interaction with those of the household of faith. Many modern Christian leaders, while acknowledging that God certainly *can* balance the odds in such challenges, are reluctant to predict that He *will*. Despite the victorious testimonies of ill-equipped heroes like Jonathan and his armor-bearer, young David and Rahab the harlot, most real-life Christian counsel today is amply infused with caution.

The message we often hear is reminiscent of the conclusions reached by the Numbers expedition—"We are not able to go up against the people. . ."—and by King Saul before David at the Valley of Elah—"Thou art not able to go against this Philistine. . . ." Both of these assessments were based on an assumption that the resources-to-challenge ratio was not realistic. The spies informed their countrymen that the Canaanites "are stronger than we," while Saul reminded David, "For thou art but a youth, and he a man of war from his youth."

Today's "bad reports" are released not by atheists or moral derelicts but by well-meaning Christian relatives, pastors and youth leaders, Bible school professors and various mission boards and committees. At the same time that weekly sermons, songs and Sunday school lessons urge us to cultivate a spirit of commitment, private conversations with spiritual leaders and role models remind us of our deficiencies, our naïveté, and all the reasons we cannot entertain a genuine hope of success or be "released" with confidence. Prevention masquerades in the name of protection.

David, as we know, went forth to meet Goliath anyway. The circumstances, the odds, the danger, didn't really matter. What did matter was that God had been defied and His people paralyzed by fear. "Is there not a cause?" asked David. In spite of being discouraged by his leader and despised by his foe, this young shepherd was granted a victory by the Holy Spirit that would be remembered down through the annals of time. Recalled less often is the fact that the normal accoutrements of battle—age, experience and training—were absent and thus had no role in David's spectacular conquest.

Spiritual inroads into enemy territory are nearly always the result of godly initiatives rather than heathen invitations. God's strategy in reclaiming His fallen creation is decidedly aggressive: Rather than wait for captive souls to petition for liberation, He dispatches His servants instead on extensive search-and-rescue missions. It is slippery and deadly serious business; for outside the perimeter of the Kingdom of God, divine emissaries are confronted immediately with the gates of hell. Fearsome in their imagery, these malevolent structures have persuaded more than one expedition to turn back for safer havens.

Those who proceed, however, do so in the double confidence that Jesus Christ has promised to go with them and that He Himself has passed through these portals before. Additional encouragement, if any is needed, is afforded in Jesus' declaration in Matthew 16:18 that "the gates of hell shall not prevail" against the Church. In glorious strokes the dynamic characteristics of the Lord's army are highlighted against the static and essentially defensive structures of the enemy. As for the supposed closed doors facing Christian believers today, the reality is that very few are the work of God. Most are deceptive barriers erected to ward off divine arrows of truth, and are therefore legitimate targets for spiritual conquest. All represent golden opportunities to prove His resources and promises afresh.

Today Goliaths stand all about us—in our society and throughout the earth. These spiritual strongmen mock us, because for decades we have displayed neither the courage nor the faith to penetrate their ramparts with the Gospel. Do we hear them? Are we, like David, shocked at their defiance of the name and honor of God? If so, the time has come for us to fulfill our duty.

Notes

1 Jamie Buckingham, "The Risk Factor," *Charisma and Christian Life*, January 1989.

2 Goethe; quote on display at exhibition on creativity at the Pacific Science Center in Seattle, Washington.

3 Freeman Dyson, "The Hidden Cost of Saying NO!", *Bulletin of the Atomic Scientists*, Vol. 31, No. 5, June 1975.

4 Aaron Wildavsky, *Searching for Safety* (New Brunswick: Transaction Publishers, 1988), pp. 2, 5.

5 1 Samuel 17:24.

Appendix

Islamic Beast Theory

Passage	Symbol	Interpretation
Revelation 13:1	Seven-headed beast rising out of sea	Human political kingdoms & systems
Revelation 13:2	Dragon gives authority	Satan controls kingdoms
Revelation 13:2	Leopard, bear & lion traits	Composite of previous systems (see Daniel 7:3–8)
Revelation 13:3	One head mortally wounded	Islamic kingdom defeated in Magog–Israel battle
Revelation 13:3	Deadly wound is healed	Islamic system recoups
Revelation 13:3	World marvels and follows the beast	Faith of global Muslim community is restored
Revelation 13:4	Who is like the beast? Who is able to battle him?	Tributes of faith after the miraculous/ supernatural recovery of Islamic empire
Revelation 13:5–8	Beast blasphemes God and makes war on the saints for 42 months	Islamic "inquisition" takes the lives of those who refuse allegiance to Islam (probably concerns the great Tribulation)
Revelation 13:11	Another beast rises up out of the earth, looking like a lamb but speaking like a dragon	Islamic *Mahdi* or Expected One
Revelation 13:12–15	Exercises authority of first beast, and causes earth to worship beast whose deadly wound was healed	As embodiment of Islamic eschatology, this miracle-worker gives credibility to Islamic system

• Revelation 13:16–18	• The mark of the beast	• Islamic identity system (likely a more fanatically applied version of similar systems that exist already in several Islamic countries)
• Revelation 17:3–6; 18	• The scarlet woman on the scarlet beast (also called Babylon the Great—that great city that reigns over the kings of the earth)	• Seductress symbolizing human power, wealth and sexual indulgence (the spirit of materialism)
• Revelation 17:9	• The seven heads are seven mountains on which the woman sits	• The seven continents of the earth
• Revelation 17:10	• The seven kings—five fallen, one is, and the other not yet come	• Given the time frame of John's revelations, these fallen kings probably refer to the empires of Egypt, Assyria, Babylon, Persia and Greece. The present one is likely the Roman Empire; the one to come, either Russia or the Western alliance
• Revelation 17:11 (8)	• The beast that was and is not (who is of the seven) and is going to perdition	• Essentially an end-times description of the final judgment of earthly political systems
• Revelation 17:12–13	• Ten horns/ten kings who give their authority and power to the beast	• Ten-nation Islamic confederacy in the last days
• Revelation 17:16	• Ten horns who hate the harlot and make her desolate	• Anti-Western, anti-materialistic crusade by Islamic confederacy

Selected Bibliography

A Fragrance of Oppression: The Church and Its Persecutors, Herbert Schlossberg (Westchester, Ill.: Crossway Books, 1991)

A History of Christianity, Kenneth Scott Latourette (New York: Harper & Row, 1953/1975)

And Signs Shall Follow, Gary Kinnaman (Tarrytown, N.Y.: Chosen Books, 1987)

Awaited Saviour, The, Ayatollahs Baqir al-Sadr & Murtaza Mutahery (London: Islamic Seminary Publications, 1979)

Called to Suffer, Called to Triumph, Herbert Schlossberg (Portland: Multnomah Press, 1990)

Closed Borders, Alan Dowty (New Haven: Yale University Press, 1987)

Charismatic Capitalism, Nicole Woolsey Biggart (Chicago: University of Chicago Press, 1989)

Christianity with Power, Charles H. Kraft (Ann Arbor, Mich.: Vine Books, 1989)

Christians As the Romans Saw Them, The, Robert Wilken (New Haven: Yale University Press, 1984)

Cosmos, Chaos and Gospel, David B. Barrett (Birmingham, Ala.: New Hope, 1987)

Countdown to A.D. 2000, ed. Thomas Wang (Pasadena, Cal.: William Carey Library, 1989)

Crescent in a Red Sky: The Future of Islam in the Soviet Union, Amir Taheri (London: Hutchinson & Co, 1989)

Culture of Narcissism, The, Christopher Lasch (New York: Warner Books, 1979)

Dictionary of Gods and Goddesses, Devils and Demons, Manfred Lurker (London: Routledge & Kegan Paul, 1987)

East Comes West, E. Allen Richardson (New York: The Pilgrim Press, 1985)

Eternity in Their Hearts, Don Richardson (Ventura, Cal.: Regal Books, 1981)

Ethnic Minorities in the Red Army: Asset or Liability?, Alexander Alexiev and S. Enders Wimbush, Rand Corporation Research Study (Boulder, Col.: Westview Press, 1988)

Faith and Power: The Politics of Islam, Edward Mortimer (New York: Vintage Books, 1982)

From Jerusalem to Irian Jaya: A Biographical History of Christian Missions, Ruth A. Tucker (Grand Rapids: Zondervan, 1983)

Four Arguments for the Elimination of Television, Jerry Mander (New York: Quill Books, 1978)

Greatness that Was Babylon, The, H. W. F. Saggs (London: Sidgwick & Jackson, 1962/1988)

Idols for Destruction, Herbert Schlossberg (Nashville: Thomas Nelson, 1983)

In the Name of God, Robin Wright (New York: Simon & Schuster, 1989)

In the Path of God, Daniel Pipes (New York: Basic Books, 1983)

Is God for Sale?, Gregory Lewis (Wheaton, Ill.: Tyndale House, 1979)

Islam in the World, Malise Ruthven (Oxford: Oxford University Press, 1984)

Islam and Revolution, Hamid Algar (Berkeley: Mizan Press, 1981)

Islam Revealed, Dr. Anis Shorrosh (Nashville: Thomas Nelson, 1988)

Islamic Messianism, Abdulaziz Abdulhussein Sachedina (Albany, N.Y.: State University of New York Press, 1981)

Jesus, Prophecy and the Middle East, Dr. Anis Shorrosh (Nashville: Thomas Nelson, 1981)

Muslims and Christians on the Emmaus Road, J. Dudley Woodberry (Monrovia, Cal.: MARC, 1989)

Occultation of the Twelfth Imam, The, Jassim M. Hussain (London: The Muhammadi Trust, 1982)

On the Crest of the Wave, C. Peter Wagner (Ventura, Cal.: Regal Books, 1983)

Operation World, Patrick Johnstone (Gerrards Cross, England: WEC Publications, 1986)

Our Globe and How to Reach It, David B. Barrett and Todd Johnson (Birmingham, Ala.: New Hope, 1990)

Overcoming the Dominion of Darkness, Gary Kinnaman (Tarrytown, N.Y.: Chosen Books, 1990)

Partnering in Ministry, Luis Bush and Lorry Lutz (Downers Grove, Ill.: InterVarsity Press, 1990)

Politics of Islamic Revivalism, The, Shireen T. Hunter (Bloomington, Ind.: Indiana University Press, 1988)

Prophecy Knowledge Handbook, The, John Walvoord (Wheaton, Ill.: Victor Books, 1990)

Republic of Fear: The Politics of Modern Iraq, Samir al-Khalil (London: Hutchinson Radius, 1989)

Revolutionary Islam in Iran: Popular Liberation or Religious Dictatorship?, Suroosh Irfani (London: Zed Press, 1983)

Russia: Broken Promises, Solemn Idols, David Shipler (New York: Penguin Books, 1983)

Russian Challenge and the Year 2000, The, Alexander Yanov (Oxford: Basil Blackwell, 1987)

Sacred Rage: The Wrath of Militant Islam, Robin Wright (New York: Simon & Schuster, 1986)

Screwtape Letters, The, C. S. Lewis (New York: Macmillan, 1982)

Searching for Safety, Aaron Wildavsky (New Brunswick: Transaction Publishers, 1988)

Seven Hundred Plans to Evangelize the World, David B. Barrett & James Reapsome (Birmingham, Ala.: New Hope, 1988)

Signs, Wonders and the Kingdom of God, Don Williams (Ann Arbor, Mich.: Vine Books, 1989)

Taking Our Cities for God, John Dawson (Lake Mary, Fla.: Creation House, 1989)

The Kingdom—Arabia and the House of Sa'ud, Robert Lacey (New York: Harcourt Brace Jovanovich, 1981)

Today's Choices for Tomorrow's Mission, David Hesselgrave (Grand Rapids: Zondervan, 1988)

Tribes with Flags, Charles Glass (New York: Atlantic Monthly Press, 1990)

Unseen Face of Islam, The, Bill Musk (London: MARC, 1989)

Virtue of Selfishness, The, Ayn Rand (New York: Signet, 1964)

Work and Leisure in Christian Perspective, Leland Ryken (Portland: Multnomah Press, 1987)

Yezidis, The, John S. Guest (London: Routledge & Kegan Paul, 1987)

The SENTINEL GROUP

A Word About the Author's Ministry: The Sentinel Group is a missions consulting organization founded by George Otis, Jr., that helps Christian agencies and individuals deploy their ministry assets—primarily prayer, finances and people—more strategically.

For information on the Sentinel Group's international research and ministry projects, or to obtain further information on the programs and services listed below, please feel free to contact

The Sentinel Group
P.O. Box 6334
Lynnwood, WA 98036
Phone: (206) 672-2989
FAX: (206) 672-3028

Ministry Programs and Services

• 20/20 Program. Meaty, monthly intelligence reports to support focused intercession.

• Global Prayer Harvest Quarterly. Quarterly record of the results of strategic-level intercessory prayer sessions around the world. Highlights significant trends.

• Frontier Insights Program. Personal exposure tours for those interested in exploring ministry opportunities on the mission frontier.

• World Overview Briefings. Regional two-day seminars providing in-depth analyses of eight world regions, practical strategy and planning tips, and insights of cutting-edge Christian thinkers.

• The Sentinel Report. Biannual publication with statistical data, field intelligence, cross-discipline trend analysis, spiritual mapping profiles, guest interviews and insights into emerging windows of ministry opportunity.